TIME
LIFE ®
BOOKS

Other Publications:

Beef & Veal

BY
THE EDITORS OF TIME-LIFE BOOKS

TIME-LIFE BOOKS/ALEXANDRIA, VIRGINIA

Cover: Its exterior crisped, but its interior kept rare and moist by careful attention to roasting times and temperatures *(page 22)*, a standing rib roast of beef warrants ceremonial carving. To make carving easier and the slices perfect, the roast has been left at room temperature for 15 minutes to rest and become firm.

Time-Life Books Inc.
is a wholly owned subsidiary of
TIME INCORPORATED

Founder: Henry R. Luce 1898-1967

Editor-in-Chief: Henry Anatole Grunwald
President: J. Richard Munro
Chairman of the Board: Ralph P. Davidson
Executive Vice President: Clifford J. Grum
Chairman, Executive Committee: James R. Shepley
Editorial Director: Ralph Graves
Vice Chairman: Arthur Temple

TIME-LIFE BOOKS INC.

Managing Editor: Jerry Korn; *Executive Editor:* David Maness; *Assistant Managing Editors:* Dale M. Brown (planning), George Constable, Thomas H. Flaherty Jr. (acting), Martin Mann, John Paul Porter; *Art Director:* Tom Suzuki; *Chief of Research:* David L. Harrison; *Director of Photography:* Robert G. Mason; *Assistant Art Director:* Arnold C. Holeywell; *Assistant Chief of Research:* Carolyn L. Sackett; *Assistant Director of Photography:* Dolores A. Littles; *Production Editor:* Douglas B. Graham; *Operations Manager:* Gennaro C. Esposito, Gordon E. Buck (assistant); *Assistant Production Editor:* Feliciano Madrid; *Quality Control:* Robert L. Young (director), James J. Cox (assistant), Daniel J. McSweeney, Michael G. Wight (associates); *Art Coordinator:* Anne B. Landry; *Copy Staff:* Susan B. Galloway (chief), Tonna Gibert, Ricki Tarlow, Celia Beattie; *Picture Department:* Alvin Ferrell; *Traffic:* Jeanne Potter

Chairman: Joan D. Manley; *President:* John D. McSweeney; *Executive Vice Presidents:* Carl G. Jaeger, John Steven Maxwell, David J. Walsh; *Vice Presidents:* George Artandi (comptroller); Stephen L. Bair (legal counsel); Peter G. Barnes; Nicholas Benton (public relations); John L. Canova; Beatrice T. Dobie (personnel); Carol Flaumenhaft (consumer affairs); James L. Mercer (Europe/South Pacific); Herbert Sorkin (production); Paul R. Stewart (marketing)

THE GOOD COOK

The original version of this book was created in London for Time-Life International (Nederland) B.V.
European Editor: Kit van Tulleken; *Design Director:* Louis Klein; *Chief Designer:* Graham Davis; *Director of Photography:* Pamela Marke; *Chief of Research:* Vanessa Kramer; *Chief Sub-Editor:* Ilse Gray; *Production Editor:* Ellen Brush

Staff for *Beef & Veal: Series Editor:* Windsor Chorlton; *Deputy Editor:* Deborah Thompson; *Picture Editor:* Anne Angus; *Anthology Editor:* Liz Clasen; *Designer:* Rick Bowring; *Staff Writers:* Norman Kolpas, Alan Lothian, Anthony Masters, Marguerite Tarrant; *Researchers:* Alexandra Carlier, Sally Crawford; *Sub-Editors:* Gillian Boucher, Nicoletta Flessati; *Permissions Researcher:* Mary-Claire Hailey; *Design Assistants:* Martin Gregory, Mary Staples; *Editorial Department:* Anetha Besidonne, Pat Boag, Deborah Dick, Kathy Eason, Joanne Holland, Eleanor Lines, Molly Sutherland, Julia West

U.S. Editorial Staff for *Beef & Veal: Series Editor:* Gerry Schremp; *Designer:* Peg Schreiber; *Text Editor:* Ellen Phillips; *Staff Writer:* Susan Bryan; *Chief Researcher:* Lois Gilman; *Researchers:* Charles Clark, Christine Dove, Eleanor Kask; *Art Assistant:* Cynthia Richardson; *Editorial Assistants:* Pamela Gould, George McDaniel

CHIEF SERIES CONSULTANT

Richard Olney is an American who has lived and worked since 1951 in France, where he is a highly regarded authority on food and wine. A regular contributor to such influential journals as *La Revue du Vin de France* and *Cuisine et Vins de France*, he also has written numerous articles for other gastronomic magazines in France and the United States, and is the author of *The French Menu Cookbook* and the award-winning *Simple French Food*. He has directed cooking courses in France and the United States, and is a member of several distinguished gastronomic societies, including La Confrérie des Chevaliers du Tastevin, La Commanderie du Bontemps de Médoc et des Graves and Les Amitiés Gastronomiques Internationales. Working in London with the series editorial staff, he has been basically responsible for the step-by-step photographic sequences in the techniques section of this volume and has supervised the final selection of recipes submitted by other consultants. The United States edition of *The Good Cook* has been revised by the Editors of TIME-LIFE BOOKS to bring it into complete accord with American customs and usage.

CHIEF AMERICAN CONSULTANT

Carol Cutler, who lives in Washington, D.C., is the author of the award-winning *The Six-Minute Soufflé and Other Culinary Delights*, as well as *Haute Cuisine for Your Heart's Delight*, a volume directed at those requiring low cholesterol diets. She is a contributing editor to *The International Review of Food & Wine* and *Working Woman* magazines, and frequently lectures about food and demonstrates cooking techniques.

PHOTOGRAPHERS

Alan Duns was born in 1943 in the north of England and studied at the Ealing School of Photography. He specializes in food, and has contributed to major British publications.
Aldo Tutino, a native of Italy, has worked in Milan, New York City and Washington, D.C. He has won a number of awards from the New York Advertising Club.

INTERNATIONAL CONSULTANTS

GREAT BRITAIN: *Jane Grigson* has written several books about food and has been a cookery correspondent for the London *Observer* since 1968. FRANCE: *Michel Lemonnier*, co-founder and vice-president of Les Amitiés Gastronomiques Internationales, is a frequent lecturer on wine and vineyards. GERMANY: *Jochen Kuchenbecker* trained as a chef, but has worked for 10 years as a food photographer in several European countries. *Anne Brakemeier* is the co-author of three cookbooks. THE NETHERLANDS: *Hugh Jans* has published two cookbooks and his recipes appear in a number of Dutch magazines. THE UNITED STATES: *François Dionot*, a graduate of L'École des Hôteliers de Lausanne in Switzerland, has worked as chef, hotel general manager and restaurant manager in France and the U.S. He now conducts his own cooking school. *Shirley Sarvis*, a freelance food writer and consultant, is the author and co-author of a dozen cookbooks. *José Wilson*, former food editor of *House & Garden* magazine, has written many books on food and interior decoration.

Correspondents: Elisabeth Kraemer (Bonn); Margot Hapgood, Dorothy Bacon, Lesley Coleman (London); Susan Jonas, Lucy T. Voulgaris (New York); Maria Vincenza Aloisi, Josephine du Brusle (Paris); Ann Natanson (Rome).
Valuable assistance was also provided by: Jeanne Buys (Amsterdam); Hans-Heinrich Wellmann, Gertraud Bellon (Hamburg); Bona Schmid, Maria Teresa Marenco (Milan); Carolyn T. Chubet, Miriam Hsia (New York); Michèle le Baube (Paris); Mimi Murphy (Rome).

For information about any Time-Life book, please write:
Reader Information, Time-Life Books
541 North Fairbanks Court, Chicago, Illinois 60611

Library of Congress CIP data, page 176.

CONTENTS

Rich Meats from a Land of Plenty

"Imagine a poor exile," wrote Mark Twain, describing a high spot of his travels in *A Tramp Abroad,* "and imagine an angel suddenly sweeping down out of a better land and setting before him a mighty porterhouse steak an inch and a half thick, hot and sputtering from the griddle; dusted with fragrant pepper; enriched with melting bits of butter of the most unimpeachable freshness and genuineness; the precious juices of the meat trickling out and joining the gravy."

By 1880, when Twain recorded this mouth-watering vision, America had already become a cattle-raising nation; and his description of prime beef still strikes a sympathetic chord. Rich and red, generously flavored, nourishing and fortifying, beef seems the archetypally perfect food.

Twain did not mention veal, perhaps because it was—and still is—more popular in Europe than in America, but it too should be prized. The taste of premium veal is subtle rather than robust; the meat has a finer texture than beef and its color is not red, but creamy pink. Yet veal, of course, comes from the same animal as beef and is cooked similarly, with some modifications of techniques to suit its special characteristics.

The first half of this book is devoted to teaching those skills you need to choose, prepare and cook both meats well. In addition, the book teaches such culinary arts as garnishing and sauce-making that are essential to finishing dishes, and it shows how to carve large cuts. When you have mastered these skills, you will be ready to choose among the scores of beef and veal recipes that compose the second half of this book. Collected from all over the world and from many eras, the selected recipes represent the traditions, discoveries, preferences and wisdom of many imaginative cooks, famous or obscure, who wrote down their procedures for others to follow.

A bit of historical background

Understanding the basic material is particularly important in cooking beef and veal. The tenderness and flavor of the meat—and therefore your choice of the best cooking method—will depend not only on the age of the animal from which it came, but also on how the animal was fed and how the carcass was butchered into retail cuts after the animal was slaughtered.

The makings of a hearty meal start with a rolled and tied beef brisket, surrounded by such culinary allies as thyme, garlic, a bay leaf, carrots, sea salt, a turnip and bouquet garni. The ale in the pitcher behind can be used to cook the beef or later to wash it down.

The ancestor of all cattle was *bos primogenitus,* a wild ox domesticated during the New Stone Age (about 10,000 B.C.) in ancient Greece and Turkey. Today, hundreds of breeds and crossbreeds are distributed over all five continents. Only a few countries, however, have the agricultural resources for large-scale beef production: chiefly Argentina, Brazil, Australia and, outranking all the others, the United States.

The development of American beef goes a long way back. The Spanish conquistadors brought the lean longhorn into what is now the Southwestern United States in the 16th Century. The Pilgrims imported heifers and a bull to the Plymouth Colony in 1624, "the beginning," as Governor William Bradford noted, "of any cattle of that kind in the land." Soon, other bulls and cows were brought to the Colonies and, during the next century and a half, the relatively small (less than 400-pound [180-kg.]) descendants of the original English breeding stock were valued, as cattle always had been, for their milk, butter, hides and especially for their capacity for work as draft animals.

As long as wild game could provide abundant meat in the New World, little attention was paid to fattening cattle for food; cows were rarely slaughtered before they were seven years old, by which time their meat was so tough that only long cooking could tenderize it. As late as 1855, a cookbook admonished its readers to put the beef "on by seven o'clock in the morning, or if not convenient, the afternoon before, and for a three o'clock dinner, it must cook slowly and steadily until about two o'clock."

We no longer have to cook beef for seven hours or more because, over the years, cattlemen learned how to produce animals with tender flesh. In the late 18th and early 19th Centuries, farmers settled in Kentucky, Ohio, Indiana and Illinois, where huge stretches of open, fertile land produced an abundance of feed grains, especially corn. These could be used to fatten herds of cattle before slaughter, a practice introduced earlier on a small scale by the Pennsylvania Dutch.

By the 1860s, the descendants of English cattle and specially imported Herefords were being carefully bred with longhorns in the newly settled West—not for milk or work but specifically for beef. The 800-pound [360-kg.] hybrid animals that resulted were grazed for two years on the Great Plains, then driven to Illinois and Iowa and fattened for a year on corn. After being slaughtered, they were sent via the railroads' new ice-packed refrigerator cars—first used in 1867 to take meat from Chicago to Boston—to the beef-hungry East.

Today the beef industry operates much the same way, with

technological refinements. Although cattle are raised throughout the country, the largest herds still are found in the West. The animals used for beef are primarily steers—males castrated because cattlemen are understandably reluctant to deal with unruly bulls. (Females, which fatten at a slower rate, are used mainly for breeding.)

When a steer is about a year old and weighs from 600 to 750 pounds [270 to 340 kg.], it is shipped to a commercial feedlot, where, along with as many as 125,000 others of its kind, it is fed for up to six months on corn plus sorghum, oats and barley. When it reaches approximately 1,000 pounds [450 kg.], the steer is ready to be slaughtered, divided into sides and wholesale cuts by a meat packer, and then shipped to butchers and supermarkets across the country.

Such grain-finished animals reach maximum size five or six months before those raised on grass and, having more fat, produce more flavorful and tender flesh; more than half of American beef is grain-fed. The United States, however, is the only country that practices grain feeding on a large scale. The beef of South America and Australia is primarily grass-fed because the corn crops in those regions are scanty.

The particular qualities of North American beef are important to remember when using foreign recipes: it rarely is so tough or lean as to necessitate the extremely long cooking time or larding (pages 56-57) specified in some European cookbooks. Our veal, on the other hand, is usually older and coarser than the European variety and may require preliminary pounding or additional cooking time to tenderize it.

Veal is more common in Europe than in America partly because beef is scarcer there. European countries, lacking both extensive pastures and land for growing feed grain in sufficient quantity, raise their herds for milk as well as meat. Most female calves are allowed to become milk producers. The other calves may be slaughtered when they are two or three months old, before weaning, or at four or five months, after a continued milk diet, to yield veal of the purest creamy pink—or they may be allowed to mature, for beef.

In the United States, where beef is the preferred meat, it is more profitable for cattlemen to raise their calves to maturity than to slaughter them early. American veal usually comes from beef-herd calves no more than three or four months old, which may have already been weaned to grass. That is why you will, from time to time, find meat that is labeled veal—or sometimes "calf"—that is red in color rather than the genuine pale pink of young veal (page 12).

Finding good meat

All beef and veal carcasses produced in the United States must be inspected for wholesomeness before they can be sold. Additionally, about 50 per cent of the beef and 10 per cent of the veal is graded for its potential tenderness and flavor by the Department of Agriculture, as described on page 12. Only an expert can recognize all the finer points in meat quality; that grading mark is, therefore, your best assurance that the meat you buy conforms to established standards. But a grading mark can not tell you all you need to know about a particular piece of meat.

If you are buying beef, you should ask the butcher if it has been aged (true veal, already tender, requires no aging). All meat ages somewhat, of course, in routine handling; but additionally, slaughterhouses, wholesalers and even butchers may hang beef carcasses from 10 days to six weeks in rooms where temperature and humidity can be rigidly controlled in order to produce the beef that is sold as "aged." During this controlled aging period, excess blood drains from the meat and excess moisture evaporates. Enzymes in the beef partially break down the fibers of the meat, with a resulting improvement in its tenderness and flavor.

Aged beef is more expensive than unaged because pound for pound there is less of it; weight is lost during the aging process and after the hardened outer flesh that aging produces has been trimmed. But it tends to cook faster than unaged beef, without as much shrinkage.

Aged or not, the quality of a piece of beef will vary according to where the meat came from on the carcass and how lean, bony or fatty it is. Bones are useful for their delicious marrow and for making stock; and meat roasted with the bone in will be juicier and more flavorful than boned meat, since cutting out the bones severs the muscle fibers and allows valuable juices to escape.

The amount of fat, which varies both according to cut and according to how the cut was trimmed by the butcher, helps determine tenderness and flavor. Grain feeding produces abundant intramuscular fat—marbling—that melts during cooking to baste the meat and keep it tender. The fat on grain-fed beef is a creamy white; yellowish fat is a sign that the meat comes from a grass-fed animal or a steer that may have been grain-fed but was past its prime when slaughtered.

Fat trimmed from meat need not always be discarded. Suet, the crumbly white fat from around beef kidneys, can be used in the pastry for a meat pie or for frying. External beef fat, cut into thin slices, can be used to bard, or wrap, very lean roasts that have little fat of their own (page 22).

By contrast with beef, the young bones of a veal calf are rich in gelatin for stock-making, poaching or braising, but contain less marrow than a steer's bones would. And a veal calf's fat, which should be ivory colored, is too meager to be worth trimming for pastry-making or barding.

The most important factor in tenderness and flavor, however, is not fat and bone but the meat itself. If you know what part of the animal your beef or veal comes from, you will know how to cook it, since each part has particular qualities that make it suitable to some cooking methods and not to others. The diagrams on pages 8-11 locate the wholesale or primal sections and explain which of these sections produce different roasts, steaks, chops and other retail cuts.

You may need to recognize retail cuts by sight, because their names can vary widely from one region of the country to the next, or from one butcher to another, even in the same town. Thus, a top-loin steak is called a New York strip steak in Kansas City, but a Kansas City strip in Manhattan. In the future, all of the names may become uniform; the meat industry is making a concerted effort to standardize them, and the diagrams shown in this volume follow the industry's recommendations.

Veal from the lower leg, shoulder and breast profits by poaching or braising, which moistens the meat and softens its tough connective tissues. The fragile flesh of the calf's back and hindquarters—the ribs, loin and rump—may be cooked by dry heat, but this should be done gently, since the meat will toughen and dry out if subjected to high heat.

In beef cattle, the most exercised and therefore the most developed muscles are found in the legs, brisket, flank, neck and shoulder. Cuts from these richly flavored muscles require long hours of braising or poaching in water, wine, beer or stock at low temperatures to prevent the lean meat from drying out before it becomes tender. The least hard-worked parts of the steer are the muscles of the back—the ribs, loin and rump. Cuts from these muscles are naturally tender, but their flavor is slightly less pronounced than that of the tougher meat. They require fairly brief roasting, broiling or frying at high temperatures to bring out their flavor while preserving their juices.

The muscles of some parts of a steer's shoulder and hind-quarters are neither so sinewy as the legs and neck nor so tender as the back. These cuts can be roasted at moderate heat and they yield good steaks for frying or broiling; but they also can be braised or pot roasted, since their flavor and muscle structure are strong enough to withstand long, moist cooking processes without disintegrating.

The demonstrations that follow underline the simplicity of the relatively few methods required to cook different cuts. And the anthology of recipes that begins on page 89 illustrates dramatically the almost limitless range of dishes the demonstrated methods can produce. Together, they present the practical and unsensational attitude once expressed by the famous French chef and editor, Prosper Montagné, compiler of the monumental food encyclopedia, *Larousse Gastronomique*. When a guest asked him: "Well, Monsieur Montagné, have you managed to produce a miracle this evening?" Montagné replied, "Miracle? No, simply good food."

Choosing the Right Wine

Good beef or veal is never better than when accompanied by good wine. Most beef dishes are best with red wine; veal goes with either red or white.

But the choice of a particular wine depends less on the meat itself than on the other elements in the finished dish. For example, a simple beef roast—unaltered by marinades, herbs or garlic—may, because of its intrinsically robust and uncomplicated flavor, profit from being eaten with a venerable French red wine, one that is elegant, subtle and intricate. The great Bordeaux possess these virtues; so does a well-aged Côte de Nuits—a Chambertin, for example, or a Musigny.

On the other hand, the concentration of mingled flavors in a braise would overwhelm an old Bordeaux, but would be well supported by a robust, relatively young wine—one of the Rhône Valley reds, such as Châteauneuf-du-Pape, Gigondas, Saint-Joseph or Cornas, or an Italian Barolo, or one of the better Zinfandels from California.

A more delicate dish, such as scallops of veal sautéed in a butter sauce, would be overpowered by one of the preceding wines. Select a fruity, light-bodied red such as a Beaujolais or Napa Gamay. Or, for an Italian wine, pick one of the clean, pleasant ones made from grapes harvested in the Chianti Classico area.

If white is your preference, choose a round and full, yet dry, white wine: Graves from Bordeaux or Sancerre from the Loire; Châteauneuf-du-Pape or a white Hermitage from the Rhône Valley; a Pouilly-Fuissé, Mâcon-Villages, Viré or Saint-Véran from the Mâconnais. Or select a Chardonnay, Chenin Blanc or Colombard from California. One of the great white wines that comes from the Côte de Beaune—Meursault, Montrachet, Puligny-Montrachet or Corton-Charlemagne—can be appreciated to the fullest when it is served as an accompaniment to a moist and perfectly done veal roast.

Apart from simple roasts and broiled meat, the classic braises—veal fricandeau and beef à la mode for example—are the best vehicles for the presentation of any fine red wine with a certain amount of maturity and complexity. Wines that satisfy these demands include the floral Volnays and Pommards from the Côte de Beaune, the Hermitages and the Côtes Rôties from the Rhône Valley or, among the Bordeaux, any of the Médocs, red Graves, Pomerols or Saint-Émilions.

California produces a number of Cabernet Sauvignons, Petite Sirahs and a few Pinot Noirs that easily hold their own with an old-fashioned braise.

There are cooking ingredients that taste better with one type of wine than with another. Most cream sauces, especially those containing egg yolks, do not provide a very complementary background for red wines, whereas a full-bodied white—a Chardonnay, perhaps, or one of the dry white wines of respectable age from the classified Graves growths—is very much at home with a blanquette or fricassee of veal.

Tomatoes mute the finesse of a red wine, but many full-bodied whites go well with them. The whites and rosés from Provence, a Gamay rosé from California, and certain white wines from Italy, such as Orvieto secco, the Veneto's Soave, or Frascati from the hills around Rome, stand up well to the tomatoes' acidity. Tomatoes are an important element in the cuisine of these wine-growing regions and the food of any region usually is best when accompanied by wines from the same area.

On the other hand, it is rare that the cuisine of a nonwine-drinking country tastes good with wine. The powerful aromatic elements in Oriental and tropical beef dishes tend to clash with wine. The best solution often is to drink beer with those dishes, although such highly perfumed, somewhat spicy and not too dry white wines as a Gewürztraminer or some of the Rhine wines will complement a spicy beef or veal dish.

A Guide to Beef Cuts

To estimate how tender or flavorful a cut of beef will be, it helps to know what part of the carcass it comes from. Meat along the backbone is the most tender; that from the front and rear sections, the tastiest. Carcasses are split at the slaughterhouse into "sides" that are subdivided into the large cuts shown at center; each yields the smaller retail cuts. The common ones illustrated are identified by the meat industry's terms for them rather than by any of their regional names.

Rib Roast

Rib Steak

Rib-Eye Roast

Boneless Rib Steak

Rib-Eye Steak

Short Ribs

Rib. Removing the short-rib ends produces a tender seven-rib roast that may be divided into smaller roasts or steaks, all of them bone-in or boneless; those nearest the short loin are tenderest. After boning, the eye muscle of a rib roast may be stripped of fat and sold as a rib-eye roast or as steaks.

Shoulder Steak

Blade Steak

Arm Steak

Chuck Short Ribs

Stew Beef

Cross-Rib Roast

Ground Beef

Chuck-Eye Roast

Neck

Blade

Chuck

Arm and Shoulder

Rib

Foreshank

Brisket

Plate

Chuck. Much of this tough, fibrous cut becomes boneless shoulder, bone-in blade and bone-in arm steaks or roasts, as well as boneless cross-rib and eye roasts — all of them filled with connective tissues and best cooked in liquid. The rest produces ground beef, stew beef or lean short ribs, which may be sold in sections of up to five rib bones or cut into individual ribs.

Plate. The top part of this tough section is sold as short ribs, which are usually cut into individual portions, each containing one bone. The rest is used for stew beef or ground beef.

Shank. Tough, flavorful meat from the animal's front or hind legs is cut up for stews or sliced into marrow-filled shank crosscuts for braising or making stocks.

Brisket. Usually sold in halves, this section includes layers of meat and fat. The flat, oblong "first cut" has less fat; the pointed "front cut," more flavor.

Short Ribs

Stew Beef

Stew Beef

Shank Crosscuts

Brisket First Cut

Brisket Front Cut

Ground Beef

Top-Loin Steak

T-Bone Steak

Boneless Top-Loin Steak

Tenderloin Steak

Porterhouse Steak

Tenderloin

Pin-Bone Sirloin Steak

Flat-Bone Sirloin Steak

Round-Bone Sirloin Steak

Wedge-Bone Sirloin Steak

Boneless Sirloin Steak

Short loin. When this section is sliced crosswise, the bone-in steaks get more tender as they near the sirloin — improving from top loin to T-bone to porterhouse. When divided lengthwise, the bottom part is the tenderest of beef — tenderloin, which may be sliced into steaks. The top part, or shell, produces bone-in or boneless top-loin steaks.

Sirloin. The closer the steaks sliced from this cut are to the short loin, the smaller their bones. They can be distinguished by the shape of their bone sections: pin-bone sirloin is nearest to the loin, followed by flat-bone, round-bone and wedge-bone sirloin. Boneless sirloin may be cut from any of these.

Round. This section produces bone-in or boneless round or rump roasts or steaks, or is divided into boneless top-round steaks and roasts, boneless bottom-round roasts or steaks, and cubed steak. Top-round meat is the more tender. The eye-of-round and the heel yield tough meat that usually is ground or, if left whole, must be braised.

Short Loin

Sirloin

Rump

Round

Round

Tip

Heel

Tip

Flank

Hindshank

Boneless Rolled Rump Roast

Round Steak

Ground Beef

Top-Round Steak

Bottom-Round Roast

Heel-of-Round

Cubed Steak

Flank. The lean and boneless flank steak comes from the inner wall of this cut; the steak may be scored to tenderize it. The meat that surrounds the steak is ground for hamburger.

Tip. Shown here in two pieces, the tip usually comes from the round but may also come from the sirloin. It produces boneless roasts or steaks; the rest is cut into cubes for kebabs or stews.

Flank Steak

Ground Beef

Tip Roast

Tip Kebabs

Eye-of-Round Roast

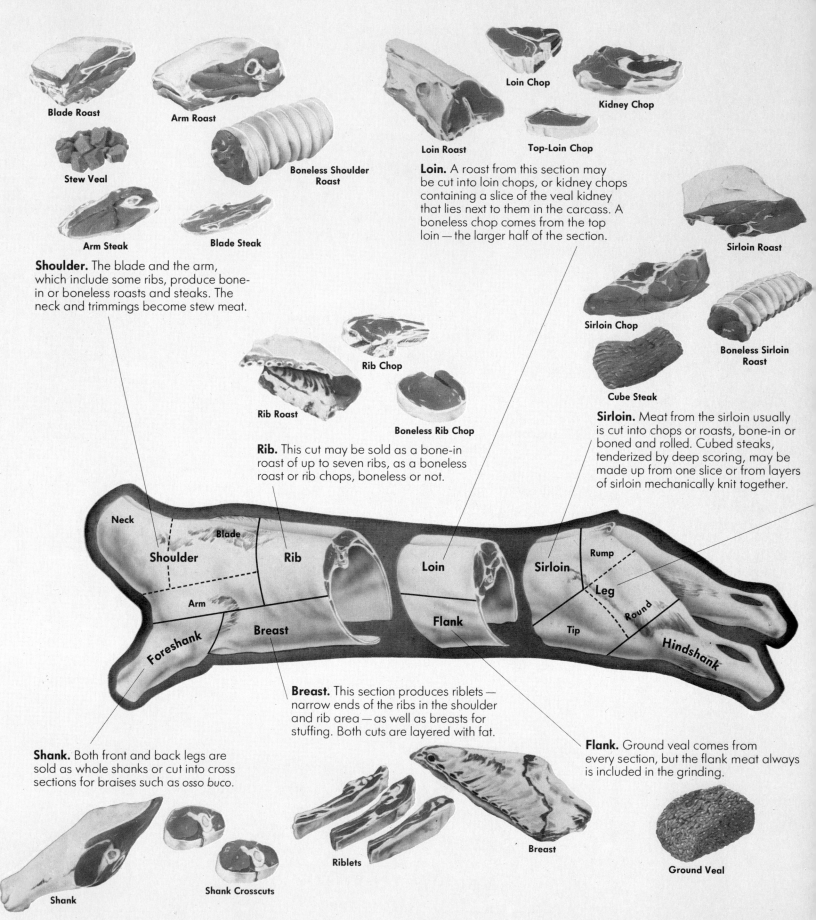

Blade Roast

Arm Roast

Stew Veal

Boneless Shoulder Roast

Arm Steak

Blade Steak

Loin Chop

Kidney Chop

Loin Roast

Top-Loin Chop

Loin. A roast from this section may be cut into loin chops, or kidney chops containing a slice of the veal kidney that lies next to them in the carcass. A boneless chop comes from the top loin — the larger half of the section.

Sirloin Roast

Sirloin Chop

Boneless Sirloin Roast

Cube Steak

Shoulder. The blade and the arm, which include some ribs, produce bone-in or boneless roasts and steaks. The neck and trimmings become stew meat.

Rib Chop

Rib Roast

Boneless Rib Chop

Rib. This cut may be sold as a bone-in roast of up to seven ribs, as a boneless roast or rib chops, boneless or not.

Sirloin. Meat from the sirloin usually is cut into chops or roasts, bone-in or boned and rolled. Cubed steaks, tenderized by deep scoring, may be made up from one slice or from layers of sirloin mechanically knit together.

Neck

Blade

Shoulder

Rib

Arm

Foreshank

Breast

Loin

Flank

Sirloin

Rump

Leg

Tip

Round

Hindshank

Breast. This section produces riblets — narrow ends of the ribs in the shoulder and rib area — as well as breasts for stuffing. Both cuts are layered with fat.

Shank. Both front and back legs are sold as whole shanks or cut into cross sections for braises such as *osso buco*.

Shank

Shank Crosscuts

Riblets

Breast

Flank. Ground veal comes from every section, but the flank meat always is included in the grinding.

Ground Veal

A Guide to Veal Cuts

Retail cuts of veal resemble miniature cuts of beef; a wholesaler, however, may divide the entire carcass into three parts, as shown here, or split it in half either lengthwise or crosswise. The butcher then finishes the cutting.

Because veal comes from young animals with underdeveloped muscles, all the meat is tender. However, since young animals store little of the fat that keeps meat moist during cooking, all veal cuts except the scallops, cutlets and chops must be either larded before roasting or braised to preserve tenderness.

Leg. Rump and round roasts—sold bone-in or boneless — come from the leg. So do steaks, sliced from the round or tip and thin, boneless veal cutlets. The thinnest cutlets, containing only one muscle, are called scallops.

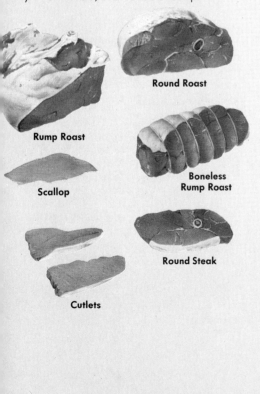

Round Roast

Rump Roast

Boneless Rump Roast

Scallop

Round Steak

Cutlets

Beef Bones: A Dividend of Marrow

Many beef bones contain marrow, but only the heavy leg bones yield a usable quantity for cooking and garnishing foods. A pale, fatty substance, marrow is highly nutritious, and has a smooth texture and a slightly meaty flavor. Marrow may be extracted raw *(below, left)* or cooked *(below, right)*. For easy handling at either stage, the bones should be sawed—by the butcher— into 3- to 4-inch [8- to 10-cm.] sections.

Raw marrow can be chopped up for use in dumplings *(recipe, page 130)*, lean hamburgers *(page 42)* or stuffings *(page 64)*. Precooked marrow can be sliced to form a garnish for steaks *(page 39)* or to serve on toast. Just before serving, poach the slices in salted water for a minute or two until they are heated through and translucent.

Cutting out raw marrow. Loosen the marrow from the bone with a small knife and prize it out whole. Raw marrow can be wrapped and stored in a refrigerator for 2 to 3 days or in a freezer for up to 2 months.

Extracting cooked marrow. Simmer the bones for a few minutes in lightly salted water to cover. When the marrow is heated, drain, then shake each bone gently over a plate until the marrow slides out.

Calf's Foot: A Rich Source of Gelatin

Calf's feet are one of the richest sources of natural gelatin. A single calf's foot will yield enough gelatin to give body to as much as 4 quarts [4 liters] of poaching broth or to make a pint [½ liter] of braising liquid that will turn into firm jelly as it cools.

Although not always readily available at the butcher's, calf's feet usually can be special-ordered. If you cannot get them, use pig's feet *(page 58)*. Two pig's feet will take the place of one calf's foot, and they will not need the disjointing or splitting shown at right.

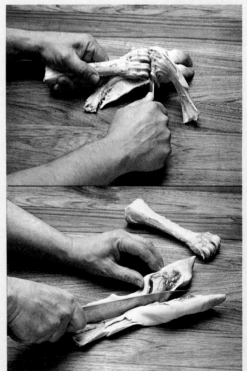

Preparing a calf's foot. Remove the shank bone at the joint if the two are still attached *(right, above)*: the gelatin in the bone is less soluble than that in the foot and would be released at a slower rate. (Keep the shank bone, though, for making stock *(pages 16-17)*, or other broths.) Split the foot in half *(right, below)* so it will fit into the pot easily and surrender its gelatin quickly.

Signs of Quality in Retail Meat

Carefully examine any beef or veal you buy for indications of its quality. Marbling in beef *(above right)* is desirable, but thick layers of fat, like large bones, may add unnecessarily to the price. Color is the most important criterion in judging veal *(below right)* and the best guide to freshness in either beef or veal.

Both meats look purplish when freshly cut; beef turns red and veal turns pink with exposure to air. The plastic wrapping on supermarket meats is porous enough so that chemical action between air and meat continues as it would in unwrapped butcher's meat, first brightening the color of the flesh, then, if the meat sits for a day or so, darkening it.

Besides making visual tests of freshness and quality, check the label or the counter sign to learn what grade of meat your butcher sells. In most cases, it will be "choice," although you can choose between "prime," "choice" and even "good" meat grades if you shop carefully. The top-ranked prime grade, however, is usually snatched up by restaurants, and much meat that might have been graded as good is not graded at all.

Stamps of Approval

Meat markings. The round seal — bearing the abbreviated words, "inspected and passed" and the code number of the processing plant — guarantees that the carcass was disease-free and properly handled during slaughtering. The shield-shaped grading stamp describes the quality of the meat.

The Marbling Test for Beef

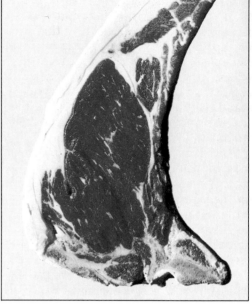

Rich marbling. This rib steak has fine-textured flesh with borders of firm white fat and the heavy streaks of internal fat, or marbling, that characterize prime and choice beef. Marbling bastes meat from within as it cooks, keeping it moist and adding to its flavor.

Scanty marbling. The lack of fat streaks in this rib steak signals beef that is usually graded "good" — and is tougher than a well-marbled piece. Such beef, however, has fewer calories and less saturated fat than higher grades and is often recommended by nutritionists.

The Color Test for Veal

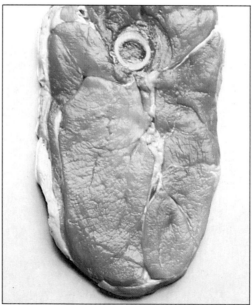

Milk-fed calf. In addition to the pale pink-white color that indicates a milk-based diet, the creamy white fat and fine texture of this veal round steak are clues that the calf from which it came was young — probably only three to four months old — and that its meat will be tender.

Grass-fed calf. Reddish-gray meat and yellow-tinged fat are signs that the calf had a grass diet, and was old enough for muscular activity to have toughened its flesh. Although much of this meat sells as veal, some experts prefer to call it calf meat.

Taking Full Advantage of Large Cuts

Whole carcasses or sides of beef *(pages 8-9)* or large sections often are advertised as bargains for those who have the freezer capacity to take advantage of them. For those who cannot benefit from such offers, it is a good idea to buy smaller, subprimal cuts—such as the tenderloin, standing-rib section and sirloin tip illustrated on this and the following pages—when they are on sale.

Such cuts will have been trimmed of much of their bone and fat when you buy them. The butcher may even be willing to cut them up for you, though probably at some additional cost. But there should be no hesitation about doing the cutting at home; it will allow you to portion your meat exactly as you wish.

All you need to produce roasts and steaks from these subprimal cuts are a cutting board, a sharp butcher knife and a boning knife. After the meat has been trimmed of fat and a thin blue-gray membrane called the silver skin *(right, Steps 1-3)*, the long, club-shaped tenderloin will yield a small roast as well as the tenderloin steaks known in France, depending on their location and thickness, as chateaubriand, filet, filet mignon and *tournedos*. The standing rib *(page 15)* is traditionally served as a bone-in roast, but it may be cut into a boneless roast or sliced into rib-eye steaks. And the inexpensive and tougher sirloin tip *(overleaf)* may be divided into two roasts or into one roast and a set of steaks and kebabs.

However you intend to divide up the meat, be sure first that it is very cold—and therefore firmer and easier to cut than meat at room temperature. When you finish butchering, freeze any of the cuts that you do not plan to cook within a day or so. See the chart on page 15 for the length of time that the meat may be kept in the freezer.

Sectioning a Whole Tenderloin

1 Removing the fat. Place the tenderloin fat side up on a cutting board. With a boning knife, peel off the yellow exterior fat that runs the length of the meat and the layer of white fat beneath it, and discard them. This will expose the membrane, or silver skin. It is easiest to work from the narrow end, or tip, of the tenderloin to the wide end, or butt.

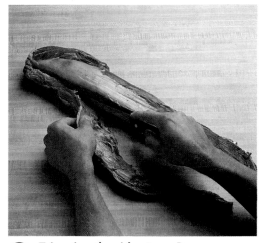

2 Trimming the side strap. Remove the side strap—the fat-encased meat along one side of the tenderloin—by pulling at it with your hand and using a boning knife to sever the connective tissue. Cut the side strap into strips for use in sautés. Cut away the fat on the opposite side of the tenderloin, but do not sever the piece that forks off the butt.

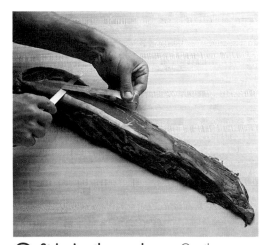

3 Stripping the membrane. Gently slide the blade of the boning knife across the tenderloin into the membrane, or silver skin, so that you catch it on the blade. Then slide the blade down to the tip end, freeing a ribbon of membrane. Hold the ribbon end taut and slice in the opposite direction to free the entire strip of membrane. Use the same method to remove the rest of the membrane.

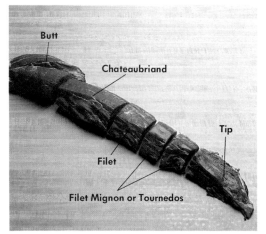

4 Butchering. Using a butcher knife, slice across the grain, or muscle fibers, of the tenderloin about 4 inches [10 cm.] from the butt to make a roast; tie it as described on page 14. Cut off the next 5 or 6 inches [13 or 15 cm.] as a chateaubriand for two. Then cut one or two filet steaks about 2 inches [5 cm.] thick. Next, cut 1- to 2-inch [2½- to 5-cm.] *tournedos* or filet mignon steaks, and slice the tip thinly for sautéeing.

Dividing a Sirloin Tip

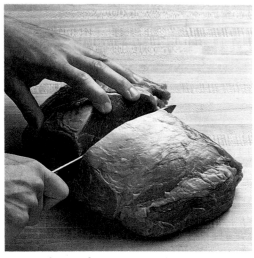

1 **Removing the fat.** Place the sirloin tip on a cutting board, fat side up. Pull away the thick top layer of fat, using a boning knife to sever the connective tissue *(above)*. Be careful not to slice into the meat beneath. Cut out the cap meat at the center of the fat layer and save it for ground beef or kebabs.

2 **Splitting the piece.** Working parallel to the muscle fibers, cut the meat across its width, roughly in the center. The thicker and meatier piece *(top, left)* may be sliced into steaks or used, with or without tying, as a roast. The thinner piece, which is made up of loosely connected muscles, must be tied into a roast, lest it fall apart during cooking.

3 **Tying a roast.** Loop string around one end of the meat — here, the thinner piece — and knot it *(above)*, leaving a long end of string. Draw the long end across the meat and hold a short section flat. Loop the string around the meat and tie it to the short section. Repeat across the roast. Draw the string under the roast and tie it to the first knot.

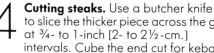

4 **Cutting steaks.** Use a butcher knife to slice the thicker piece across the grain at ¾- to 1-inch [2- to 2½-cm.] intervals. Cube the end cut for kebabs.

5 **The divided sirloin tip.** In addition to steaks, a roast and kebabs, a sirloin tip yields scraps of beef *(far right)* that you can chop or grind for hamburgers.

Butchering a Rib Section

1 **Freeing the bones.** Ask the butcher to saw off the chine bone and cut away the feather bones from the broad end of the standing ribs. Place the meat rib side up on a cutting board. With a butcher knife, slice between the outer tips of the ribs and the meat.

2 **Removing the bones.** Lifting all the ribs in a single unit as you work *(above)*, continue slicing — making successive small cuts between the bones and the meat. Keep the knife blade tilted up toward the ribs to avoid gouging the meat. Reserve the bones for barbecued ribs or for stock.

3 **Trimming the fat.** Turn the meat fat side up. Starting at the thick end, pull at and gradually cut away the layer of fat that covers the meat *(above)*. Then slice off the fat-streaked, tapered end.

4 **Cutting steaks.** The trimmed rib section may be roasted whole as a rib eye or cut into steaks with a butcher knife. A three-rib section such as the one shown here will yield six steaks, each about 1 inch [2½ cm.] thick.

Refrigerating and Freezing Meat

The chart below shows how long different cuts of raw beef and veal may be refrigerated or frozen. Meat stored too long in a refrigerator will spoil. Meat kept in a freezer beyond the recommended period will lose flavor and become flabby as ice crystals formed by meat juices rupture its cells.

Wrap meat for freezer storage in freezer paper and seal it airtight with freezer tape. Label each package and date it in indelible ink. Thaw the meat, in its package, in the refrigerator for the time recommended below. In that way the ice crystals will melt slowly so that the meat tissues reabsorb them.

Type of Meat	Refrigeration Limit at 40° F. [4° C.]	Frozen Storage Limit at 0° F. [-18° C.]	Thawing Time in the Refrigerator
Beef roasts	5-8 days	6-12 months	4-7 hours a pound
Beef steaks	3-5 days	6-12 months	8-12 hours a pound
Veal roasts	5-6 days	6-9 months	4-7 hours a pound
Veal chops	2-4 days	6-9 months	8-12 hours a pound
Ground meat	1-2 days	3-4 months	8-12 hours a pound
Stew meat	2-3 days	6-12 months	8-12 hours a pound

Making and Storing a Basic Veal Stock

Pure veal stock, produced by simmering bones and meat in water with aromatic vegetables *(recipe, page 169)*, has a subtle flavor and smooth body that make it indispensable to certain dishes—and a welcome enrichment to many others. The bony, cartilaginous veal best for making it is relatively inexpensive and so well endowed with natural gelatin that as the stock cools it sets into a clear jelly.

To make stock, choose veal shoulder, breast and leg cuts with plenty of meat left on the bones; add a shank for its high gelatin content. You can retrieve the meat to eat after 1½ hours of cooking.

Veal stock should be cooked slowly and gently to draw all the flavor into the broth. Start the meat and bones in cold water, and allow time for the liquid to come to a boil over low heat—it may take up to an hour. Foamy scum will appear on the surface as proteins in the exposed surfaces of the meat coagulate and are drawn out by the rising temperature.

To achieve stock that is pure in flavor and appearance, the scum must be re-peatedly skimmed off *(below)*. And all fat that appears on the surface in the later stage of cooking must be removed *(box, page 51, and right)*.

The liquid will reduce in quantity during the cooking. To make the most of the lengthy process, pick the largest stockpot you have and prepare more stock than you need for one recipe. Any stock that you do not use immediately can be kept refrigerated safely for a few days or stored in the freezer for several months.

1 Removing scum. After putting the veal pieces into the stockpot, add cold water to cover them by about 1½ inches [4 cm.]. Bring slowly to a boil. With a large spoon or ladle, carefully remove the gray scum that rises to the surface.

2 Retarding the boil. If the liquid boils vigorously, its turbulence will prevent coagulated proteins from forming scum. When boiling starts, add a dash of cold water to keep the liquid just below the boiling point.

3 Finishing the scumming. Remove the scum that continues to form on the liquid's surface. Add more cold water when the liquid returns to a boil. Repeat once or twice until only a white froth appears on the surface *(above)*.

4 Adding vegetables. Put aromatic vegetables into the pot for flavor. Here, carrots, onions—one stuck with cloves—and an unpeeled garlic bulb are used along with a bouquet garni of celery, leek, bay, thyme and parsley.

5 Salting. Season the stock with salt. Because the liquid will reduce in quantity while it simmers, you need relatively little salt. A tablespoon [15 ml.] or so of salt—here, coarse salt—is enough for 5 quarts [5 liters] of stock.

6 Bringing to a boil. After adding the vegetables, and thus lowering the temperature of the liquid, allow the stock to return slowly to a boil. Skim off traces of surface scum that appear. Reduce the heat to a simmer *(above)*.

7 **Adjusting the temperature.** Cover the pot, setting the lid slightly ajar *(above)* to keep steam from building up and raising the temperature of the liquid. Simmer for at least 4 hours, repeatedly checking to be sure that the surface is rippled only by gentle bubbles.

8 **Straining.** Spoon off any fat from the surface. Strain the stock *(above)* through a colander set in a large bowl. When the meat and vegetables are drained, strain the stock again through a sieve lined with a double layer of dampened cheesecloth or muslin.

9 **Degreasing.** Refrigerate the stock for 8 to 12 hours. When the stock is firmly jelled, scrape off the congealed fat *(upper picture)*. Dab away the last particles of fat with a paper towel wrung out in hot water *(lower picture)*.

10 **Storing the stock.** Spoon convenient quantities of the cold jelled stock into small plastic bags *(right)* for freezing. Or store the stock in a covered bowl in the refrigerator. To increase the storage life of refrigerated stock to a week or more, bring it to a boil every few days to kill any bacteria and return it, still hot, to the refrigerator.

1
Roasting
Choosing the Right Temperature

Roast beef has signified feast and celebration since ancient times, when the adventurers whose wanderings are chronicled in Homer's *Odyssey* made heroic meals of stolen oxen on island beaches.

For most of culinary history, beef was seared and cooked over hot coals or before an open fire; today, an oven normally furnishes the necessary dry heat. No cooking method is less complicated; yet no method arouses more controversy about procedure. The arguments revolve around the question of temperature: is beef best roasted at high heat, at low heat or at some combination of the two?

Devotees of high-heat roasting insist that the flavor of their beef is unsurpassed and point to the delectable crust produced by searing in a hot oven. Supporters of gentler cooking methods point out that high heat shrinks meat because it evaporates the juices, and they rest their case on the inevitable tenderness of beef cooked at lower temperatures. Proponents of searing the beef at a high temperature then cooking it with milder heat believe that their method combines the advantages of both the other techniques. In fact, the proper choice of procedure often depends on the cut of meat.

Tender beef cuts *(chart, pages 8-9),* such as rib or tenderloin, and premium-grade beef roasts from the round, are best suited to high-heat roasting, or to a method that starts the roasting at a searing heat and continues it at a more moderate one. This is because the very best beef does not need long, slow cooking to make it perfectly tender; it is naturally so and can stay in a hot oven just long enough for the penetrating heat to bring it to the right degree of doneness. Less tender cuts, such as chuck roasts, or beef grades that are only lightly marbled, profit from gradual, steady cooking that softens their tougher tissues; low-heat roasting will prevent them from drying out before the tenderizing action of the cooking has taken effect.

Veal, too, must be treated gently. Delicate and close-textured, veal should be roasted at no more than moderate heat to cook it through without drying it out. To bring out the mild flavor of the young meat, veal is invariably served well done—though it should never be overcooked—and, like many of the leaner cuts of beef, it needs to be wrapped in additional fat to protect it from the drying heat of the oven.

A well-sharpened knife and a two-pronged fork deal out neat slices of a boneless chuck-eye roast. The even color of each slice is the result of slow roasting at a low temperature, which tenderizes the meat without destroying its natural succulence during its long period in the oven.

19

High Heat to Sear Tender Meat

The principle of high-heat roasting is to sear the outside of the meat and bring the interior to the desired degree of doneness as rapidly as possible. But only a beef cut less than 5 inches [13 cm.] across—eye of round, tenderloin, sirloin tip or rib eye—can be cooked at continuous 500° F. [260° C.] heat without burning. (Even so the oven will be splattered with fat that will smoke at this temperature.)

Larger cuts, such as a rump or the rib roast shown here, require a modification of the method: combining an initial searing at 500° F. with prolonged roasting at a lower temperature of 350° F. [180° C.]. A rib roast with protective shields of bone and fat is ideally suited to combined-heat roasting. The bones, however, necessitate special carving (below)—a simple process if the butcher removes the thick chine bone at the base of the ribs.

Whatever the size of the roast, use the chart on page 22 to estimate its cooking time. Take it from the oven while slightly underdone; the roast will continue cooking—its internal temperature rising as much as 5° F. [3° C.]—as it rests.

1 Preparing the roast. Oil the surfaces lacking natural fat coverings. Season the meat. With a rib roast, as here, place it rib side down in a small pan to keep drippings from spreading and charring. The bones form a natural rack that keeps the meat from stewing in its own juices. With other roasts, use a metal rack to raise the meat in the pan.

2 Roasting the meat. Place the meat in a preheated 500° F. [260° C.] oven. After 15 minutes, reduce the heat to 350° F. [180° C.]. Roast until the meat is done. You can test for doneness by gingerly poking a lean surface (above). If the flesh yields readily, the meat is rare; more resistant meat is medium rare and firm meat is well done (page 29).

5 Cutting the first slice. Stick your carving fork into the porous, wedge-shaped end of the top rib bone. Make horizontal slices ½ inch [1 cm.] thick by cutting from the fatty side toward the bone (above). At the inside edge of the first rib bone, make a vertical slit along the bone to free that slice.

6 Cutting the second slice. When you cut the next horizontal slice, stop carving just short of the now-exposed rib. Then make a vertical cut (above) along the length of the rib as close to the bone as possible. Make the cut the full depth of the rib—approximately 1 inch [3 cm.]—and lift away the slice.

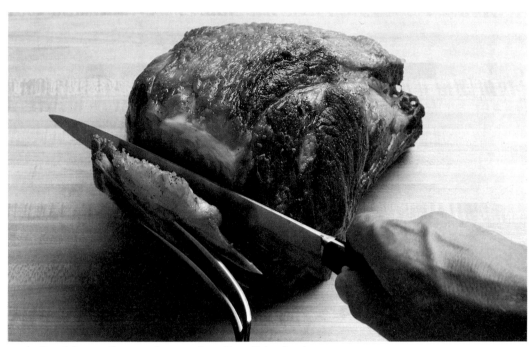

3 **Lifting out the roast.** With a rib roast, stick a large fork into the fatty, tapered end. Using the fork as a lever, tip the meat upward just enough to wedge another fork underneath to brace the roast without piercing it. Using both forks, lift the roast onto a cutting board. For other roasts, slide two firm-bladed spatulas underneath and lift.

4 **Readying a rib roast for carving.** Cut off the feather bones — oval slivers jutting off the rib bones *(above)* — left attached to the backbone so that juices would not escape during the cooking. Remove the excess fat above the tapered end of the roast. Stand the roast on its broader end to rest for 15 to 20 minutes.

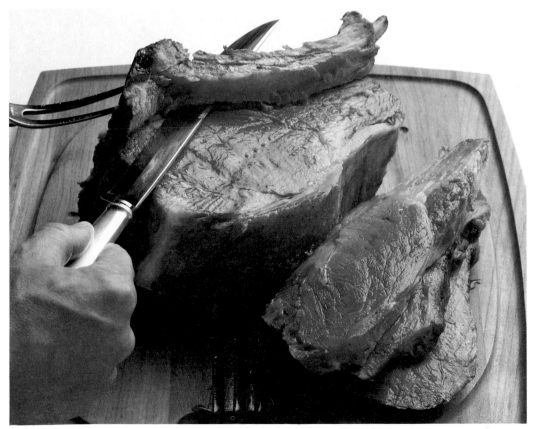

7 **Removing the rib bone.** Cut along the bottom edge of the rib bone *(above)* to free it from the roast. Put aside the bone and continue carving until all your guests are served. A three-rib roast like this one will produce up to 12 ½-inch [1-cm.] slices; figure two generous servings for each rib when you order the roast.

Advantages of Slow Roasting

Roasts of beef cut from the chuck, rump, round or sirloin tip *(pages 8-9)* have excellent flavor and—if prime or choice grade meat—will yield juicy slices when roasted at a steady, moderate heat. And premium roasts, such as standing ribs, shrink much less than they would if fast-roasted at high heat.

Since slow-roasted beef cooks through at an even rate, this method does not achieve the much-admired combination of a crusty brown exterior with an inviting red interior. But you can produce moist, medium-rare beef if you do not insist on a seared surface—or you can achieve a temptingly browned exterior if you do not mind having relatively well-done beef within.

When the cooking time is long, the heat must be mild or the meat will dry out. Some cooks advocate a steady temperature as high as 350° F. [180° C.] and some as low as 250° F. [120° C.] for minimum drying and shrinkage. A temperature of 325° F. [160° C.] is probably a satisfactory average, but with experience you will form your own ideas.

Rump, round and tip roasts generally have very little external fat or marbling. To keep them tender and moist you can bard them—cover them with a sheet of fat—before roasting *(box, below)*. If the barding makes it difficult to test the meat for doneness by pressing it *(page 20)*, a meat thermometer inserted before roasting will ensure that the beef will be done to your taste. The internal temperature of meat is 120° to 125° F. [50° C.] when rare, 135° F. [55° C.] when medium and 150° F. [65° C.] when well done. Suggested cooking times and oven temperatures are given in the chart below.

Let the meat rest for 15 minutes or so after you take it from the oven and before you carve it. This allows the flesh to become firmer, making it easier to carve and retaining more of its juice.

Matching Time and Temperature

The roasting chart below gives appropriate temperatures and approximate cooking times in minutes per pound [½ kg.]. A dash indicates where a process is deemed not advisable: tenderloin is always cooked at high heat and never served well done; chuck is always cooked slowly and is never served rare. Multiply the number of minutes shown by the weight of your roast to find the total time. The times for the combined heat method *(fourth column)* include 15 minutes at 500° F. [260° C.]. Undercooking can be corrected, overcooking cannot: all times shown are minimum. Check doneness before taking the roast from the oven.

ROAST	DONENESS	MINUTES A POUND [½ KG.]		
		500° F. [260° C.]	500° F. [260° C.] 350° F. [180° C.]	325° F. [160° C.]
Standing rib	Rare	—	15	—
	Medium	—	20	25
	Well done	—	25	30
Rib eye	Rare	10	15	—
	Medium	15	20	25
	Well done	20	30	30
Tenderloin	Rare	7	—	—
	Medium	10	—	—
	Well done	—	—	—
Sirloin tip, eye of round	Rare	7	8	—
	Medium	10	10	20
	Well done	—	—	25
Rump	Rare	—	12	—
	Medium	—	15	20
	Well done	—	—	25
Chuck, top round, bottom round	Rare	—	—	—
	Medium	—	—	30
	Well done	—	—	35

Adding Fat to Lean Beef Cuts

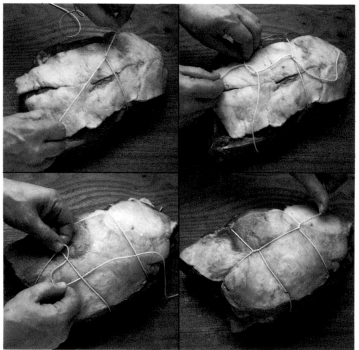

Barding and tying a roast. If you are roasting a lean cut of beef with little external fat of its own, bard it by covering it with a sheet of fat that will help protect it from the drying heat of the oven. Ask the butcher for thinly sliced beef or pork fat, making sure you get flexible sheets cut from the outside cover of a roast, not crumbly kidney fat. Trim the bard to fit over your beef and set it in place. Using a long cotton string, tie a loop crosswise around the meat at one end and then make another loop at the opposite end to secure the fat *(top, left and right)*. Turn the roast over and loop the string lengthwise around the meat *(bottom, left and right)*, finishing with a double knot at the first tie.

1 **Preparing the beef for roasting.** Tie a boned cut, such as the cross-rib roast shown here, into a compact shape that will cook evenly and put it in a roasting pan or ovenproof dish; a rack will prevent the meat from sizzling in its own juices. (A cut with the bone in needs to be tied only if you add extra fat, as shown in the box at left.) Preheat the oven to 325° F. [160° C.] and put the meat in.

2 **Salting the beef.** After the meat has roasted for an hour or so its surface will be firm. Now is the time to salt the beef — salting it beforehand would only draw out the juices, since the slow-roasting method does not initially sear the meat. Turning the roast with a pair of wooden spoons, season all the outside surfaces. Put the beef back in the oven to finish roasting.

3 **Completing the cooking.** Test for doneness by pushing a finger against the center of a lean surface. If you are using a meat thermometer, remember to remove the meat from the oven while its temperature is still about 5° F. [3° C.] below the level you want, since it will go on rising for 15 to 20 minutes. As soon as the beef has been taken out of the oven, snip off the trussing string and remove the barding fat (above).

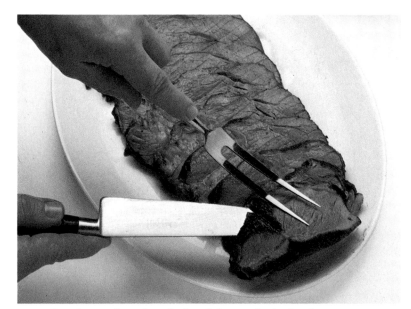

4 **Carving and serving the beef.** Set aside the beef to rest in a warm place. Spoon off the fat from the juices left in the roasting pan, add a little liquid such as water, stock or wine to the meat juices and reduce this gravy over high heat to the consistency you prefer. Slice the beef as thickly or thinly as you prefer and serve it with the hot gravy.

How to Keep Veal from Drying Out

Roasting veal presents a special challenge. The best veal comes from a "milk-fed" animal a few months old. Its pale pink meat, the result of an iron-free diet, has a mild flavor that does not develop unless the veal is cooked through; veal must not be served underdone. At the same time, veal is one of the most delicate meats, and high heat will leave it dry and tough, especially if the cut is small. To produce a veal roast that is fully cooked but still juicy, choose a piece that weighs at least 3 pounds [1½ kg.] and roast it in a moderately slow oven (325° F. [160° C.]) for 25 minutes a pound [½ kg.]. The shape of the cut may affect the timing, however, so check that the veal is ready by the technique described for roast beef on page 20. Veal is finished when its internal temperature reaches 165° F. [75° C.].

Lean veal cuts suitable for roasting—such as rump, loin or the round roast shown here—need extra fat to keep them moist. Smear your veal on all sides with butter before roasting; or, better still, bard it *(right)* with fat that will partly melt and baste the meat as it roasts. Fresh pork fat, which is mild and smooth-textured, is the best material; a calf has not developed enough fat of its own to provide extra barding pieces, and the flavor of beef fat is too strong to be used in barding veal. Cut the barding fat in ½-inch [1-cm.] strips and lay it over the top of the roast in a crisscross pattern. The patterned barding serves to baste the veal and also to decorate it: after roasting, barding strips form a crisp, golden lattice around the meat.

A classic way to add interest to roast veal is to finish it with mustard and cream *(recipe, page 147)*. For the version shown here, coat the meat when it is three-quarters cooked with a mild mustard such as Dijon, which is sharp enough to contrast with the veal, but not so powerful as to overwhelm its flavor. Cream poured over the mustard blends with the pan juices to make a luxurious sauce—and forms an appetizing glaze on the roast's surface as it finishes cooking.

1 **Barding the veal.** Cut strips of pork fat ½ inch [1 cm.] thick and ½ inch wide, and space them over the roast. Here, lengths of pork fat create a lattice design. Enclose the sides of the veal with broader slices of fat *(above)*.

2 **Tying and roasting the veal.** Tie the fat around the meat with cotton string. Place the veal on a rack in a roasting pan and roast the meat in a preheated 325° F. [160° C.] oven until it is three-quarters done and the juices run pink when the meat is pierced. Transfer the roast to a platter, spoon off the fat in the pan and deglaze the pan *(page 38)* with white wine.

3 **Coating the veal.** After removing the string, return the roast to the pan and spread the meat's surface evenly with Dijon mustard *(top)*. Then spoon heavy cream over the mustard coating *(above)*. Return the veal to the oven and increase the heat to 400° F. [200° C.].

4 **Serving the veal.** During the last 30 minutes or so of roasting, baste the veal repeatedly with the pan juices until a rich glaze forms on its surface and the liquid in the roasting pan reduces to a thick sauce. Transfer the veal to a warmed serving platter. Slice the roast thickly and serve immediately with the sauce spooned over it *(above)*.

2
Broiling and Grilling
Methods that Call for Tender Cuts

The perfect steak . . .
. . . and how to carve it
A basic guide for timing
Improving a barbecue
Five degrees of doneness
Adding final sauces

Because broiling is a relatively brief, dry-heat process, it is suitable only for naturally tender meat—not for cuts that need the gentling of long, moist cooking. Steaks, of course, are ideal candidates for broiling. From a large slab of rib steak to a neat slice of tenderloin, from flank to sirloin, from porterhouse to top loin, steaks provide a considerable range of flavor and texture. For further variety, you can broil cubes of beef round or chuck, marinated until tender and then threaded on skewers to make kebabs; ground beef or veal hamburgers; and thick veal cutlets or chops from the veal loin or rib.

Whether you broil these meats on an outdoor grill over hot coals, under an oven broiler or in a pan on the stove, the process remains the same: they should be tossed onto a preheated metal surface and seared rapidly on both sides, then cooked to doneness at a lower heat. Despite what many cookbooks say, searing does not seal in juices. It is the briefness of the process that conserves the natural juices in the meat; the searing produces firm, rich brown crusts and the distinctive flavor and aroma that signal perfectly broiled steak.

Searing is more difficult to achieve when meat is placed under the relatively low heat of a broiler than when dropped on a hot grill over a bed of charcoal or wood embers, or when thrown into a fiery skillet. (Home broilers heat up to only 550° F. [290° C.] compared with the 700° to 1,000° F. [360° to 540° C.] attained by those in restaurants.) But the problem usually can be overcome by preheating the oven broiler with its rack and pan in place, then setting the meat on the hot rack, which will brand the bottom while the flame or broiler unit sears the top—first on one side, then on the other.

After the initial searing, the broiling process becomes a matter of controlling the intensity of the heat—and learning to judge when the meat has reached the right degree of doneness *(pages 28-29)*.

Although purists may prefer to broil meat with nothing more than a little oil rubbed on the meat to keep it from sticking to the hot metal, many variations are possible. You can marinate steaks or kebabs before cooking, baste them with the marinade or a sauce during the broiling, or give extra fragrance to the smoke of the charcoal fire—and extra flavor to the meat—by dropping into it sprigs of fresh herbs.

Branded by a hot charcoal grill, these beef and veal cuts are the best choices for broiling. Clockwise from top left: flank, sirloin, tenderloin, boneless top-loin, porterhouse and rib steaks and a hamburger surround a thick veal chop.

Judging When a Steak Is Ready

As heat penetrates from the surface of a steak to the interior, it progressively alters the protein structure of the meat so that the color changes and some of the moisture evaporates. Such terms as rare, medium and well done are informal definitions for meat at different stages of doneness, from almost raw to completely cooked. These stages are illustrated at right in photographs of similar 2-inch [5-cm.] rump steaks that have been broiled for different lengths of time.

The chart on the opposite page can serve as a guide to approximate times for broiling, but you must adjust the figures to reflect your own experience and cooking method. Plainly, the thickness of a steak is the most important consideration for timing: the thicker the steak, the longer the heat will take to penetrate it. But other factors are important, too: oven broilers and charcoal grills vary greatly in efficiency, and various cuts will cook differently. For example, boneless steaks (listed first on the chart) take a little less time than those that include a bone. Also, if you broil tougher cuts of meat, such as sirloin tip steaks, you must add time to that listed on the chart; they take longer to cook than tender meat, such as tenderloin.

To ensure that a steak is cooked to your taste, begin testing it for doneness two or three minutes before the end of the cooking time listed on the chart. The simplest test is a quick pressing of the meat with your finger—and it has the advantage of not piercing the meat, which would allow juices to escape. The same principle applies as when you test a roast by pressing it: the softer the meat feels, the rarer the steak (box, opposite, below).

Another way to gauge doneness—provided you are broiling over, rather than under, the heat source—is by the color of the meat juices. When red droplets appear on the steak's already seared upper surface while the second side is still cooking, the meat is medium rare. Pink juice means the steak is medium. Clear juices mean well done, but by the time meat reaches the well-done stage, it will be so dry that you must make a tiny slit in it to see the color of the juice.

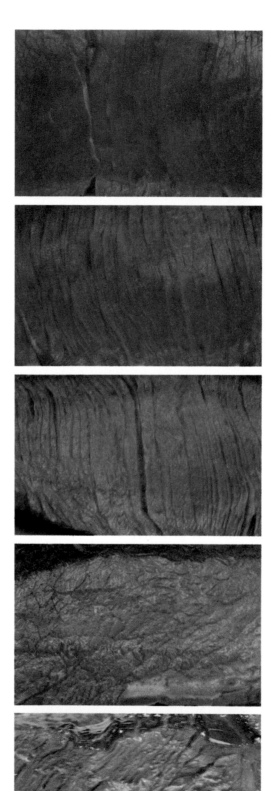

Very rare steak. After searing and a couple of minutes' cooking on each side, the outer surfaces of this 2-inch [5-cm.] steak are browned, but the internal temperature has not risen enough to alter the color.

Rare steak. After about 3 minutes of cooking on each side following the searing, most of the steak is still quite red inside. (Flank steak should always be kept rare; otherwise it will be tough and dry.)

Medium-rare steak. Another minute or two raises the interior temperature of the steak and brings it to the stage shown here: the outer cooked layers are thicker and the center, though still moist, is a paler red than before.

Medium steak. After searing and an additional 10 minutes' cooking time, only the center of the steak retains any pinkness. The outside is richly brown but the meat is still running with pale pink juices.

Well-done steak. After a total cooking time of about 18 minutes, the steak is evenly done throughout. Further cooking can only dry it up. Never serve tenderloin steaks well done: they will be dry and flavorless.

Criteria for Timing

The chart on the right suggests approximate times for broiling beef and veal to the different degrees of doneness illustrated opposite. Where a stage of doneness is not advisable for a particular cut, the chart so indicates with a dash.

The figures shown represent the total cooking times for both sides of the meat, including 1 minute's initial searing at high heat on each side. If your steak or chop varies from the dimensions given here, increase the cooking time for each side by about half a minute for each additional ½ inch [1 cm.] of thickness. The chart is based on the cooking times required for prime or choice grade meat that has been brought to room temperature and cooked, after searing, at a distance of 3 to 5 inches [7 to 13 cm.] above a bed of coals or 1 inch [2½ cm.] below a preheated gas or electric broiler. Pan-broiled meat *(page 32)* cooks in about half the time shown here.

Because there are so many variables in meat cuts and degrees of heat, the figures given here cannot be more than guidelines. For meat done exactly to your taste, check for doneness as described on the opposite page and below.

Type of Meat	Thickness	Total Cooking Time in Minutes				
		Very Rare	Rare	Medium Rare	Medium	Well Done
Beef						
Tenderloin	1 inch [2½ cm.]	3-4	4-5	5-6	6-7	—
	2 inch [5 cm.]	5-6	6-8	8-10	10-12	—
	3 inch [7½ cm.]	7-8	8-10	10-12	12-15	—
Boneless rib, top loin	1 inch [2½ cm.]	4-5	5-6	6-7	7-10	10-12
Flank	1 inch [2½ cm.]	3-4	4-5	5-6	—	—
Rump, top round	1 inch [2½ cm.]	4-5	5-6	6-7	7-10	10-15
	2 inch [5 cm.]	6-7	7-8	8-9	9-12	12-18
Hamburger	1 inch [2½ cm.]	2-3	3-6	6-10	10-12	—
	2 inch [5 cm.]	4-5	5-8	8-12	12-14	—
Porterhouse, T-bone, bone-in top loin	1 inch [2½ cm.]	4-6	6-7	7-10	10-13	13-16
	2 inch [5 cm.]	6-8	8-9	9-12	12-15	15-18
Sirloin	1 inch [2½ cm.]	5-6	6-8	8-12	12-16	16-22
	2 inch [5 cm.]	7-8	8-10	10-14	14-18	18-25
Bone-in rib	1 inch [2½ cm.]	8-11	11-12	12-16	16-20	20-26
Veal						
Chop, cutlet	1 inch [2½ cm.]	—	—	—	—	12-15

A Handy Test for Doneness

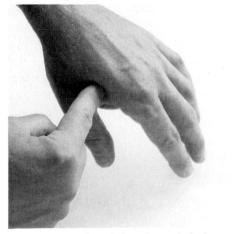

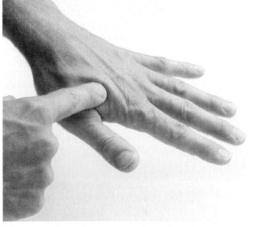

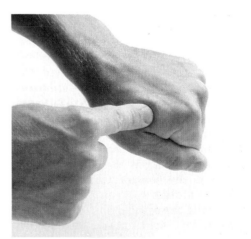

Rare. Let your hand dangle and shake it gently to relax it. Touch the side of your hand between thumb and index finger *(above)*. The muscle will feel like rare meat — soft and wobbly, yielding to the slightest pressure.

Medium. Stretch out your hand and tense your fingers. Touch the muscle again *(above)* and you will feel the springy firmness that develops as meat cooks. Medium steaks have the same resistance.

Well done. Now ball your hand into a fist and touch the muscle *(above)*. It should feel hard and unyielding, with all springiness gone. When the surface of a steak feels the same way, the meat is well done.

Choose: Oven, Barbecue or Pan

You can broil a steak in a matter of minutes, but the best results require some preliminary planning—to prepare both meat and heat source.

Whether you are pan broiling, oven broiling or barbecuing outdoors, always give the raw meat time to reach room temperature so that it will cook evenly.

Trim away excess fat—good steaks have enough streaky marbling to keep them tender while they are broiling. Oil the meat very lightly to ensure that it does not stick to the grill or pan and to help it brown well. Never season a steak until it has been seared; salt draws out juices and retards browning.

Searing forms an appetizing crust on the meat, but must be done quickly, which means that you should fire up your heat source well in advance. Preheating a skillet for pan broiling requires only a few minutes. Broilers should be heated with their racks in place so that the steak sears as quickly as possible.

Oven broilers—electric or gas—need about 15 minutes to reach the proper temperature. Outdoor gas cookers take about 10 minutes to warm up; electric patio units about 25 minutes. Charcoal and wood fires take at least a half hour to burn down to the ash-covered coals needed for broiling.

When your preparations are complete, follow the directions for different broiling methods on this and the following pages. Never broil steaks thinner than 1 inch [2½ cm.]; the interiors tend to cook through before the meat is seared. Steaks up to 1½ inches [4 cm.] thick can be broiled an inch below the heat of an oven broiler or about 3 inches [8 cm.] above a charcoal grill.

Bigger steaks, which may be up to 3 inches [7 to 8 cm.] thick, can be seared at the same distance, but should be moved farther from the heat or cooked at a reduced heat in order to keep the outsides from burning while the centers cook to your taste. Any steak that you pan broil should be carefully watched to keep from overcooking; pan broiling will cook meat twice as quickly as the other methods. But you pay a price for speed: pan broiling creates a lot of smoke, making an exhaust fan a must. The chart on page 29 provides timing for different cuts.

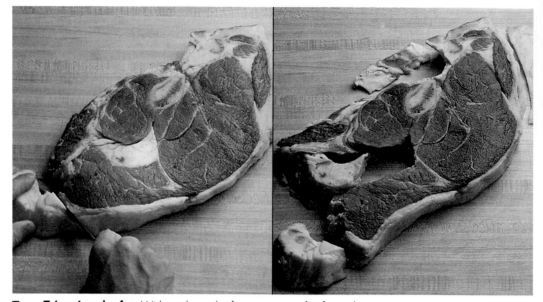

1 **Trimming the fat.** With a sharp knife, cut excess fat from the edges of the steak *(above)* until a strip only ¼ inch [6 mm.] thick remains. Be careful not to cut through the fat into the interior of the meat; this would cause juices to escape from the edges during cooking. Then cut any large, solid pieces of fat from the inside of the steak; they would melt during cooking and burn on a skillet, giving the meat a charred taste. In oven broilers and charcoal grills, melted fat close to open flames can cause flare-ups.

2 **Skewering the meat.** Push skewers through the steak *(above)* to close any gaps left by the removal of large pieces of fat. Wooden skewers are better than metal ones: wood will not conduct heat into the interior of the meat. They require soaking in water for at least 10 minutes ahead of time to keep them from burning.

3 **Oiling.** If you are oven broiling or barbecuing, coat a platter that is large enough to hold the steak with a very thin film of oil. Dry the steak thoroughly and put it flat on the platter. Then put a few drops of oil on top of the meat and spread them across the surface with your fingers *(above)*.

The Oven: Convenience in the Kitchen

1 **Searing the steak.** Preheat the broiler to its highest setting, with the broiler pan rack about 3 inches [8 cm.] from the heat source if your steak is no more than 1½ inches [4 cm.] thick. For a thicker steak, set the rack 4 inches [10 cm.] from the heat. Put the oiled steak on the preheated broiler rack and wait for the upper surface of the meat to turn brown, indicating that it is seared.

2 **Turning the meat.** Season the seared surface with salt and pepper. Then turn over the steak, using tongs (above) or, if the steak is small enough to lift easily, a fork inserted into the fatty border. But be sure to avoid piercing the meat and allowing its juices to escape. When the second side of the steak is seared, season it, too.

3 **Final cooking.** If the steak is as thick as the 1½-inch [4-cm.] sirloin shown here, lower the rack 2 inches [5 cm.] to finish cooking the meat. Thinner steaks will be ready almost immediately after searing; if not, cook them just a moment more without adjusting the rack.

The Barbecue: Fair-Weather Feasting

1 **Searing the steaks.** Spread the red-hot charcoal evenly over the bottom of the grill pan, knocking off the ash that covers it. If the grill is adjustable, position it 3 inches [8 cm.] above the coals. Place the oiled steaks on the grill. When small red beads of juice appear on the top surface (above), turn the steaks with long-handled tongs and season the seared sides.

2 **Cooking the steaks.** Sear the steaks on the second side until juice rises to the surface again — about 2 minutes. Reduce the heat by closing the grill dampers, by spreading the coals farther apart or by raising the grill so that it is 5 inches [13 cm.] above the coals. Continue grilling until the steaks are done to your taste. Test for doneness as described on page 29. Remove the steaks and salt and pepper the unseasoned sides.

The Skillet: Speedy But Smoky

1 Oiling the meat. If the steak has a bone, remove it so that the meat will lie flat in the pan. Dry both sides with paper towels. Brush one side of the steak — here a flank cut — with a film of cooking or salad oil *(above).* Leave the second side unoiled so that when you sear the first side, beads of red juice will rise readily to the exposed surface.

2 Searing the first side. Preheat a large, heavy skillet until you can feel heat radiating from the bottom when you pass your hand slowly above it. Place the steak in the skillet, oiled side down, and press the edges flat so that no part of the meat will go unseared.

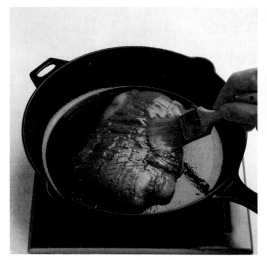

3 Oiling the second side. Sear the steak over high heat until drops of juice appear on top, signaling that the bottom side of the steak is browned and the meat is ready to turn. Immediately brush the top with a thin film of oil.

4 Turning the steak. If any of the steak's fat has melted in the pan, pour it off to keep the steak from frying. Then turn the steak with tongs *(above)* to sear the newly oiled side.

5 Final cooking. After the second side browns, reduce the heat. When the meat is almost done, turn the steak again *(right)* to ensure even browning. Season the surface after the last turning, then test for doneness *(page 29).*

Carving — Not Just Cutting — a Steak

When well executed, carving a steak ensures that everyone gets the tenderest portion possible. To make the task easy, you need a firm work surface, plenty of elbow room, a sharp knife and a two-pronged fork to hold the meat. An incised carving board, like the one below, keeps the meat steady, and collects juice you can spoon over each serving.

The carving techniques vary with the texture and structure of a steak. T-bone, sirloin or porterhouse *(top row, below)* have a nugget of tenderloin, separated from the rest of the meat by a bone. To include some tenderloin with each portion, remove the bone and slice across the two sections with one stroke.

For tougher steaks, such as round, rump or flank *(bottom row, below)*, carving across the grain of the meat will result in short, chewable bits. And the thinner the slice, the more tender the meat will seem. If you angle the knife as you carve to cut diagonally, even thin steaks can be made to yield broad slices.

Carving porterhouse steak. Steady the steak on the carving board with the back of the tines of a carving fork. Using a well-sharpened knife, separate the meat from the T-shaped bone between the tenderloin section, shown at the left side of the porterhouse in the pictures above, and the rest of the steak. Carve along its edges, then lift the bone out. Make two or more cuts at roughly equal intervals across both sections of steak *(above right)* to produce equal portions, each having a slice of tenderloin.

Carving flank steak. Press the back of the tines of a carving fork onto the thick end of the steak to hold it firmly. To begin the first cut, lay the knife blade almost flat against the steak about a third of the distance from the tapered end. Carve at a slight diagonal to the end *(above left)* and shave off a slice about ⅛ inch [3 mm.] thick. Begin each successive cut at about ⅛-inch intervals *(above right)*. The first and last slices will be somewhat wedge-shaped, but all those in between will be of uniform thickness.

Kebabs: The Virtues of Trimming and Marinating

Kebabs are a Middle Eastern speciality that has been enthusiastically adopted throughout the world. The most popular version consists of cubes of meat that are marinated, skewered and then grilled over hot coals or broiled in the oven. The marinade in the recipe on page 95 contains wine, which tenderizes the meat, so you need not use costly cuts of beef. The chuck steak used here gives excellent results, as does round steak, provided you trim the meat scrupulously.

To complement the meat and help complete the meal, you can alternate vegetables with the meat on the skewers. Middle Eastern cooks often use pieces of parboiled peppers, and raw tomatoes and onions. Other possibilities are the mushrooms, bay leaves and bacon added here.

1 Removing the excess fat. To remove the layer of external fat from chuck or round steak, slice away the thin, tough membrane that lies between the fat tissue and the meat, pulling the fat away from the meat as you cut.

2 Trimming the meat. Pare away any membrane from the surface and cut the meat into 1½-inch [4-cm.] cubes, trimming them of any fat or gristle. Marinate the cubes in oil, wine and herbs for 2 or 3 hours at room temperature or overnight in a refrigerator.

3 Preparing the vegetables. Cut all vegetables into chunky sizes and shapes that will fit neatly on the skewer. But be sure to quarter the onions by cutting them vertically (above). Do not slice them horizontally or they will fall into rings when put on the skewer.

4 Assembling the kebabs. Use square or flat-bladed skewers; on round skewers, kebabs slip when they are turned and may cook unevenly. Thread the skewers with the meat and vegetables arranged alternately. Then lay the skewers in a flat dish and pour the reserved marinade over the kebabs.

5 Cooking and serving kebabs. Grill or broil them for 10 to 15 minutes, rotating the skewers a quarter turn at regular intervals. Baste frequently with the marinade. Use a fork to slide the kebabs off the skewers and onto the serving plates (right).

Two Classic Accompaniments

Beef served hot from a grill, with the taste of the wood embers on its surface, needs no more seasoning than salt, pepper and butter. But you may also present the meat—whether grilled outdoors or broiled in the kitchen—with béarnaise sauce or an equally classic accompaniment known as a compound butter: a blend of softened, unsalted butter with herbs or other ingredients.

Béarnaise sauce, like hollandaise, is a smooth emulsion of egg yolks and butter. What gives it a piquant taste is the addition of tarragon, shallots and chervil cooked in white wine and vinegar (*recipe, page 168*).

Compound butters may incorporate any of a variety of ingredients, depending on your taste. Among the possibilities are chopped parsley with lemon juice, mustard, pounded garlic cloves or anchovy fillets, grated horseradish root, puréed almonds or blanched tarragon leaves. Demonstrated below is a *beurre marchand de vins* ("wine merchant butter") that includes shallots precooked in red wine (*recipe, page 168*).

1 **Starting a béarnaise sauce.** In an earthenware pot over a fireproof pad or in a double boiler, simmer finely chopped shallots, tarragon, chervil sprigs and a chili in white wine and vinegar until the mixture is syrupy—about 15 minutes. Remove the seasonings.

2 **Adding eggs and butter.** Reduce the heat to low. Whisk egg yolks into the liquid *(above)*. Cut butter into bits and add them gradually, whisking. If the sauce threatens to curdle, take it off the heat; mix in a teaspoon [5 ml.] of ice water before continuing.

3 **Finishing the sauce.** Whisk the sauce until it is as thick as heavy cream. Add finely chopped tarragon and chervil leaves. Then season the sauce with salt and pepper. If you use a double boiler, the sauce can be kept for up to an hour over the warm water.

1 **Starting the butter.** Simmer finely chopped shallots in red wine for about 30 minutes until they are soft and the liquid is reduced by two thirds. Cool, then add the mixture to softened cubes of butter. Add chopped parsley, salt and pepper, and blend with a whisk.

2 **Blending the ingredients.** Work the butter and seasonings together to combine them. You will have to stir and press down on the cubed butter slowly at first, but as the mixture becomes softer you can start to beat it firmly with the whisk.

3 **Completing the butter.** Continue to whisk until the seasonings are evenly distributed throughout the butter and the mixture has a firm, creamy consistency. Do not refrigerate the butter before serving; it should be soft enough to spoon onto a steak.

Frying
A Variety of Attractive Options

Seasoned with freshly ground black pepper, pan-fried boneless top-loin steaks lie ready for serving. The meat juices that remain in the pan after the excess fat is discarded will become the base of a simple sauce when whisked with water, wine or stock.

Frying always means cooking in hot oil or fat, but the quantity of fat employed can vary widely. A steak may be sizzled in a heavy pan that has been filmed with rendered beef fat; veal scallops may be sautéed gently in a generous swirl of butter; breaded cutlets may be dropped into deep, hot oil and fried until their coatings are crisp and golden.

Although hot fat is, of course, a liquid, frying is technically a "dry" cooking method, since no part is played by water, wine, beer, stock or other moisteners. Just as in grilling, only tender, quick-cooking cuts of beef and veal are suitable because frying usually requires high heat, at least in the first stage, and is a relatively brief process. Overfrying can make even the finest cuts of meat stringy and leathery.

In deep frying, the oil or fat itself is the cooking medium. Veal, sliced thin enough for the heat to penetrate rapidly and protected with an outer coating, is perfect for the method. But veal is always cooked until well done, while most people prefer beef in its rare stage. So beef is better suited to pan frying, where the temperature can be adapted to the thickness and size of the cut.

In pan frying, the meat is first seared by contact with the coated surface of a preheated pan, then cooked over reduced heat until done. The fat used to coat the pan—lard, beef fat, butter or oil—prevents the meat from sticking to the metal and adds flavor. The method works admirably for steaks and hamburgers, and is the ideal way to prepare the delicate slices from the veal leg called scallops. In a pan, with plenty of butter to moisten and protect them, such slices can cook gently, retaining their juiciness. With the veal, as with the beef, pan frying yields a valuable dividend by releasing meat juices into the pan; these can be readily transformed into a sauce *(page 38)*.

In all frying, the size of the pan is crucial. For deep frying there must be plenty of room and plenty of oil in the pan, so that when the food is put in to fry it does not lower the temperature of the oil too much. In pan frying, however, the pan must be of a size that will hold the meat snugly, but not too snugly. Crowding traps meat juices in the bottom of the pan and the meat stews instead of searing. Leaving the pan half-empty, on the other hand, allows the fat and juices to burn in the areas where the meat does not cover them.

A Bonus of Sauces from Steaks

Whatever kind of steak you pan fry, the basic procedure is the same: start with a very hot pan lightly coated with fat or oil; sear the meat on each side to brown the outside surfaces; then lower the heat to finish the cooking.

Simple though this method is, perfect results depend on attention to details. Before the beef is cooked it should be at room temperature; otherwise, the outside may be overdone before the center has finished cooking. The meat surfaces should be patted dry, since moisture will delay searing and make the meat brown

unevenly. Finally, the pan must be a heavy one that you can get hot enough to make the steak sizzle when you put it in.

The cooking time will depend on the steak's thickness and on the degree of doneness you prefer. As a guide, a 1¼-inch [3-cm.] cut is cooked rare by the time both sides have been seared—about 4 minutes in all. Frying each side for another 1½ to 2 minutes produces a medium steak, and a total cooking time of 9 to 10 minutes results in a well-done steak.

To test for doneness, press the meat with your finger as explained on page 29. Or check it visually after you have seared

one side of the meat and turned it to sear the other: at the moment the first pearl of red juice appears on the seared surface, the beef is medium rare. After longer cooking, pierce the steak with a knife tip: if the juices that flow out are light pink, it is medium; if clear, it is well done.

Fried steaks can be enhanced with a sauce made from the pan juices (box, below). For a further refinement, sauté chopped shallots in the pan before deglazing it with red wine (top, opposite) or give the steaks a peppery coating before frying (bottom, opposite).

Deglazing: The Treasure Left in the Pan

When you pan fry either beef or veal, the heat makes juices ooze from the meat. In the hot pan, moisture evaporates from these juices, leaving a residue of solid protein deposits that coagulate on the pan as the frying continues. You can take advantage of this resource of flavor by diluting the residue with liquid over heat to make a sauce—a process called deglazing.

The deglazed juices usually form the

foundation of a sauce to dress a pan-fried steak or a veal scallop. But the deglazing process is not limited to pan frying. Braised meats are often given a preliminary browning in a frying pan, and the pan deposits left behind can be deglazed as an enrichment for the braising liquid (pages 52 and 53). During roasting, too, meat juices that form a glaze in the bottom of the pan are the natural starting point for a gravy.

If you want to preserve the meat flavor, deglaze with water or, for extra

richness, with stock. Wine is a frequent deglazing liquid and it lends its flavor to a pan sauce, gravy or braising liquid. Be sure, however, to boil a wine-based mixture intensely for a few minutes to evaporate the alcohol. Other deglazing liquids suit different dishes. Lemon juice, for example, contributes a piquant edge to a sauce for pan-fried veal (pages 44-45), and cream smooths the bite of a pepper-crusted beefsteak (opposite).

Incorporating pan deposits. Carefully pour off the fat from the pan, stopping before any darker meat juices escape. Return the pan to high heat and immediately pour in a generous splash of liquid — here, veal stock (left). Stir the liquid as it comes to a boil, scraping up the pan deposits with a wooden spatula to incorporate them into the liquid. To make a sauce or gravy, use a beurre manié — equal parts of butter and flour kneaded together — to thicken the liquid (center). Whisking vigorously, add the beurre manié bit by bit, boiling each addition for one minute until the sauce reaches a light, syrupy consistency (right).

A Wine-and-Marrow Topping

1 **Frying the steaks.** Heat the thin layer of fat or oil in the frying pan. When it is very hot, sear the steaks — here, boneless top loin — for about 2 minutes on each side. Turn them with tongs or use a fork, as here, carefully inserting it into an outside edge. Reduce the heat and cook to the desired doneness.

2 **Frying the shallots.** Remove the steaks to a warmed platter. Pour any excess fat or oil from the pan, leaving only a thin film. Evenly distribute the shallots — finely chopped so they will cook quickly — in the pan (above). Cook over moderate heat, stirring occasionally, for a minute or so until they are soft but not colored.

3 **Finishing the dish.** Deglaze the pan with red wine. Simmer to reduce the liquid to the consistency of a thin sauce. The steaks may also be garnished with bone marrow that has been pried out of the bone (page 11), then sliced and poached in salted water until translucent. Put a slice on each steak and then pour on the sauce.

A Peppery Crust and a Creamy Coating

1 **Peppering the steaks.** Half an hour before cooking, crush the coating mixture — allspice berries and peppercorns, here — with the edge of the bottom of a heavy skillet. Spread out the spices and press the steak — boneless top loin, here — onto the spices (above) to encrust the bottom of the steak; repeat on the other side.

2 **Frying the steaks.** Heat the fat or oil in the frying pan. When it is hot, sear the steaks for a minute or two on each side. To turn the meat, use a fork inserted at the side so as not to dislodge the pepper. Reduce the heat and continue cooking, without turning, until the steaks are done to your taste.

3 **Making a sauce.** Pepper steaks may be served with the crust left on, or scraped off for a less spicy taste. They can also be dressed with a contrasting sauce — here, Cognac and cream (recipe, page 98). Deglaze the pan with Cognac, boiling it to evaporate the alcohol. Then add cream and reduce the liquids. Pour the sauce over the steaks.

How to Chop Meat by Hand—and Why

Ground beef or veal is an old standby of many popular dishes, but it cannot begin to match meat that has been chopped by hand. The texture alone makes the extra effort involved worthwhile and elevates any dish made from such meat. Hamburgers, for example, are unusually delicious and juicy when the beef has been coarsely chopped and cooked, preferably rare, with the same respect you would accord a prime steak. For meat loaves and meatballs, which need to cook longer, a small proportion of fat chopped with the meat will flavor the beef or veal and help keep it moist while it cooks.

Tartar steak *(page 80)* is another dish that benefits when the beef is hand-chopped. By selecting the piece of beef yourself and making sure that it is free of all fat and gristle, you control quality. And by chopping it as close to serving time as possible—ideally within minutes—you guarantee the freshness and flavor of the dish.

Chopping your own meat has other advantages. You can control the proportion of fat to lean, and you can pick the beef or veal that is the best buy in terms of flavor, economy and the recipe you have chosen. Careful trimming and chopping will tenderize even inexpensive cuts.

The best equipment for chopping is a pair of heavy chef's knives of the same length and weight. With two matched knives, you can easily achieve a chopping rhythm that will permit the heft of the cutlery to do most of the work. If you lack such knives, do not try to improvise; a single knife will do the job better than two that are out of balance. But whether you use two knives or one, make sure each blade has a scimitar-sharp edge; a dull edge will mash the meat into pulp instead of cutting it cleanly.

To make quicker work of chopping meat, you can use an electric food processor. Trim the meat as shown at right, cube it and process it in small batches, controlling the process by turning the machine on and off rapidly as it chops to avoid reducing the meat to purée. A home food grinder, although useful for many chores, is not recommended; it can mash and mangle meat fibers so that their juice is lost.

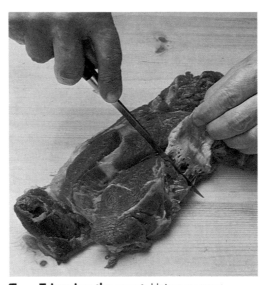

1 **Trimming the meat.** Using a very sharp knife, cut the meat away from the bone, if any. Then divide the meat along the muscle seams into lean sections, paring away all sinewy tissue. The cut being trimmed here is chuck—a good choice for hamburgers or tartar steak, since its flavor is excellent and chopping tenderizes it.

2 **Cubing.** Trim off every trace of fat and membrane from the meat *(above)*, and cut the trimmed sections of lean meat into fairly small cubes. The chopping will proceed more swiftly if you start with meat pieces that are roughly uniform in size.

3 **Chopping.** Spread the cubed meat in a single layer *(above, left)* and chop it with a matched pair of heavy, sharp chef's knives, moving them alternately and rhythmically, as if beating a drum. Work with a loose-wristed action, holding the knives more or less parallel with a relaxed grip and letting their weight do most of

Assessing the Fattiness of Ground Beef

When you buy commercially ground beef, the key to quality is fat content. Some stores guide you by labeling beef as regular, lean or very lean. Others label different grades as ground round (which contains about 15 per cent fat), ground sirloin (about 20 per cent) and ground chuck (about 22 per cent).

But terms and definitions tend to vary widely from market to market so examine the meat itself to gauge the amount of white fat embedded in the lean red meat. The lighter the color of ground meat, the more fat it contains and the more your hamburgers or meat loaves will shrink in cooking.

Regular. A patty like the one above contains about 25 per cent fat. An inexpensive choice for meat loaves, this ground beef calls for draining after cooking.

Lean. Specks of fat visible in this patty add up to about 15 per cent of its total weight. The fat binds the lean together so that meatballs or hamburgers hold their shape.

Very lean. Less than 10 per cent of this patty is fat, but you may have to ask your butcher to grind it specially for you from already lean cuts of beef in his stock.

the work for you. As the chopping progresses the pieces will begin to spread out. Stop from time to time and use one of the knife blades to flip the edges of the pile back into the center, turning the mass over each time. This helps to achieve a consistent texture. Continue chopping until the texture is as fine as you wish.

Dressing Up the Plain Hamburger

According to one of many accounts, the hamburger began in Baltic Russia as a dish of raw, chopped beef. It was brought to Hamburg and introduced in cooked form by German traders. German immigrants supposedly brought it to the United States in the 19th Century, and by the 20th Century the grilled ground-beef patty—served in a bun—had become as much a symbol of America as the cowboy. Although the hamburger has suffered rough treatment at the hands of snack-bar cooks, at its best—made from good quality beef, cooked juicily rare—it can compare in taste with steak.

A lean cut of beef, such as round, is ideal for hamburgers. The less expensive cuts—chuck, for example, or flank if carefully trimmed of all of its connective tissue—are also excellent; they have a good flavor and, when suitably ground, cannot be tough. For a really juicy hamburger, with the kind of texture you prefer, chop the meat by hand, as explained on the previous pages.

Many people like the flavor and moistness imparted to hamburgers by the inclusion of some fat with the meat *(page 41)*. But undercooked beef fat is hard to digest; so if you like rare hamburgers, use lean meat and mix it with a little butter or—even better—raw beef marrow *(page 11)*. Season the mixture before cooking, but lightly; you want to bring out the flavor of the meat, not conceal it. Shape the patties gently; a loosely formed hamburger cooks more evenly and has a more appetizing texture than a compact patty, but the meat mixture must be firm enough to hold together while it cooks.

The hamburger patty can actually be grilled, broiled or fried. Grilling—especially over charcoal or wood embers—adds flavor, but the meat needs skillful treatment so that it does not dry out; the cut edges of the patty can exude a lot of moisture unless the hamburger is effectively seared *(page 27)*. Broiling *(page 31)* requires similar careful searing. In pan frying, any juices that the hamburger yields remain in the pan and can be recaptured by deglazing *(page 38)*, then used for a sauce.

Fry the hamburger just as you would a steak *(page 39)*. Turn it once, using a spatula to prevent the meat from crumbling. When cooked, the hamburger can be served with any of the sauces or garnishes used for steak, and even patties that are destined for the traditional bun may profit from a sauce made with the deglazed pan juices.

1 **Seasoning the beef.** Using your fingers, lightly toss the ground meat together with whatever seasonings you are using. Chopped fresh dill is shown above, but you can substitute any other fresh or dried herb that you prefer, as well as grated cheese, fried onion or minced capers.

2 **Shaping the patties.** Divide the meat into balls. Flatten each ball, but do not squash it. For a rare hamburger, make the patty as thick as 2 inches [5 cm.]; for a well-cooked hamburger, scale down the thickness to no less than 1 inch [2½ cm.] so the outside does not dry out before the middle is done.

3 **Searing the hamburgers.** Heat a film of oil in a frying pan set over high heat. When the oil is hot, add the patties and fry them for 3 to 5 minutes. Turn over each one and sear the second side. Lower the heat and finish cooking to your taste.

4 **Deglazing the pan.** Serve the hamburgers — on toasted French bread, as here, or on buns, if you like. Pour off excess fat from the pan, add a dash of water or wine and stir briskly to dissolve the juices. Pour the sauce over the hamburgers *(right)*.

Adding a Surprise Stuffing

One way to vary hamburgers is by mixing the raw ground beef with other ingredients. Use fresh herbs, such as the dill shown on the opposite page, or try fresh or dried marjoram, chervil, thyme or even mint. Another way to lend variety is to conceal a stuffing of contrasting texture and flavor inside the hamburger patty *(right)*.

A nugget of soft cheese is a good basis for a hamburger stuffing. The Roquefort cheese shown here has a sharp enough flavor of its own; but you might prefer Cheddar, or farmer or cottage cheese, accented with capers or chopped anchovies, chives, dill or olives. The possibilities for improvisation are almost limitless. Try enclosing a pocket of chopped cooked vegetables, such as mushrooms or buttered carrots, in the hamburger. To produce a distinct contrast in texture, add a crunchy stuffing: one good combination is a mixture of chopped nuts with parsley and onions.

1 **Filling the patties.** To stuff a hamburger, simply press a cavity in the middle of it with your thumb, add a small ball of whatever filling you have chosen and close the meat around it with your fingers. Shape the patty carefully and cook it in the usual way.

2 **Finishing touches.** In this hamburger, the Roquefort cheese center comes as a creamy contrast to the ground beef. You could use a harder cheese such as Cheddar, sliced or grated, for a different flavor, or you could add chopped chives or scallions, mashed together with a soft cheese.

Veal Scallops with a Butter Sauce

Veal is never served rare, so the temperatures and timings for pan frying it are determined only by the thickness of the meat. Chops that are cut ¾ inch [2 cm.] thick or more must be briefly seared over high heat, then cooked very slowly to prevent the outside from becoming tough and dry before the inside is ready. But thinly sliced veal scallops or boneless cutlets, rarely more than ½ inch [1 cm.] thick, are best fried briefly over moderate heat as shown here, so that the veal will cook through before it has time to toughen or lose its moisture.

Both thick and thin cuts of veal should be fried in a pan just large enough to hold them without overcrowding; wide gaps between the pieces may cause the fat to burn, while overlapping meat will not sear properly. And both kinds of cuts should be fried in enough butter or oil—or a mixture of the two—to cover the bottom of the pan generously. Butter's fine flavor suits veal well, and butter will not burn at the moderate temperatures suitable for frying this meat.

Before frying, the veal must be completely dry. After it is done, it can be set aside while the pan is deglazed (page 38) to take up the rich, meaty deposits.

Here, white wine and lemon juice are used for the deglazing liquid, and butter thickens the sauce; but you could finish the dish with stock, cream or one of the sauces described in the box at far right.

Pounding Veal: Pro and Con

Many cooks pound veal cutlets or scallops before cooking them, in order to break down the muscle fibers, thereby tenderizing the meat. But heavy-handed pounding will render juicy veal dry and lifeless.

Only two circumstances may justify vigorous pounding. In recipes such as the *olivette di vitello alla pesarese* on page 149, where the scallops enclose a bulky filling, you may have to pound the meat to stretch it. And if the scallops you unwrap at home do not seem as tender as they did at the butcher's, pounding helps make the best of a bad situation. Otherwise, well-cut veal needs no such treatment.

Even the best veal, however, will benefit from a gentle pressing to smooth it out, thus ensuring that each piece measures about ¼ inch [6 mm.] in thickness, lies flat in the pan and cooks evenly. Before pressing scallops, trim off any fibrous connective tissue; it would shrink on contact with the hot fat and cause the meat to curl up. Place the slices on a chopping board and flatten each one by pressing it down with the flat of a knife, a meat mallet or even the heel of your hand.

1 Frying veal scallops. Heat the butter and oil over moderate heat. Slip the scallops into the pan, and sprinkle them with salt and pepper. Cook them about 3 minutes, giving the pan an occasional shake to prevent sticking.

2 Turning the scallops. When the scallops are lightly browned on the bottom, turn them with a fork (below). There is no need to test for doneness; they will be ready when the second side has turned golden. Set the scallops on a platter and keep them warm.

3 **Deglazing the pan.** Add liquid — here, white wine and the juice of half a lemon — to the pan. Scrape up the meat residues from the bottom and, stirring constantly, reduce the sauce over high heat to give it body and concentrate the flavor. Then turn off the heat and stir or swirl in a handful of small butter chunks *(above)*.

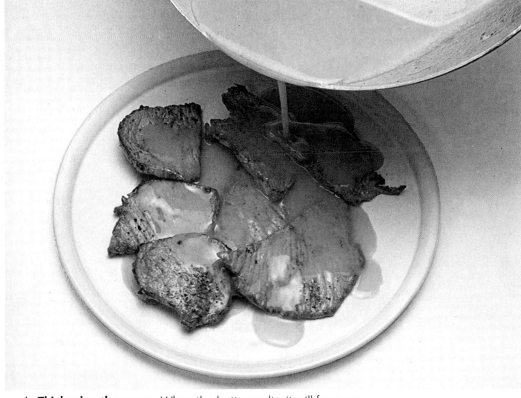

4 **Thickening the sauce.** When the butter melts, it will form an emulsion with the lemon juice and lightly thicken the sauce. This sauce will separate if it boils, so pour it immediately over the meat *(above)*; do not return the pan to the heat.

Touring the World of Veal

Pan-fried veal chops, scallops and cutlets are so easy to prepare that they invite elaboration — and the subtle flavor of veal blends superbly with a variety of sauces. The versatility of pan-fried veal has made it a popular dish in many parts of Europe, where first-class veal has been available for centuries. Some famous variations, favorites of home cooks and restaurateurs alike, are briefly described below. Recipes for these and other veal dishes appear on pages 147-152. Many of the recipes feature scallops — also known as escalopes, collops, *scaloppine* or *schnitzel* — but most can be easily adapted for either cutlets or chops.

Italy has a long tradition of veal dishes that were evolved to make the most of prime local ingredients. One simple version is *frittura piccata* — veal scallops sauced with the butter in the pan combined with lemon juice and parsley. *Scaloppine al Marsala* has a sauce that is based on the dark, sweet wine of that name. For *saltimbocca* — literally, "leap into the mouth" — prosciutto and fresh sage leaves are placed on top of each piece of veal.

France has always made much of veal. Prepared *à la crème,* the veal is simply smothered in thick cream flavored with lemon juice; *à la Provençale,* the veal is enhanced by anchovy fillets and tart gherkins. In *escalopes de veau Normande,* the veal is finished with a rich, ivory-colored sauce made from cut-up apples, heavy cream and Calvados, the apple brandy of Normandy.

Other celebrated veal dishes, including *Wiener schnitzel* from Austria, and *cotolette alla Milanese* from Italy, call for the crisp coating of eggs and bread crumbs demonstrated on the following page.

Cutlets with a Cheese-and-Crumb Crust

Breaded, deep-fried veal cutlets are favorites of several cuisines *(recipes, pages 150-152)*, and in every case, success depends on completely coating the meat with a layer of egg and bread crumbs. In the hot cooking oil, the coating forms a crusty seal that prevents meat juices from leaking out, and gives a crunchy contrast to the softer texture of the meat.

To form an effective seal, the coating must stick firmly to the cutlet. To ensure that it does, the surface of the meat must be dried before it is dipped in egg and rolled in the bread crumbs. The usual method of drying is to cover the meat with a film of flour.

A more ingenious way is to use grated Parmesan cheese, as shown here, for the undercoat. The cheese holds the egg as well as flour does, and—as a bonus—lends its pleasant flavor to the cutlets. The flavor of the cutlets can be further enhanced by marinating them ahead of time—but be sure to blot off the marinade afterward *(below, left)*. If the surface of the veal is wet, neither the cheese nor the egg will adhere evenly.

1 Marinating the veal. Flavor the cutlets by marinating them at room temperature for about an hour—here, in olive oil, lemon juice and fresh herbs. Pat the cutlets dry with a towel *(above)*, but do not wipe off the herbs: their flavor improves the dish.

2 Coating with cheese. Grate Parmesan cheese into a shallow bowl or plate, then coat both surfaces of each cutlet by lightly pressing them into the cheese. The cheese provides a good surface for the egg to cling to and melts during frying.

3 Preparing the egg mixture. Add a little cold water to the eggs to keep them from coating the meat too thickly. Beat the egg-and-water mixture with a fork until the whites just blend with the yolks; overbeating will make the eggs adhere less well.

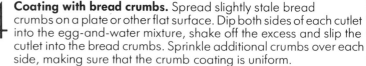

4 Coating with bread crumbs. Spread slightly stale bread crumbs on a plate or other flat surface. Dip both sides of each cutlet into the egg-and-water mixture, shake off the excess and slip the cutlet into the bread crumbs. Sprinkle additional crumbs over each side, making sure that the crumb coating is uniform.

5 **Scoring the cutlets.** Tap both
sides of each cutlet with the dull edge of a
heavy knife to make crisscrossing
lines through the coating *(left)*. The
indentations allow the coating to
shrink as it cooks without breaking. Let
the cutlets stand at room temperature
for an hour before deep frying so that the
coating will dry and cohere better.

6 **Frying the cutlets.** In a heavy
skillet, heat several inches of oil to a
temperature of 375° F. [190° C.]. (Test
the temperature by dropping in a bread
cube: it should sizzle on contact but
take 10 to 20 seconds to brown.) Fry the
cutlets, turning them once, for 3 to 5
minutes, until golden on both sides. Lift
them out with a wire strainer *(left)* and
drain them on paper towels. Fry the
cutlets in batches if necessary to avoid
crowding the pan and lowering the
temperature of the oil. Keep them
warm on a platter in a slow oven, but
leave the oven door ajar.

4
Braising
Using Moisture to Meld Flavors

The importance of degreasing
Imaginative uses for bony cuts
Basting from the inside out
Garnishes and stuffings
A pure sauce and how to achieve it

The gleaming fricandeau of veal shown opposite, which any 18th Century French aristocrat would have been proud to display on his banqueting table, is a braise. So is a simple stewed steak *(page 50)*. Braising is the general term for all those cooking processes in which meat is very slowly simmered in the liquid and vapor of a tightly enclosed vessel. The long, slow cooking produces a gradual and subtle melding of flavors through the medium of the simmering liquid. By altering ingredients or proportions, the cook can vary the technique almost without limit.

The cuts of beef and veal best suited to braising are the firm ones from the animal's working muscles—such as the leg, shoulder or neck. The lengthy cooking process breaks down the tough connective tissue that makes these cuts unsuited to more rapid methods, while it slowly releases their gelatin, making the meat succulent and the liquid velvety. The meat is usually browned briefly before braising to produce coagulated residues that will enrich the flavor, body and color of the dish. Then aromatic vegetables are added, and frequently a bouquet garni—thyme, bay leaf and parsley wrapped in cheesecloth or tied in a leek leaf. The bouquet garni is removed when cooking is done. The vegetables may be replaced with fresh ones toward the end of the process.

The quantity and quality of the liquid used are all-important to the character of the finished dish. Meat may be braised in only a few spoonfuls of liquid—or it may be completely immersed. The less liquid you add, however, the more the flavors will concentrate. Always choose a braising vessel that holds the ingredients snugly, thereby minimizing the amount of liquid you need. If your liquid is a good gelatinous stock, your braise will certainly have body. But if you use a thin moistening agent, such as water or wine, the consistency of the sauce will be improved if you include a thickening element such as flour or a particularly gelatinous cut such as pig's foot. Or you can boil the cooking liquid in a separate pan to reduce and thicken it just before serving.

When the meat is cooked, always take the trouble to purify the braising juices *(pages 51 and 59)*, to remove as much as possible of the fat that detracts from both flavor and appearance. Thus purified, the finished dish—whether simple or ambitious—will do justice to one of the most rewarding methods in the cook's repertoire.

Studded with larding fat, a braised piece of veal *(page 62)* develops a beautiful chestnut-colored glaze under repeated basting with the rich veal stock in which it has simmered for hours.

The Fundamental Steps

A typical braise is a simple two-step procedure: first the meat is browned in fat, then it is simmered to tenderness in a liquid. The braising liquid becomes a sauce that need only be skimmed of surface fat before serving. Adding a few extra steps to the preparation and to the finishing of the braise—as shown here for Swiss steak *(recipe, page 118)*—will produce an even more robust dish, irresistible to the most critical diners.

For this braise, flour is pounded into the surfaces of the meat—here a piece of chuck steak—before it is browned. The flour gives the meat an even coating that browns to a crust during the preliminary searing; pounding it into the meat ensures that the flour coating is a generous one. The browned crust contributes both color and flavor; and as the flour disperses through the simmering braising juices, it helps to thicken the sauce to the right consistency for serving as soon as the meat is done.

Every braise can be improved by adding aromatic vegetables to the cooking liquid. For this Swiss steak, a mixture of onion, carrots and celery is chopped to a coarse dice to form the classic vegetable flavoring known as a mirepoix. Feel free to vary the vegetables as you like and to sprinkle on whatever fresh or dried herbs appeal to you. Tomatoes, fresh or canned, are especially valuable. Together with a little water, tomatoes can furnish just enough liquid to surround the meat.

In all braises, it is essential to cover the pan or pot with a lid, and then to simmer the meat slowly—on top of the stove or in the oven, whichever you prefer. When gently cooked, the braise will emerge fork-tender, saturated with rich, ready-made sauce and with the mingled flavors of the accompanying vegetables.

1 **Pounding in flour.** Trim any fat or membrane from the meat. Spread seasoned flour on your work surface and over the meat. Pound the flour into the meat with the dull edge of a large knife *(above)*. Turning the steak over repeatedly, pound until both sides of the meat are almost stiff with flour.

2 **Assembling the braise.** Warm a shallow layer of oil in a heavy pan set over medium heat. Add the floured meat and brown it well on both sides. The browning will take about 30 minutes. Add chopped vegetables, parsley and mixed herbs. Pour in enough water *(above)* to surround the steak.

3 **Sieving the tomatoes.** Drain canned tomatoes of about half their juice, pour the contents of the can into a sieve held over the pan and press the tomatoes through the sieve with a pestle *(above)* or a large spoon. Raise the heat under the pan until the liquid bubbles, then lower the heat to maintain a gentle simmer, and cover the pan.

4 **Cooking and serving.** Cook for 1 to 2 hours, turning over the steak once or twice. When you can pierce the meat easily with the tip of a sharp knife, remove the steak to a warmed platter. Degrease the braising sauce *(box, opposite)*. Slice the steak and dress it with the vegetable-laden sauce *(above)*.

Four Ways to Degrease

Fat plays a valuable role during braising. Internal fat—whether it is part of the meat or inserted in the form of lardons *(pages 56-57)*—improves the flavor and helps to keep the meat moist while it is cooking. And during the preliminary browning, additional fat is often used to keep the meat and vegetables from sticking to the pan.

When the braise is completed, however, liquid fat, which is lighter than water or stock, floats to the surface of the juices and must be removed to ensure that the sauce will taste good and will not be greasy.

The quantity of fat that needs to be removed will vary widely. A simple, unlarded braise—such as the steak on the opposite page or the beef *carbonnade* on pages 52-53—produces relatively little fat, especially if you trim the meat carefully before you cook it. On the other hand, a larded braise, such as a beef daube *(recipe, page 116),* will develop a thick layer of surface fat as the lardons soften and melt.

While the braising juices are still hot, you can collect the fat from the surface with any suitable spoon or ladle *(top right)*. Take care, though, to avoid stirring the floating fat back into the juices beneath. Then discard the fat that has been skimmed off. If there are any remaining traces of fat you cannot capture with a spoon, you can remove them by blotting them up with several thicknesses of paper towel *(bottom, right)*.

When time allows, a simpler way to degrease a braise is to let the dish cool overnight in the refrigerator. The fat will congeal on the surface as the liquid cools; when it has hardened, you can lift the fat away without difficulty *(bottom, far right)*. You may, however, find that a little new fat melts out of the meat and appears on the surface when you reheat the dish. In that case, dispose of it with a spoon or paper towels.

Spooning away shallow fat. Put the tip of a large spoon into the braising liquid. Tilt the bowl enough to allow the fat to flow into the spoon, without draining off any of the braising juices underneath. Discard the fat. Repeat until no more fat can be removed.

Ladling off a deep fat layer. Tilt the side of a large ladle, preferably a basting ladle *(above),* downward into the braising juices. Let the fat flow into the ladle until its bowl is about half full. Empty the fat into a container. Repeat the procedure as often as necessary.

Blotting up fat. Fold several thicknesses of paper towels together. Holding the towels by the edges, lay the center section over the surface of the liquid briefly. Lift up the towels the instant they become saturated. Repeat the procedure as necessary, using fresh paper towels every time.

Lifting solidified fat. Slide one edge of a metal spoon under the bottom of the layer of chilled, solid fat. Carefully lift it up and remove the detached section of fat from the braise. Repeat as necessary.

Using Pan Residues to Enrich the Braise

After meat is browned in fat, some particles of it, as well as its coagulated juices, will remain on the bottom and sides of the braising pan. When the pan is deglazed, these deposits provide the base for a rich braising liquor. The deglazing process that amalgamates these juices and bits into the braising liquid of your choice *(box, opposite page)* is the same as for pan frying *(pages 38-39)*. But in braising the process is a preliminary to the main cooking period: instead of reducing the deglazing liquid immediately and pouring it over the cooked meat before serving, use the liquid as the medium in which to stew the meat to tenderness.

In the *carbonnade*—a beef and onion stew—demonstrated here *(recipe, page 113)*, first sliced onions and then slices of beef contribute to the pan deposits that will be deglazed. The oil or fat in which the onions are cooked is drained and re-used to brown the beef; as cooking proceeds, the oil takes on an increasingly rich flavor and color. The sugar in the onions turns naturally to a caramel that adds a hint of sweetness to the flavor—a hint bolstered here by the addition of a little brown sugar.

Trim the sliced beef of all fat, but do not flour it before browning; the pan deposits will build up more cleanly without flour. If you want a thicker braising liquid, you can blend a little flour into the pan juices after the meat has been browned.

For an authentic Belgian version of *carbonnade*, the braising liquid should be beer, augmented with a little stock. The slight bitterness of the beer will balance—but not overwhelm—the sweetness of the onions. Any type of beer will do; flat beer works as well as fresh. But a dark beer, such as stout or porter, will give a characteristically rich color and flavor to the braise.

1 **Coloring the onions.** Using a large, heavy pan and a minimum of oil, cook the sliced onions, covered, over low heat until they are caramel-colored. This may take up to an hour, but rapid cooking over high heat would burn some of the slices. Pour the cooked onions into a sieve placed over a bowl *(right)* to catch the oil that drains from them.

2 **Browning the beef.** Return the oil to the pan, adding fresh oil if necessary. Salt the beef slices, a few at a time, and brown them rapidly on both sides. Transfer each browned slice to the sieve to drain, saving the oil and meat juices. Return the oil to the pan as needed to brown the rest of the beef.

3 **Filling the braising dish.** In a casserole, arrange the beef and onion slices in alternate layers to ensure that their flavors mingle. The first layer should be beef and each layer of onions should be topped with a bay leaf and a sprinkling of mixed herbs.

4 **Caramelizing and deglazing.** Add brown sugar *(inset, left)* to the pan and stir over low heat while the sugar melts to a caramel. You then may add a little flour, stirring until the mixture is smooth and lightly browned. Increase the heat, slowly pour in beer and scrape up all of the rich pan deposits.

5 **Moistening the braise.** Stir a little stock into the beer mixture. Bring the liquid to a boil and pour it over the beef and onions *(above)*. Add more beer, stock or water if necessary, until the meat is barely immersed. Cover the casserole and bake for about 3 hours. Degrease the sauce *(page 51)* before serving.

A Choice of Braising Liquids

Liquid is essential to any braise: it surrounds the meat to hold in moisture, and it fills the upper part of the braising vessel with steam, which bathes any ingredients that are not immersed.

Water will suffice for this purpose, but braising liquids with flavor, body or color enrich the final product and increase the possibilities of variations on a basic braise. Some braising liquids seem to suit white meats, others dark. A veal stock *(pages 16-17; recipe, page 169)*—pure yet rich in body and flavor—is superb for braising both beef and veal. Certain dishes—such as the glazed fricandeau of veal demonstrated on page 62—depend upon veal stock for their richness. A beef stock, on the other hand, is too strong-tasting for use with veal and is best reserved as an enrichment for such beef dishes as German *rouladen (recipe, page 119)*.

Tomatoes can contribute part of the moisture you need and at the same time complement the flavor of either beef or veal. Tomatoes are especially useful because they will disintegrate when they cook and thus will thicken the braising liquid *(page 54)*.

Wines, which are often used in combination with stock, are also eminently suited to braising. They require long cooking to eliminate acidic overtones from their taste. Simmered for hours along with the meat, a wine will surrender all its aroma to the dish even as the alcohol in it evaporates.

A good dry red wine acts as a sympathetic medium for beef—witness such classic dishes of French wine-country cooking as *sauté de boeuf à la Bourguignonne (recipe, page 114)*. A light, dry white wine is traditional with veal in such dishes as pot-roasted veal, Swiss-style *(recipe, page 154)*. But the whites may also be used with beef—or, indeed, the reds with veal—to give different but equally rewarding results.

Osso Buco: Meat and Marrow

Braising can turn the fibrous toughness of the less expensive cuts of veal into an asset: the long, slow cooking softens the meat, melting its gelatin into the braising liquid to make a thick, luxurious sauce. Cuts from the rump, the breast, the round and the shoulder are all good braising material (recipes, pages 152-162). But the shank, if sawed into cross-sections, has an advantage: the core of the bone is filled with delicious and nutritious marrow. When the meat is done, you can scoop out the marrow with a small fork or spoon and eat it. Cuts from the foreshank have a little marrow, but a hindshank has much more. Ask your butcher to cut the shank crosswise into 2-inch [5-cm.] slices, each of which will contain a good-sized portion of marrow.

As in most braises, preparation begins with a preliminary browning of the meat in fat or oil. Before cooking shanks, however, slit the thin membrane that surrounds each slice; otherwise, the membrane may shrink when it touches the hot fat and distort the shape of the meat beneath it. Once the meat has colored, you can add chopped aromatic vegetables such as onions, carrots, celery and garlic before deglazing the pan with wine.

For the braising medium, plain stock or water will serve. However, in the renowned north Italian creation called *osso buco* (hollow bone)—shown on the right—the stock is frequently supplemented with tomatoes, which cook down to thicken the sauce and give it extra body. Fresh ripe tomatoes are best, but when they are not available, you can substitute canned plum tomatoes, if you first carefully drain off all their liquid. In any case, you should add a sprinkling of sugar at the time you stir in the tomatoes: sugar will counter the tomatoes' acidity.

To elevate the braise into a real *osso buco alla Milanese (recipe, pages 158-159)*, garnish it just before serving with the *gremolata* described on the opposite page—a fine example of a simple finishing touch that can transform a basic dish into a memorable one.

1 Browning the veal. Heat a film of oil or fat in a heavy pan over moderate heat, then brown the veal. Turn the veal pieces so that they color evenly on both sides but keep them upright as you turn them to prevent the marrow from falling out. Reduce the heat and stir in finely chopped aromatics such as onion, carrots, celery, garlic and parsley.

2 Deglazing the pan. When the aromatics have softened and colored, add a little white wine and scrape up meat residues from the base of the pan. Use a flat spatula to scrape under the meat pieces. Continue scraping until the wine has almost completely evaporated.

3 Adding tomatoes. Stir two or three tomatoes — peeled, seeded and chopped — into the pan and cook gently for 5 to 6 minutes. When the tomatoes give off juices, add veal stock or water until the liquid almost immerses the veal. Cover the pan and simmer gently for 1½ hours, until the meat is ready to fall from the bone.

4 Finishing the dish. When the meat is cooked, degrease the sauce (page 51) and prepare a *gremolata* garnish (opposite page). Sprinkle the garnish on top of the veal shanks. Replace the lid for a minute or two before serving; the heat in the pan will release the full flavor of the garnish.

Assorted Garnishes to Flavor Braises

Braising, more than most other methods of cooking beef and veal, offers the opportunity to make a garnish an integral part of the finished dish. Of course, separate garnishes frequently accompany braises: a veal fricandeau, for example *(page 62),* is particularly good with braised sorrel. But integrating a garnish into the braise gives the dish extra dimensions of flavor and texture.

A perfect case in point is the *gremolata* sprinkled over the finished veal shank braise shown opposite. This garnish is simplicity itself: a fragrant combination of chopped parsley and garlic, with grated orange and lemon peel added *(below, left).* When the mixture is warmed by the heat in the braising vessel, its aromas immediately suffuse the dish, setting the veal and tomatoes in sharp relief. Chopped garlic and parsley by themselves—a *persillade*—can enhance a finished braise in the same way.

A quickly made garnish for a braise that provides a crisp contrast in texture is small bread cubes, sautéed in butter until they are golden brown. Scatter the cubes over the dish at the last moment, so that they do not have time to get soggy with the sauce.

Vegetables provide a wide range of garnishes. Select the ones that your instinct and experience tell you will best suit the meat you are braising. You can garnish almost any dish, for example, with a mixture of whole onions and chunks or olive-shaped pieces of carrot. They will refresh the flavors contributed by the chopped vegetables that have braised for hours with the meat.

In a classic beef braise, such as beef à la mode shown on pages 58-59, turnips can make a distinctive contribution. The more subtle flavors of either artichoke hearts or fennel have a greater affinity with veal.

If you cook the garnish vegetables separately before adding them to the braise, treat them in whatever manner is most appropriate to their individual characteristics. For example, before you add a garnish of onions or root vegetables, peel, parboil and drain them. Then stew the vegetables in butter *(below, center).* Add them to the braise for the last 15 minutes of cooking so that they will take on the flavor of the dish without losing their own personalities.

Delicate vegetables such as spring peas, small green beans or peeled broad beans should first be parboiled briefly in lightly salted water. After draining, the vegetables are tossed in butter and added to the braise at the last minute. Immersion in the cooking pot for any time would dull their colors and destroy their freshness.

Mushrooms should be quickly sautéed in butter *(below, right)* before being incorporated into the braise.

Preparing a gremolata. Finely chop garlic and parsley, and grate over the mixture the peel of a lemon, taking care not to include the bitter white pith beneath the peel. Then add a little grated orange peel *(above),* more or less of it as you prefer.

Precooking root vegetables. In lightly salted water, parboil small white boiling onions for 5 minutes, along with carrots and turnips cut to a similar size. Drain, and cook gently in butter for 10 minutes *(above)* before adding them to the casserole; or simmer them separately in the braising liquid until tender—about 5 minutes.

Sautéing the mushrooms. Leave small mushrooms whole; halve, quarter or slice larger ones. In a skillet, sauté the mushrooms in a small amount of butter over medium heat until their moisture evaporates and they brown lightly. Add the mushrooms directly to the braise— here, a veal casserole roast *(page 63)*— for the last 15 minutes of cooking.

Three Ways to Baste Lean Meat from Within

The beef and veal cuts usually used for braising tend to be better endowed with flavor than with the internal fat that is so important for keeping meat from drying out during cooking. One way to ensure a succulent finished dish is to introduce fat into the meat. This can be done through larding—a process that enables you to take advantage of less expensive, lean cuts such as shank *(opposite, below)*.

In larding, strips of fresh pork fat—known as lardons—are inserted through the raw meat with the aid of a knife or one of the special larding tools demonstrated here. During braising, the strips melt, thus basting the meat from within. And the melted fat that runs into the braising liquid rises to the surface in the pan or pot, so that it can be skimmed off *(page 51)* before you serve the liquid as soup or turn it into a sauce. The remnants of the lardons left in the meat will

also checker it attractively when it is sliced for serving.

For the best lardons, use firm, white fat from the belly or loin, and cut it into strips as wide as they are thick *(right)*. Allow about 1½ ounces [60 g.] of fat to 1 pound [½ kg.] of lean meat.

If you coat the lardons with seasonings, they will carry flavor right into the heart of the meat. You can marinate them first in an aromatic mixture of herbs and wine, or dip them in fresh or dried chopped herbs. Take care to insert the strips of fat with the grain of the meat, not across it. That way, the lardons will show up attractively in the slices that you carve against the grain. When larding a large piece of meat, arrange the lardons in a symmetrical pattern; this will give an extra distinction to the final appearance of the dish, as well as distribute the fat evenly throughout the meat.

Cutting the lardons. Trim the rind from your pork fat, then slice it into lardons ¼ inch [6 mm.] wide and thick. The fat will be easier to handle while you are cutting the strips if you first chill it well in the refrigerator to firm it.

Larding a Large Cut

Larding the interior. Use a *larding knife*: a tool with a U-shaped groove along the top edge. Thrust the point through the meat — here, a beef bottom-round roast — following the grain. Let the tip protrude well beyond the opposite side of the meat. Lay a lardon, shown at left, into the groove. Pull back the knife until the lardon fills the channel made by the point. Ease out the knife, leaving the lardon in the meat. Repeat, spacing lardons evenly. Trim the ends of fat close to the meat surface *(above)*.

Larding at the Surface

Stitching with lardons. Use a hinged larding needle for this technique. Close the toothed clip at the handle to clasp the end of the lardon securely *(above)*. Push the point of the needle under the surface of the meat — here, veal round. Draw the lardon through the meat just far enough to make a single stitch *(right)*. Release the clip and snip off the surplus fat, leaving the short length. Rethread the needle and repeat, making one stitch at a time, in neat rows.

Larding a Small Cut

Inserting flavored lardons. With the tip of a small, sharp knife *(right)* pierce the center of each piece — in this case beef shank. With your fingers push a short lardon into the hole *(far right)*. Here, the lardons are seasoned first by rolling them in a *persillade* of chopped fresh parsley and garlic. After larding, each chunk of beef will contain a nugget of fat and flavor.

Beef à la Mode: A Grand Braise

A large, whole cut of meat produces as tempting a braise as smaller pieces do. And when that cut simmers along with pork rind, or calf's or pig's feet, which gradually surrender their gelatin in the cooking process, the meat can be served either hot, with a translucent and velvety sauce, or cold and enveloped in the jelly that forms as the sauce cools.

A classic example of such a braise is the beef à la mode shown on these pages. This favorite of French family cooking has almost as many variations as there are cooks *(recipes, pages 106-107,109)*. Generally, however, the phrase "à la mode" signifies larded beef cooked with wine and carrots.

Larding a lean cut such as this bottom-round roast serves to baste it internally during its long period of cooking. Trussing keeps the lardons in place and holds the meat in a compact shape that will fit snugly into a casserole, where it will cook through evenly.

Marinating in wine helps to tenderize the meat, and the wine becomes the basis of the herb-flavored braising liquid. Red wine is a traditional complement to beef because of its full flavor and rich color; but a dry white wine—used in this demonstration—is also well suited to a marinade. White wine is lighter-tasting than red, and when the finished cooking liquid jells, it will be amber-colored and milder in flavor than if made with red wine.

Beef à la mode does not necessarily require advance browning. The aromatic vegetables for the braise, instead of being softened in fat, can be "pinched"—that is, baked covered for 30 minutes or so in a hot oven without any added fat or moisture, until they begin to caramelize at the edges. Their flavor will be purer and there will be less fat to cleanse from the sauce after braising.

A special virtue of beef à la mode is that sliced leftovers can be decoratively coated with the jelly *(box, page 60)* and the dish made to do double duty. (If you like, you can, of course, serve the whole braise jellied.) But the need for a limpid jelly to set off the cold beef calls for one last refinement: a scrupulous cleansing of the braising liquid *(box, opposite)*.

1 **Trussing.** After larding the beef with fresh pork-fat lardons, as shown on pages 56-57, form it into a compact shape. Using a single piece of kitchen string approximately 3 feet [1 meter] long, tie up the meat securely just as you would a parcel.

2 **Marinating the meat.** Place the meat in a bowl with the dry ingredients of the marinade — in this case, onion, celery, bay leaf, parsley, garlic and mixed herbs — that have been mixed with olive oil. Turn the meat to coat it, then add white wine to cover. Marinate for several hours at room temperature.

3 **Preparing the rind and feet.** Cut pork rind into 1-inch [2½-cm.] squares. Put them into a pan with 1 inch of cold water. Add the pig's or calf's feet. Bring to a boil, and boil for 3 minutes to extract the albumin that rises from the meat as foam, which will ensure a clear jelly. Then rinse the meat in cold water.

4 **Preparing the aromatics.** Dice the vegetables — here, carrots and onions. Spread them in a heavy casserole that will hold the meat snugly. Cover the casserole and place it in a 425° F. [220° C.] oven for 30 minutes until the vegetables begin to color *(above)*. Uncover for the last 5 minutes to allow the moisture to evaporate.

5 **Deglazing the casserole.** After removing the meat, pour the marinade through a strainer into the casserole with the aromatics *(above)*. Discard the marinade seasonings left in the strainer. Then use a wooden spoon to loosen any vegetables that have stuck to the bottom of the casserole.

6 **Assembling the braise.** Center the meat on the vegetables; pack in the pork rinds and the pig's feet. Add just enough stock *(above)* to cover the meat. Slowly bring the liquid to a boil on top of the stove. Cover and cook in a preheated 300° F. [150° C.] oven until tender — about 2 hours. Baste often and turn the meat once or twice.

A Simple Procedure for a Pure Sauce

While a braise gently cooks, its liquid draws flavors from the vegetables and meat, making the resultant sauce an integral part of the finished dish. But the long cooking also coaxes out fats and impurities, some of which remain in the liquid, spoiling its clarity and muddying its flavor. You can easily remove these impurities by cleansing the liquid after the meat is done.

First strain the liquid into a saucepan and degrease it as usual *(page 51)*, then bring it to a simmer. The impurities will rise to the surface, as will much of the remaining fat; both will be trapped by a skin that gradually develops around them. The skin can be lifted off with a spoon *(right)*. Do not hurry; give the skin time to form firmly.

After removing the first skin, let the liquid continue to simmer until another skin forms, and so on. It may take some 30 minutes of careful, repeated skinning before a top forms that is clear of impurities. At this point the sauce is ready to serve.

Cleansing the liquid. Bring the liquid to a boil in a saucepan. Reduce the heat and move the pan half off the heat. When a firm skin forms on the cooler side of the liquid, draw it aside with a spoon *(above)* and lift it off. Repeat until only a thin, clear skin forms. Boil the sauce, if necessary, to reduce it to a coating consistency.

7 **Serving the hot beef.** Put the meat on a warmed platter. Cut away the string and slice as much beef as you plan to serve. Surround it with pork rinds, meat from the pig's or calf's feet and garnish vegetables *(page 55)*. Cover the platter to keep the meat and vegetables warm. Cleanse and reduce the braising liquid *(left)* and glaze the meat with the resultant sauce.

Molding a Braise in Its Own Jelly

Beef braised with gelatinous pig's or calf's feet and rinds, as shown on the preceding pages, offers a splendid bonus: whatever is not eaten hot can later be served cold in the jelly that readily forms from the leftover sauce. Indeed, many people think of beef à la mode primarily as a cold, molded dish.

The natural gelatin that is in the sauce should be enough to ensure the right consistency—but if you find that your chilled sauce has not set, reduce it by boiling it briskly over high heat. The sauce will be the proper consistency when a spoonful dribbled onto a chilled saucer congeals after 15 minutes in the refrigerator. At room temperature it will have a liquid, syrupy consistency that makes it easy to pour as you coat the mold and the beef.

You can use any of the original garnish vegetables in the mold with the meat and jelly, and you can give it a decorative surface *(below)* by arranging colorful cooked vegetables—strips of carrot, for example, or a handful of green beans—in an attractive pattern at the base of the mold.

1 **Preparing the mold.** Pour a shallow layer of liquid sauce into the bottom of a bowl or a plain mold and chill only until the sauce begins to jell, or set. Arrange in it a pattern of vegetables, perhaps freshly parboiled carrot strips and leftover garnish vegetables. Chill until the jelly is firm enough to hold the vegetables in place.

2 **Packing the mold.** Line the mold with beef slices, pork rind and the meat from the pig's or calf's feet. Fill up the center with the remaining beef and vegetables. Pour on enough liquid sauce (cooled, so it will not melt the jellied sauce on the bottom of the mold) to cover the contents. Let the dish set overnight in the refrigerator.

3 **Serving.** Run the point of a knife around the edge of the mold to loosen the jelly. Dip the mold in hot water for 5 seconds to soften the outer jelly layer. Put a plate over the mold, and invert mold and plate together to release the beef. Serve it cold, not chilled *(left)*, and carve it into thin slices *(above)*.

Meat Slices, Stuffed and Rolled

An attractive way to make meat go further is to cut it into thin slices, roll each one around a stuffing and then braise the rolls. These neat parcels go by many names: *paupiettes* in France, *rollini* or *rollatini* in Italy, *rouladen* in Germany, "olives" or "birds" in Britain and America, and "blind finches" in the Netherlands *(recipes, pages 119 and 160)*.

Whatever the name, all are assembled in basically the same way. The best meat for rolling is a solid piece that gives slices without any connective membranes that might give way during braising. For beef rolls, choose bottom round (shown here), top round or rump; for veal, use rump or loin—or scallops. If the slices are not roughly rectangular, trim them and flatten them with a meat mallet.

Stuffings may range from economical bread mixtures to imaginative combinations of meats, cheeses, sweet or sour pickles and seasonings. But any stuffing you use should always include some element of fat—chopped bacon or ham, for example, or simply a little butter—to baste the meat from within.

To keep the rolls from opening as they cook, tie them with kitchen string.

1 **Stuffing the rolls.** Flatten each slice slightly with a meat mallet. Near one end, arrange a neat pile of stuffing — in this case, blanched salt pork, hard-boiled egg, capers, parsley and an anchovy fillet *(recipe, page 119)*.

2 **Rolling the slice.** Start rolling at the end nearest the stuffing. To help hold the stuffing in place, tuck in the edges of the meat on both sides as you roll up the meat into a compact package *(above)*.

3 **Trussing each roll.** Tie a piece of string about 1 foot [30 cm.] long around the middle of the rolled meat. Then cross the string and loop it lengthwise around the roll, ending with a double knot. Trim off the excess string *(above)*.

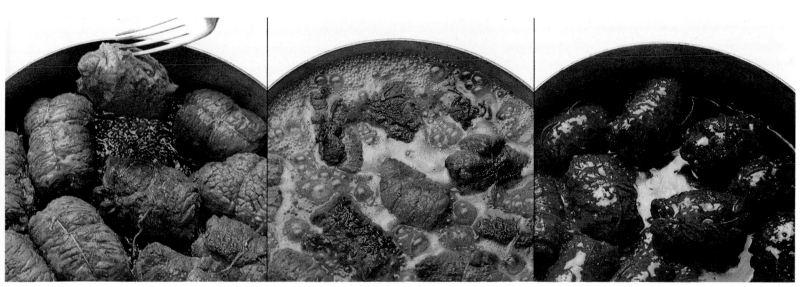

4 **Braising the paupiettes.** In a pan just large enough to hold all the rolls snugly, heat a thin coat of fat or oil. Put in the rolls and cook them over moderate heat, turning them *(above, left)* so that they brown evenly. Add liquid — here, veal stock — until the meat is about two thirds covered. Bring the liquid to a rapid boil *(above, center)*, then reduce the heat to a bare simmer and cover the pan. Cook until tender, basting and turning the meat regularly. Leisurely braising — for 2 hours or longer — concentrates the juices, and the basting will yield a rich glaze *(above, right)*. Cut off the strings before serving.

Two Ways to Prepare a Large Cut of Veal

A Golden Fricandeau

Slow and gentle braising is a rewarding treatment for large cuts of veal and—as demonstrated by the two dishes shown here—it can be done in various ways. The veal fricandeau on this page is a classic braise. The veal is first larded with strips of pork fat *(pages 56-57)* to keep it from drying out while it is cooking, then simmered for about 5 hours in plenty of rich veal stock and a little white wine.

The braise on the opposite page, a homely pot roast, uses the smallest possible quantity of liquid, most of it the juices the meat itself exudes during cooking. And while the fricandeau is carefully protected against evaporation for most of its cooking time, the juices that bathe the pot roast are reduced until they form rich, brown, crusty bits.

For the fricandeau *(recipe, page 153)*, choose a large, solid cut such as a veal round roast. If you arrange the lardons of fat in the traditional, symmetrical rows and trim them so that their ends protrude a little from the meat, they make a handsome pattern on the glazed surface of the finished dish.

During the first and longest phase of braising, the fricandeau requires almost no attention as it cooks gently in a tightly lidded pot inside the oven. Later, the oven heat is increased and the lid removed so that the veal will color. Now it needs frequent basting to give it a gleaming, even glaze. During the basting, the lardons and the veal will deepen from pale gold to a clear amber.

When the veal is done, the basting liquid, thoroughly degreased and cleansed, becomes a sauce for the meat. The long hours of cooking give the meat a texture so soft it can be carved with a spoon—the traditional way of serving it.

Braised sorrel is an ideal accompaniment, as is the spinach shown here. Or you can serve the fricandeau with a purée of potatoes, turnips, or celery root, or a mixture of these.

1 Preparing the veal. Trim fat, gristle or surface membranes from the veal, leaving a layer of fat on the bottom. Lard the veal. Put chopped carrots and onions in the pot and place it, covered, in a hot oven for 30 minutes; check to see that the vegetables do not burn *(pages 58-59)*. When they have colored, set the veal on top of them *(above)*.

2 Adding stock. Return the braising pot, uncovered, to the oven for about 10 minutes until the meat firms a little and turns white. Then transfer the pot to the top of the stove. Add white wine to a depth of ½ inch [1 cm.] and boil it for a few minutes to reduce it by half before pouring in enough hot veal stock *(above)* to cover two thirds of the meat.

3 Basting. Cover the veal with buttered parchment paper, put a lid on the pot and place it in a moderate oven. The paper ensures that rising moisture falls back continually to baste the meat. For the last hour of cooking, increase the oven temperature and uncover the pot so the veal will begin to color. Baste it frequently with the braising juices.

4 Glazing and serving. Half an hour before cooking time is up, transfer two thirds of the braising liquid to a saucepan and reduce it to a syrup over high heat. Baste with this syrup to give the meat an amber glaze. When the meat is done, remove it to a heated platter and cover with foil to keep it warm while cleansing the liquid in the pot *(page 59)* to serve as a sauce for the fricandeau.

A Simple Pot Roast

A pot roast is a braise done with a minimum of liquid; no roasting is involved. The meat cooks in moist heat inside a closed casserole, not in dry oven heat. The method suits both beef and veal, particularly gelatinous round and shoulder cuts—such as the veal rump roast shown here—that will yield a rich sauce.

Begin a pot roast *(recipe, page 152)* by tying the meat into a compact shape for even cooking. Season it and place it in a heavy pot with oil or butter and aromatic vegetables. In the early cooking stages, the meat exudes its juices. Later, these juices gradually evaporate and caramelize; and as they do, the meat begins to color. Add a little water periodically to dissolve the coagulated juices. A rich sauce gradually forms, small in quantity but concentrated in flavor, and the meat acquires a color as rich as if it had been roasted in dry oven heat.

Separately cooked vegetable garnishes *(page 55)*, such as the mushrooms shown here, complement this preparation. And to provide a bed for the rich sauce, surround the finished roast with another vegetable, such as mashed potatoes.

1 **Filling the casserole.** Tie up the meat, salt it all over, then put it in the casserole with some melted butter. Add halved, peeled carrots *(above)* and, if you like, some sliced salt pork. Cover the casserole and set it over low heat, or put it in a moderate oven.

2 **Turning the meat.** After the first half hour, turn the meat at 30-minute intervals to ensure that it cooks—and later, browns—evenly on all sides. Cooking time will be about 3 hours for a 2- to 3-pound [1- to 1½-kg.] roast. Use a carving fork and a large spoon to turn the piece, and work carefully so that the hot fat does not splatter.

3 **Reducing and deglazing.** When the juices coagulate and the meat begins to brown, add 2 to 3 tablespoons [30 to 45 ml.] of water—no more—and scrape the casserole to loosen the brown, crusty bits. Replace the lid. Repeat the process every 45 minutes until the veal is done.

4 **Incorporating a garnish.** Remove the veal, strain and degrease the juices, and return them, with the veal, to the pot. Add a garnish such as the mushrooms shown here. Cook gently for 15 minutes. Untie and slice the veal, and serve it with the juice and the garnish.

Loving Care for a Neglected Cut

The sinewy meat of an oxtail responds particularly well to braising. The gentle, lengthy cooking softens and partly melts the gelatinous tendons that extend the length of the tail, thus keeping the meat moist and succulent and producing juices that can be reduced to a velvety sauce. To be sure, oxtail is a particularly bony cut, but its price is low and its flavor more than compensates for the diners' task of picking the meat off the bones.

Recipes for oxtail stews are, therefore, legion and so are other, less usual ways of presenting this rich, dark meat (recipes, pages 125-127). Two imaginative techniques are demonstrated on these pages: broiled oxtail (above, right) and boned, stuffed oxtail (below).

For broiling, oxtail pieces of any size will do. If your butcher cannot supply cut-up oxtail, you can disjoint it quickly (right). Then you simply tenderize the pieces with a preliminary braising, cover them with an undercoating of mustard and a top coating of bread crumbs, and brown the oxtail under the broiler. The result will be tender, juicy meat in a spicy, crunchy crust.

For stuffing, a whole oxtail is essential, and you will want to get the largest one you can find to make boning it easier. That job can take an hour or more if you are new to it, but boning the tail needs no special skill: just a small, sharp knife and patience. Work slowly, following the intricate contours of the bones with the knife tip. Try to avoid piercing the outer membrane; a few small slits in it will not matter, however, since they will seal as the meat contracts during the cooking.

Stuff the boned oxtail, then braise it in two stages: first wrapped in cheesecloth to help it keep its shape and then unwrapped until the meat is tender (recipe, page 127). After unwrapping, transfer the oxtail to a smaller pot; it will have shrunk during the first stage of the cooking and a snugly fitting pot is essential if the oxtail is to remain partly immersed in the minimum of concentrated juices. Finish the braising in the oven with the lid off, basting frequently to give the oxtail a beautiful glaze.

Broiling as a Finishing Touch

1 Disjointing an oxtail. To divide a whole oxtail into cross sections, slice down through each of the slight indentations in the surface that mark the cartilage between vertebrae. The tip of the tail — the last four or five vertebrae — has little meat; keep the tip for the stockpot.

2 Assembling the braise. Stand the oxtail pieces on end in a deep casserole lined with chopped vegetables — here, carrots and onions. Barely cover the meat with stock, water or wine. Put a lid on the casserole and simmer slowly in the oven, or on top of the stove, for 3 to 4 hours, until the meat is tender.

Boning and Stuffing a Whole Oxtail

1 Boning the oxtail. Lay the oxtail with its underside toward you and make a slit in the flesh along the length of the tail. Using a small, sharp knife and working from the base of the tail toward its tip, detach the meat from each bone in turn and carefully peel it back until all of the meat is separated in one flat, boneless piece.

2 Stuffing the tail. Pile the stuffing in a compact mound in the middle of the meat; the stuffing used here is a mixture of chopped, parboiled spinach, bread crumbs, bone marrow and herbs, bound with egg. Fold the narrow end of the tail over the mound of stuffing, pinch the two sides of the meat together over the fold and run through them a trussing needle threaded with about 3 feet [1 meter] of string.

3 **Coating oxtail pieces for broiling.** Drain the braised pieces and place them on a platter until they are cool enough to handle. Coat each piece first with a prepared mustard such as Dijon, then with fresh bread crumbs *(above)*. Arrange the pieces in a broiler pan with the rack removed and dribble melted butter over them. Preheat the broiler to its highest setting, set the pan in the broiler about 6 inches [15 cm.] from the heat and brown the pieces, turning them until they are crisp on all sides.

4 **Serving the oxtail.** Degrease and cleanse the braising juices *(pages 51 and 59)*, then boil them until they reduce to a syrupy consistency. Trickle the juices over the oxtail pieces and serve them with a hearty accompaniment, such as braised red cabbage, glazed carrots or a purée of vegetables.

3 **Sewing up the oxtail.** Draw the edges of the meat over the stuffing and sew them together up the length of the tail. Do not pack in the stuffing too tightly; while the meat is cooking, the stuffing will expand and at the same time the meat will contract.

4 **Wrapping the oxtail.** To help the tail hold its shape until the meat is firmed by cooking, wrap it in a piece of clean muslin or a double thickness of cheesecloth and tie securely with string *(above)*. Put the oxtail in a close-fitting pot, cover it with stock and simmer for 2 hours. Spoon off the fat from the surface of the liquid, remove and unwrap the meat and let it drain while you cleanse and reduce the juices.

5 **Completing the braise.** Put the drained, unwrapped oxtail on a bed of aromatic vegetables in a smaller pot that fits its reduced size. Add enough cleansed and reduced stock to cover it by half. Bring the stock to a simmer, cover the pot, and braise the meat in the oven for 2 more hours. Uncover for the last hour and baste often to form a glaze. To serve, strain the sauce and spoon it over the sliced oxtail *(above)*.

5
Poaching
Gentle Simmering for Tougher Cuts

Added during the last moments of cooking, a lush liaison of egg yolks and cream enriches the bouillon produced as veal and vegetables simmered *(pages 70-71)*. The finished dish exemplifies the elegance that can be achieved through simple poaching.

Cooks have been boiling meat for as long as there have been pots to boil it in. Almost every country has its traditional favorite—the boiled beef and carrots of the English, pot-au-feu for the French, *bollito di manzo* for the Italians, New England boiled dinner in the United States. Yet "boiling" is really a misnomer: if these were really boiled, they would not be the popular dishes they are.

The boiling point for water is 212° F. [100° C.], too high for meat. Beef or veal cooked at a rolling boil becomes stringy and dry because the extreme heat alters the protein structure and dissolves away fat that would otherwise serve to baste the meat internally. But a barely bubbling simmer of about 175° F. [80° C.] softens the connective tissues so gradually that meat becomes tender without losing its shape or texture. Poaching is the name for this gentle treatment.

The best cuts of meat to use for poaching—as for braising—are working muscles that are richly flavored but might be tough unless given a long, moist cooking. Beef round, chuck or flank and veal shoulder or breast will all produce excellent results.

Almost any liquid can be used for poaching, and many cooks favor stock used alone or flavored with wine. But water is usually the best and most economical choice. Water allows the flavor of the meat to develop naturally, and is itself transformed into a fragrant bouillon, which in some dishes—the pot-au-feu on the next page, for example—is as much of an attraction as the meat and vegetables cooked in it. The bouillon can be presented as a light and nourishing soup, reserved for stock, or, when thickened and enriched, used as a sauce for the finished dish.

When meat is poached, part of its protein is coagulated and drawn out as the liquid heats up during the first few minutes of cooking. This protein appears as scum on the surface of the liquid. Some cooks leave scum untouched—to dissolve slowly into the liquid, or sink to the bottom of the pot—so as not to lose nutrients; but most cooks skim it off scrupulously, since their aim is a clear bouillon.

Once the scum is dealt with and aromatic vegetables are added to the liquid, the meat can be left to poach undisturbed. The best cooks, however, first devote up to half an hour to adjusting and readjusting the heat to achieve just the barest simmer inside the pot.

A Soup as well as a Main Course

The classic French dish known as pot-au-feu *(recipe, page 129)* is honest and economical. It produces two dishes from a single pot: the clear broth can be served as a bouillon for the first course or it can be reserved as a stock for poaching tender cuts *(box, opposite);* the finished beef and vegetables will provide a handsome main course. Since both the broth and the meat are equally important, you must carefully control the cooking time. The beef must be poached long enough to flavor the cooking liquid, but not so long that it becomes overcooked and loses its taste.

To satisfy these demands, the beef you choose should have flavor to spare and enough natural gelatin to prevent it from drying out during cooking. The convenient way to achieve this is to tie together two cuts—a gelatinous one, such as shank, and a meaty piece of short rib, rump or top round *(chart, pages 8-9).* If you use a single piece of lean meat, add to the pot several crosscut sections of veal or beef shank, wrapped in cheesecloth so that the marrow does not slip out. For a particularly well-flavored broth, add a piece of oxtail to either combination.

Aromatic vegetables such as carrots, onions and turnips, sometimes supported by dried mushrooms, are indispensable to the quality of the broth. A fresh batch of garnish vegetables often is added near the end of the cooking time. Cored turnips, carrots, onions and potatoes as well as cabbage quarters are used here. The aromatic vegetables are exhausted by the long cooking, but they can be chopped and offered with the broth, which may also be garnished with rice or pasta, or served with toast and sliced beef marrow or a sprinkling of cheese.

1 **Tying the meat.** Select two cuts — here, some short ribs and a boned shank *(inset, left)* weighing at least 2 pounds [1 kg.] each. To preserve their shape and form a compact parcel for poaching, tie the two pieces of meat securely together with a length of cotton string.

2 **Skimming the pot.** Put the meat in a pot and cover with water. Heat the water, removing the scum that forms as it comes to a boil *(page 16).* When froth but no scum appears, reduce the heat until the water barely simmers.

3 **Adding the vegetables.** Put the prepared vegetables into the pot: here, onions — 1 stuck with 3 cloves — turnips, carrots, an unpeeled bulb of garlic and a bouquet garni. To counter any fatty taste, add a whole apple. Salt the water lightly.

4 **Preparing mushrooms.** Soak dried mushrooms, such as the cepes shown here, for 30 minutes in cold water. Strain the water through cheesecloth into the pot; add the cepes. Simmer, partly covered, for three hours.

5 **Serving the broth.** Remove the vegetables. Strain most of the broth into a tureen, leaving enough in the pot to moisten the meat. Ladle the broth into bowls over a bread slice; serve with grated Parmesan cheese.

6 **Serving the main course.** For the last 30 minutes of the cooking time, simmer the garnish vegetables in the broth with the meat. (The cabbage quarters are cooked separately in some of the pot-au-feu broth because of their dominating flavor.) Present the vegetables, then carve the meat.

Some Surprising Candidates

Tender cuts such as beef tenderloin may seem to be unlikely candidates for poaching, but they are delicious when cooked in stock until rare. The heat of the liquid seals the roast's surface, keeping the interior succulent, while the brief immersion in the stock—preferably a rich bouillon from a pot-au-feu—reinforces the tenderloin's subtle flavor.

1 **Poaching the tenderloin.** Truss the meat, leaving a long, loose end of string. Suspend the meat in boiling stock; tie the string to the pot handle or to a wooden spoon laid across the top. Return the stock to a simmer and poach the tenderloin 8 to 10 minutes for each pound [½ kg.].

2 **Serving the tenderloin.** Draw the meat out of the pot by the string to avoid piercing the surface and losing juices. Cut off the trussing strings and slice the meat. Serve with vegetables cooked separately in bouillon.

From Poaching Liquid to Velvety Sauce

Poached in liquid for an hour or so, low-priced cuts of veal—such as breast, riblets, shank or cuts from the shoulder—emerge as tender as the most expensive scallops. But the young cells of veal release their protein much more easily than those of beef and, as the meat comes to a boil, a considerable amount of scum forms. Special care must be given to removing the scum from the surface of the poaching liquid *(page 16)*.

Since the meat has a delicate flavor, the poaching liquid for veal is usually water and the flavorings should be mild, such as the carrots, clove-studded onion and bouquet garni shown here. This liq-

uid can be made into a creamy sauce that becomes an integral part of the finished dish. The sauce is made in two stages, each a basic culinary technique in its own right. The result is a smooth white stew, or blanquette *(recipe, page 163),* that suits this meat to perfection.

The first step *(below)* is to thicken the strained poaching liquid with a roux—a paste of flour and butter—to produce a smooth sauce known as a velouté, a term meaning "velvety." A flour-bound sauce such as this should always be carefully cleansed *(below)* to remove unwanted fats held in suspension—a 20-minute process that also helps to banish the pasty taste of undercooked flour. In the meantime, the veal pieces are kept warm

in the original cooking vessel, along with separately precooked garnish vegetables (the small boiling onions and the button mushrooms shown here are the traditional accompaniment to a blanquette).

The lightly thickened velouté is then added to the veal and its garnish. After an additional 15 to 20 minutes of gentle simmering to mingle the flavors and to complete the cooking of the velouté, the sauce receives a final binding of egg yolks and cream. This classic addition, demonstrated opposite, must always be made at the last minute—and, to prevent the egg yolks from curdling, the sauce must never be allowed to boil.

1 **Poaching the veal.** Arrange the veal pieces snugly in a pot and just cover with lightly salted cold water. Bring to a boil, carefully skimming off the scum. When no more scum appears, add aromatic vegetables and herbs. If mushrooms are the garnish, boil them briefly in lemon juice, water and butter and strain the cooking liquid into the pot *(above)*. Cover and adjust the heat so that the pot barely simmers for 1½ hours.

2 **Making a roux.** Strain the cooking liquid into a bowl. Return the meat and vegetables to the pot and add the garnish vegetables. In a saucepan, mix butter and flour; cook for a minute or so over low heat, stirring constantly. Pour in all of the poaching liquid *(above)* and whisk rapidly until it boils.

3 **Cleansing the velouté.** Position the uncovered pan half off the heat and keep the sauce at a light boil for about 20 minutes. Remove the skin that will repeatedly form on the cooler side of the liquid's surface; it will take fatty impurities with it, leaving the sauce lightened and purified. When no more skin forms, pour the cleansed sauce over the veal and its garnish vegetables.

4 **Preparing the final binding.** Partly cover the pot and simmer the veal and the vegetables in the sauce for 20 minutes. Meanwhile, in a bowl blend 2 or 3 egg yolks with about 2 tablespoons [30 ml.] of heavy cream per yolk. Season with pepper — and add a pinch of grated nutmeg, if you like. Warm the mixture by stirring into it a ladleful of hot liquid from the veal.

5 **Adding the egg yolks and cream.** Turn off the heat and pour the egg mixture over the veal and vegetables, stirring slowly. Heat the pot again gently for a few minutes, but take care that the contents do not approach a boil: low heat partly coagulates the yolk protein and thickens the sauce smoothly; high heat will coagulate the protein completely and curdle the sauce.

6 **Finishing the sauce.** Tilt and shake the pot to complete the mingling of the ingredients — constant stirring could damage the meat. Lemon juice added at this stage will bring subtle vivaciousness to the sauce. As soon as the liquid assumes a custard-like appearance, serve the blanquette.

Stuffing a Breast of Veal

At first glance, a breast of veal is an unprepossessing cut—flat, shaped irregularly, and lined with rib bones. But when boned, rolled around a stuffing and gently poached, it yields a dish (*opposite page*) as decorative as it is delicious.

You may buy either a whole or a half veal breast. Buying the whole one, which usually weighs about 9 pounds [4 kg.], is the better idea; you can divide it yourself, thereby ensuring yourself a piece long enough—about 1 foot [30 cm.]—to make a good-sized roll. The extra meat, too short a piece for stuffing, can be cut up for sautés or for the blanquette of veal demonstrated on pages 70-71.

If you buy only half a breast, you may find a pocket already cut into the meat. Ignore it; such a pocket was made by the butcher so the breast could be stuffed flat like an envelope with the bones still in-

side the meat. The pocket will not interfere with the different stuffing method demonstrated here.

Boning the breast is not difficult. It requires only sharp butcher and boning knives and some careful cutting: you should be able to pull the rib section away in one piece. Reserve the ribs for stock making, or set them aside to use in the bottom of the poaching pot. In the pot, the ribs will serve as a rack for the veal, allowing the poaching liquid to baste the bottom of the meat as it cooks; the gelatin that melts out will enrich the broth.

Stuffing adds flavor and color to the veal roll, and you may use any combination of ingredients so long as they do not dominate the subtle flavor of the meat. Chard, mild cheese, chopped eggs, onion and prosciutto are all possible ingredients. Or try the stuffing used here—a mixture of shallots and spinach, spices, ground pork and beef, bread crumbs and

an egg for binding (*recipe, page 157*).

Recipes often produce far more stuffing than needed for the roll, which usually requires only two or three cupfuls, but the extra stuffing may be cooked and served as a side dish. Warm it for 20 to 30 minutes in a double boiler or, if the stuffing mixture includes raw pork, bake it in a greased casserole in a 375° F. [190° C.] oven for half an hour or so in order to eliminate any possibility of trichinosis.

Since the stuffing will flavor the meat, you may wish to poach the veal roll in water with aromatic vegetables and seasonings only; the resulting broth will be light and pure. If you like a more assertive taste, you can add white wine to the water or substitute veal stock for all or some of the water. In any case, you will want to use the poaching broth to moisten the carved veal roll.

1 Dividing the breast. Place the meat, bone side up, on a cutting board. Cut a section six to eight ribs long from the wide, rectangular plate end of the meat. The six-rib piece being cut above will serve four people amply; an eight-rib section would serve six.

2 Freeing the ribs. Working from the outer tip of the rib bones, use a sharp boning knife to cut close under the bones and free them from the meat. Keep the blade pointed toward the bones so that you do not pierce the meat. Pull up the bones as you loosen them (above) so that it will be easier to see what you are cutting.

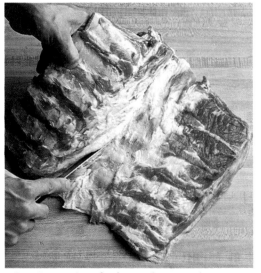

3 Removing the breastbone. When the rib section is freed from the meat underneath, it will still be connected to the breastbone. Roll the rib bones away from the meat as if opening a book. Cut under the exposed breastbone (above), pulling it back from the meat until you cut it free. Trim away any excess fat and cartilage, including the flap that covered the ribs. Save the flap for stock.

4 **Stuffing the breast.** Spoon stuffing in a line down the center of the boned side of the meat *(above)* and shape the breast into a compact cylinder 3 or 4 inches [8 or 10 cm.] across. The outside of the cylinder will have a uniformly grained surface that will give the finished roll an attractive exterior.

5 **Sewing the roll.** Close the long sides of the meat over the stuffing so they overlap, then sew the seam *(above)* with a trussing needle and cotton string. Tuck in and sew the ends. All stitches should be at least ¼ inch [6 mm.] from the edges to prevent tearing during cooking. Allow some slack for the meat to shrink without wrenching the seam.

6 **Poaching the veal.** Put the meat on top of its bones in a pot with liquid to cover. Bring to a boil and skim off the scum. Reduce the heat so the liquid simmers, then add a bouquet garni and aromatic vegetables — carrots are used here. Simmer, covered, for 1½ to 2 hours, adding liquid periodically *(above)* to keep the meat submerged.

7 **Carving the roll.** Take the meat out of the poaching broth and carefully remove the stitches. Let the meat rest on a cutting board for 15 minutes before carving it into thick slices. Arrange the slices and the uncut section of the roll seam side down on a serving platter. Surround the meat with separately cooked garnish vegetables — perhaps boiled carrots sprinkled with parsley, as here — and moisten each slice with broth *(opposite)* before serving.

Corned Beef—a Lasting Favorite

Before modern refrigeration, beef—like other meats—was preserved by "corning" it—coating it with dry salt—or soaking it for several days in a flavored salt brine. The salt used in Anglo-Saxon times was crushed into granules the size of wheat kernels—"corn" to the British—which provided the name for the process. Although corning is no longer a necessity, the curing gives meat a hearty taste that has earned for salt, or corned, beef a lasting place in many cuisines.

Corned beef can be bought ready to cook from your butcher, of course, but if you cure the meat yourself *(box, below)*, you can choose whatever cut or quality of beef you prefer and prepare it to your own taste. Brisket, with its natural interlarding of fat, and coarse-grained bottom round are traditionally used for corning.

Before cooking corned beef, soak it in cold water for several hours or overnight to draw out excess salt. Then truss it into a neat shape and poach it in water—perhaps with a discreet addition of hard cider, as in the demonstration at right. Gentle simmering allows the characteristic flavor of the beef to emerge and tenderizes even the toughest cuts.

1 **Skimming the corned beef.** Place the soaked and trussed beef in a pot, cover with cold water and bring to a boil, removing the scum *(page 16)*. When no scum appears, reduce the heat and simmer. If the liquid is salty after 10 minutes, start again with boiling fresh water. Add aromatics—here, onions and a bouquet garni. Skim any other scum and simmer for 2 to 3 hours.

2 **Completing the poaching.** Transfer the beef to a clean pot and add fresh garnish vegetables—here, onions, sliced turnips and carrots cut into chunks. Strain, cool and degrease the poaching liquid *(page 51)* and pour it over the beef. Add some hard cider if you like. Poach for about 1 hour more—or until you can pierce the beef easily with a skewer.

A Briny Bath for Brisket

To corn a 5-pound [2- to 3-kg.] piece of brisket *(right)* or bottom round, prepare about 4 quarts [4 liters] of pickling brine *(recipe, page 129)*, or enough to cover the meat completely. Saltpeter (sodium nitrate) is often added to lend a rosy hue to the beef, which otherwise may become grayish. But saltpeter will harden the meat and may, according to health officials, be a health hazard; it was therefore not used in this demonstration. How long to leave the meat in the brine is a matter of taste: the longer the time, the more the salt will penetrate. The minimum time is about three days; the maximum is 10 days.

To prevent the meat from spoiling during the salting, make sure all your utensils are clean, and keep the beef in a cool, dark place. Use a stoneware, glass or enamel crock or pot: metal or plastic may affect the color or taste of the beef.

1 **Draining the meat.** To draw off any excess blood—and to help the brine to penetrate—pierce the beef all over with a trussing needle or skewer and place the meat in cold water for about 45 minutes. Then remove the meat, rinse it and put it in a clean crock or pot. Do not truss or roll the meat.

2 **Adding the brine.** Mix water, salt, sugar and seasonings, and boil until the sugar and salt dissolve. To test for saltiness, put a raw egg in the cooled solution; if it does not float, add salt until it does. Cool the brine and pour it into the crock over the meat, which should float in the brine.

3 **Serving and garnishing.** Remove the meat from the poaching liquid, cut the trussing strings and carve the meat into generous slices. Place them on a warmed platter. Arrange the cooked garnish vegetables around them and pile on dumplings (box, right). Sprinkle with chopped fresh parsley and serve.

Making Light Dumplings

Lightly seasoned dumplings (recipe, page 130) are the perfect complement for corned beef. You can poach them with the meat for the last 30 minutes of cooking; but the dumplings should be able to float freely, and they may break up in the crowded pot. To avoid this difficulty, cook the dumplings separately in a large pan, using some of the beef's poaching liquid, or stock or lightly salted water. Cover the pan as soon as you drop in the dumplings—and do not lift the cover for at least 15 to 20 minutes.

1 **Making the dumplings.** Mix the ingredients to a firm consistency and chill for at least 30 minutes. Wet your hands to prevent sticking, and form small, round balls. Roll them in flour for easier handling.

3 **Weighting the meat.** To submerge the beef and ensure its saturation, place a clean plate, weighted with a heavy object, on top of the meat. Use a glass, ceramic or enameled weight that will not interact with the brine — in this case, a pickling jar filled with water. Cover the crock.

4 **Removing the meat.** When the beef is corned to your taste, lift it from the crock. Do not be alarmed if the beef feels very slippery. If it has been in the brine for only three to four days, soak it a few hours in cold water before cooking. If it has been corned for a longer time, soak it overnight.

2 **Poaching the dumplings.** Half-fill a large pan with poaching liquid. Drop the dumplings into the simmering liquid, cover and poach for about 30 minutes. Transfer the dumplings to the serving platter with a slotted spoon.

6

A Medley
of Methods

Slices of tomato and green pepper slide into a skillet full of potatoes and pieces of beef that have been sautéed with onion and garlic. The colorful assembly will be stirred and cooked until the separate flavors have merged to form a fragrant hash.

This chapter deals with preparing beef and veal in ways that do not fit neatly into the orderly divisions of roasting, broiling, frying, braising and poaching. In two instances, the beef is not cooked at all. Finely chopped as tartar steak or flattened in paper-thin slices *(page 81)*, it is served raw, complemented only by carefully chosen garnishes. In another instance, the meat is cooked in an old-fashioned way: enclosed in pastry and baked in the oven to produce a savory meat pie. Suet pastry, appropriately based on beef fat, serves as an edible lid for such fillings as cut-up steak and kidney, sealing in moisture and flavor as the pie cooks.

Meat loaves are baked and meatballs are usually fried and then braised or poached, but both offer every cook the opportunity to explore a wealth of existing recipes or to invent new ones by changing the proportions, varying the meats and adding or subtracting herbs, spices and other seasonings. In addition, variations in ground-beef or ground-veal dishes can be achieved with accompaniments and with sauces ranging from the simplest kind of homemade tomato sauce *(page 86)* to a lightly sweetened sauce that is based on beer with lemon juice *(recipe, page 165)*, or even an exotic and delicious blend of eggs and yogurt flavored with caraway seeds *(recipe, page 138)*.

Many of the classic beef dishes are best prepared in large quantities, and the leftover cooked meat they provide paves the way for improvisation. Part of the pleasure of making a French pot-au-feu *(pages 68-69)* is using the extra beef and broth for a *miroton* —a traditional, oniony stew that may be transformed into a crisp-crusted gratin *(pages 82-83)*. Alternatively, pot-au-feu or roast-beef leftovers can be sliced or diced and cooked with vegetables *(opposite)* for a full-meal hash. Red-flannel hash *(pages 84-85)* is a variation on the corned beef and potato dish that traditionally comes in the wake of a New England boiled dinner. Veal leftovers, too, lend themselves well to interesting treatments, such as a molded festive pudding *(page 88)* made from the ground meat.

The wide range of possibilities underlines the most important lesson to be learned: use leftovers with as much care and attention as you bestow on the cooking of the grandest beef roast or the most delicate veal scallops, and you will be rewarded with results that are as delicious and as attractive as any more formal dish.

Making Pastry with Suet

Suet (beef-kidney fat) is the ingredient of choice for making pastry to go with beef and veal. Buy it from the butcher when you buy your meat. Combined with flour and a little water or milk *(recipe, page 168)*, suet makes a dough that will be delicately crisp when baked in the oven *(opposite)* or spongy and light when steamed *(recipe, page 133)*.

In pastry-making, the key to working with butcher's suet is to chill it before use until it is hard; that way the suet will readily crumble free from the membranes that hold it together. It will also be easier to chop into tiny pieces that mix thoroughly with the flour and liquid to produce an even-textured pastry.

To make sure your pastry is light, work quickly so the suet remains cool.

Knead and roll out the dough on a floured, cold surface—a marble pastry slab, if you have one. Cook the dough as soon as it is prepared. Unlike some pastry, suet dough should not be rested or chilled before use. To make the pastry in advance, mix the dry ingredients and refrigerate them; then add liquid and mix the pastry when you need it.

1 **Preparing the suet.** Break apart the chilled suet *(above, left)* and peel away any transparent connective tissue. Chop the suet with a large, sharp knife, occasionally sprinkling the fat with flour so that the pieces do not stick together. Continue chopping until the suet pieces are the size of coarse bread crumbs *(above, right)*.

2 **Mixing the pastry.** With your fingers, lightly mix the suet, flour and a pinch of salt *(above, left)*. With a fork, stir in cold water or milk, a little at a time *(above, right)*, until the dough masses together. Very little liquid is needed. Form the dough into a ball.

3 **Kneading the pastry.** Knead the dough lightly to complete the blending. Use the heel of your hand to press out the dough, then gather it into a ball and push it out again. Repeat until the dough is smooth and workable.

4 **Rolling out the pastry.** Divide the pastry into portions to top individual pies or make a double crust. Flour the surface and roll out the pastry *(right)* to the correct thickness for your recipe: usually ¼ to ½ inch [6 mm. to 1 cm.].

Quick and Easy Meat Pies

A quick, simple and traditional way to join beef and pastry in a single dish is a meat pie. To make it, you simply spoon braised meat into a pie dish, mounding it high to prevent your piecrust from sinking as it cooks. Cover the meat with a suet pastry or whatever other kind you prefer, cut a slit in the center so that the steam can escape and then bake the pie until the crust turns crisp and golden. These pies offer you an opportunity to experiment with different mixtures of beef or veal and vegetables, or you can use the time-honored steak-and-kidney combination *(recipe, page 133)* shown here.

If you would rather start with raw meat, so that the flavors can permeate the crust, you will have to increase the cooking time. Use tender braising meat, such as chuck, and brown it before assembling the pie. Turn down the oven heat during the latter part of the pie's cooking time and shield the crust with aluminum foil to keep it from burning.

1 **Cutting up the beef.** Any cut of beef that is suitable for braising can be used for a steak-and-kidney pie. Here, a piece of chuck steak weighing 2 to 2½ pounds [1 kg.] is cut into rough cubes about 1 inch [2½ cm.] across.

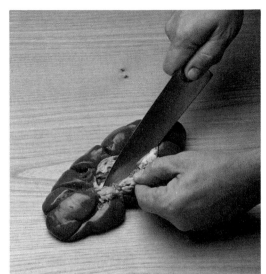

2 **Preparing the kidneys.** Cut away the fatty tissue from each kidney *(above).* Divide the kidney lengthwise, pare away any remaining white tissue and cut the meat into chunks. To diminish the strong flavor of the pieces, boil them in water for 1 minute and drain them for 15 minutes.

3 **Assembling a pie.** When the filling — here, chuck steak and kidney braised with onions in stock — is done, let it cool; a hot filling will make the pastry soggy. Roll out the pastry and cut out a lid slightly larger than the pie dish. Spoon the filling into the dish. Lay the pastry over the dish *(above, left),* crimp its edges and brush it with an egg-and-water glaze *(above, right).*

4 **Baking.** Put the pies in an oven, preheated to 400° F. [200° C.], and bake until the crust is golden (45 minutes to 1 hour). To serve each pie, cut away a portion of crust with a spoon, then serve the filling beside it *(right)* so as not to mar the pastry's crispness.

Beef at Its Natural Best

The Classic Raw Chopped Beef

Tasting the first forkful of raw beef is a happy surprise, even for people who are not usually blessed with adventurous appetites. The two raw-beef dishes shown here are most often found in restaurants, but both are easy to prepare at home. The only indispensable ingredient is superlatively fresh, top-quality, lean beef.

Tartar steak *(right)* is a chopped-beef classic, but Carpaccio steak, the thinly pounded raw beef shown opposite, is a 20th Century innovation.

The name of tartar steak reflects its presumptive beginnings: at daybreak—or so the story goes—the 13th Century Mongolian Tartars slipped slices of raw beef under their saddles; by nightfall, the beef was tenderized from the chafing of a hard day's riding. Nowadays, however, preparation of tartar steak is less strenuous *(recipe, page 136)*. The accompaniments may be prepared ahead of time, but the beef should be chopped—preferably by hand *(pages 40-41)*—at the last possible moment. Many cooks use tenderloin or sirloin steak, very tender but expensive cuts; round steak is less expensive and better flavored. Whatever cut you use, pare away every bit of fat and connective tissue; part of the quality of tartar steak resides in the perfect leanness of the beef.

Thin slices of raw beef with a piquant garnish became a celebrated dish at Harry's Bar in Venice, where they were first served to a favored customer whose doctor advised him to eat only raw meat. The dish, named Carpaccio in honor of the great 15th Century Venetian painter, was prepared by slicing chilled beef paper thin on a machine. You can produce the same effect by gently pounding small slices of beef until they are so thin they are almost translucent.

As with tartar steak, you can use beef tenderloin, or a cheaper cut thoroughly trimmed. Top round is the choice here; pounding takes care of toughness and closes any slits you make while removing streaks of internal fat. With any cut, the dish is economical: you can make a dozen servings from 1 pound [½ kg.] of beef.

1 **The presentation.** Put flattened mounds of freshly chopped — not ground — raw beef on a platter and surround them with such chopped garnishes as the parsley, onion, capers, shallots and gherkins used here. Make a well in each mound and slip a raw egg yolk into it. Set salt, pepper and olive oil at hand.

2 **The final mixing.** Give the diners two forks each to help themselves to a mound of beef and to the garnishes they like. When they have chosen the ingredients that suit their palates, they can use the forks to mix the seasonings gently through the meat.

Beef Pounded Paper-Thin

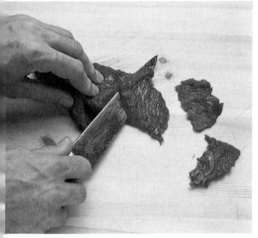

1 **Slicing the meat.** Trim away every trace of fat and connective tissue from a piece of raw steak. Then partially freeze the steak to make it easier to carve. Cutting across the grain of the meat, slice the steak into small pieces about ¼ inch [6 mm.] thick.

2 **Pounding.** Smear two sheets of clear plastic wrap with olive oil and place a slice of beef between them. Pounding gently and evenly, flatten the meat with a meat mallet. The meat will spread very little at first, but once it becomes soft, it will thin out rapidly.

3 **Peeling off the plastic.** To test the meat for thinness, hold the sheets and meat up to the light; if you can see light through the meat, it has been pounded sufficiently. When it is thin enough, remove the top sheet of plastic wrap and invert the meat onto a plate. Gently peel away the other layer *(above)*.

4 **Garnishing.** Arrange the slices of pounded beef side by side on a plate. Decorate the beef with a crisscross pattern of anchovy fillets — these silvery ones are salt-cured — parboiled and thinly sliced green peppers, capers and pickled red peppers, then sprinkle with chopped chives. Serve at once. Lemon wedges, Dijon mustard, watercress, mayonnaise and thinly sliced rye bread all go well with this dish.

A Hot Onion Sauce for Cold Meats

In a well-run kitchen, leftover beef—especially from a roast or a pot-au-feu—is usually the sign of a cook who thinks ahead. Served cold, such cuts make delicious salads and sandwiches; they are also the foundation for any number of easily assembled hot dishes. Provided the meat is not allowed to dry out during its second cooking and is presented in a form that looks—as well as tastes—delicious, a dish made of leftovers can be just as good as the original meal.

One glorious example is the French *miroton,* which is prepared by heating thin slices of leftover beef from a pot-au-feu in a sharp onion sauce *(recipe, page 140).* Although *miroton* is renowned as a working man's dish (the 19th Century French novelist Honoré de Balzac linked it memorably with Parisian concierges), its fame has spread because of its flavor, not because of its thrift.

The dish acquires its character from a sauce made by combining butter-stewed onions with stock and an enlivening dash of vinegar. You can improvise freely on this formula: one often-used embellishment is to finish the dish with a crisp gratin of buttery bread crumbs, as demonstrated here. And although onions are always the predominant flavor in a *miroton,* tomatoes, garlic and mushrooms are all possible additions. For extra bite you can use a pinch or two of grated horseradish instead of vinegar.

A true *miroton* is made with pot-au-feu beef that has already been tenderized by long poaching. This beef will be ready after only half an hour in the oven, enough time for it to absorb the sauce's flavor.

Roast beef can be treated in a similar way, but needs more thorough cooking. Since meat cooked by dry heat toughens at the beginning of a moist cooking process, allow leftover roast beef to simmer in a sauce for at least an hour. If you have no pot-au-feu stock, use any other, convenient liquid—wine, perhaps, or veal stock or a combination of the two—for the onion sauce demonstrated here.

1 **Preparing the beef.** Chill the meat well to make carving easier. Cut the thinnest possible slices of beef—here, shank and short-rib meat from the pot-au-feu shown on pages 68-69—so that the flavors from both the meat and the sauce will merge fully.

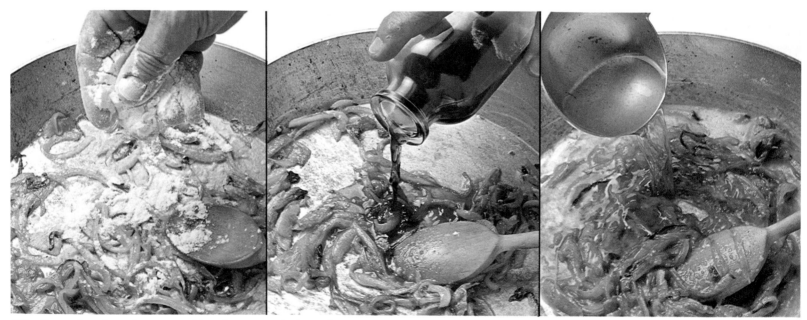

2 **Preparing the onion sauce.** Slice the onions thinly and cook them in butter in a heavy skillet over low heat. When they are golden and very soft—about 10 minutes—sprinkle them with enough flour to make a light roux *(above, left).* Stir the mixture thoroughly for 2 to 3 minutes before adding 1 to 2 tablespoons [15 to 30 ml.] of wine vinegar *(above, center).* Continue stirring and pour over enough pot-au-feu broth or veal stock to make a thin, creamy sauce *(above, right).* Bring the sauce to a boil, then lower the heat and cook the mixture at a simmer for about 30 minutes.

3 **Assembling the dish.** Pour a layer of the sauce into a shallow, ovenproof dish. Arrange the meat in overlapping slices, and cover with more sauce. Bake, covered, in a moderate oven for half an hour. If you are using roast beef, cover the dish and simmer for at least an hour before going on to Step 4. Check to make sure that the sauce does not reduce too much during the simmering; if it does, add more stock.

4 **Adding the gratin topping.** When the *miroton* has completed its preliminary cooking, sprinkle its surface with a thick coating of fresh bread crumbs. Spoon just enough melted butter over the crumbs to moisten them. Place the dish in a moderate oven for about 30 minutes, or until a golden crust forms.

5 **Serving the miroton.** If you wish, sprinkle the crusted top of the *miroton* with freshly chopped parsley and squeeze over it the juice of half a lemon. To ensure a crisp crust, serve the *miroton* at once, from the baking dish.

Adding Vegetables to Stretch Leftovers

A hash is a pan-fried mixture of sliced or chopped leftovers—meat and vegetables—plus seasonings. The word hash is derived from the French *hacher,* meaning "to chop," and the ingredients should be cut small to speed cooking. Otherwise, give your imagination free rein.

Choose any combination of ingredients that appeals to you. Vegetables make the meat go further and provide scope for improvisation; use those that were originally cooked with the meat, or add fresh ones. Sweet peppers, tomatoes and even beets contribute both color and flavor to a hash. Potatoes, cooked or raw, can stretch the hash and may account for as much as half its volume. If you use raw potatoes, moisten the hash with a liquid, such as stock or cream, and cook it slowly—or grate the potatoes so that they will be cooked by the time the rest of the hash is done. You can cook the hash either to a moist, soft consistency or to a browned and crusty crispness.

The cooking sequences illustrated here demonstrate two different approaches to hash-making. In the top panel, each element is cooked separately before it joins the assemblage. The first three steps show the preparation of a lyonnaise hash *(recipe, page 141),* redolent of onions and vinegar. Then, fried potatoes are added to the hash to make it into a more filling dish, with an edge of crispness. And finally, sweet peppers and tomatoes give the hash a Mediterranean character and add moistness. You can stop at any stage—after adding the onions or potatoes, for example—or go on to add the other ingredients suggested.

In the lower panel, all the ingredients of the hash are combined in advance and fried into a cake with a crisp outer crust. The cake illustrated here is a red flannel hash *(recipe, page 143),* which is traditionally made from the leftovers of a New England boiled dinner: corned beef, potatoes and beets. For a hash-cake mixture, cut up the meat and precooked vegetables into small pieces of uniform size so they heat evenly. But chop raw ingredients—especially onions—very fine, so that everything will mix thoroughly, enabling the cake to hold together well and cook in a conveniently short time.

Elaborating on a Lyonnaise Hash

1 **Cutting up the meat.** To produce neat pieces, make sure the meat is well chilled. Cut it into pieces that are small enough to warm through quickly and that will mix easily with the onions and other vegetables to be added later. Here, leftover boiled beef shank is cut into slices about ½ inch [1 cm.] thick.

2 **Softening the onions.** Melt butter in a skillet over gentle heat and put in the onions, a bouquet garni and a few unpeeled, crushed garlic cloves. Cover the skillet and cook the mixture gently for about 20 minutes or until the onions are soft and golden; stir regularly *(above)* to keep the onions from sticking to the pan or burning. Remove the garlic and the bouquet garni.

Crusty Red Flannel Hash

1 **Combining ingredients.** Dice the meat and the precooked vegetables — here, corned beef, potatoes and beets — and chop the raw onions finely. Put these ingredients in a bowl and add salt, pepper and a grating of nutmeg *(above)*. Mix thoroughly.

2 **Shaping the hash cake.** In a heavy pan, melt a generous quantity of butter or oil (or a mixture). When the fat is hot, spoon the hash mixture into the pan and pack it down firmly with a spatula so that an even crust forms on the bottom. Compact the edges of the cake *(above)* so that the ingredients hold together when the hash is turned over.

3 **Frying the meat.** In a separate pan over high heat, fry the meat slices in fat or oil until their edges turn a little crusty. Reduce the heat and add the softened onions; using a wooden spoon, toss them together with the meat *(above)*. Stir in a splash of red wine vinegar and sprinkle with chopped parsley to finish the lyonnaise hash.

4 **Varying the hash.** For a more substantial hash, add potatoes that have first been parboiled, skinned and sautéed in oil *(above)*. For yet another version, you can incorporate sliced sweet peppers and skinned, seeded tomatoes. Precook the peppers over gentle heat with olive oil and salt. Add the tomatoes, heat them through, then tip them into the hash.

5 **Serving the hash.** Stir or toss all the ingredients together to keep them from sticking as you warm the hash for a few minutes to evaporate some of the liquid. Then sprinkle on plenty of chopped parsley. Serve the hash directly from the skillet *(above)*, or turn it into a heated serving dish.

3 **Inverting the hash.** Fry the hash over low heat for about 8 minutes, shaking the pan regularly to make sure that the cake slides easily without sticking. When the edges are lightly crusted, it is time to turn the cake over. To turn it in one piece, start by covering the pan with a large plate.

4 **Turning out the hash.** Holding the plate firmly against the pan, quickly turn over pan and plate together. If you make certain first that the hash slips freely in the pan, the cake will unmold neatly onto the plate *(above)*. If any bits stick to the pan, scrape them off and pat them onto the top side of the cake when you put the hash back in the pan.

5 **Browning the second side.** Add more oil and butter to the pan if needed. Once the fat is hot, carefully slide the hash cake from the plate back into the pan, easing it into place with a spatula *(above)*. Fry gently for about 8 minutes more to form a crust. Serve the hash from the pan, or turn it onto a plate.

Meat Loaf: Imagination as the Key Ingredient

A meat loaf is an invitation to improvisation; you can easily devise a recipe that will be distinctly your own. You may experiment with combinations of ground meats, making the texture coarse or fine, exploring a variety of seasonings and liquids, and adding ingredients, such as chopped vegetables, bread crumbs or dry cereals, to the basic mixture.

The loaf shown here is a straightforward classic *(recipe, page 145)*; use it as a basis for your inventions. The meat is a mixture of two parts ground beef to one part each of ground veal and pork. This combination produces a light and well-flavored loaf; but you can vary the proportions freely according to your preference, allowing one meat to predominate or mixing the flavors equally into a complex whole. Moistening agents, such as the milk used here, can also be varied; try veal stock, cream, wine or beer. The important thing is that you use enough. Too lean or dry a mixture results in a loaf that is crumbly and hard to slice. In this loaf, bread crumbs add lightness. Raw eggs incorporated into the mixture—about 1 egg for every 1 pound [½ kg.] of meat—bind the ingredients together.

For the best results, shape the mixture into a well-proportioned loaf and set it in the center of a shallow baking pan. Some cooks place their loaves on racks to prevent the bottoms from becoming soggy, but this is unnecessary unless your loaf is made from very fatty meat that might burn on the bottom of the pan.

To keep the top of the loaf from drying as it bakes, either cover it with strips of bacon before putting it in the oven, or baste it regularly during the cooking. If you do the basting with a sauce, you can color and flavor the surface of the loaf. The tomato sauce used here is a simple one made by puréeing drained, canned tomatoes, then adding a large pinch of dried mixed herbs. If you are serving the loaf hot, it should be cut into fairly thick slices; when the meat is cold, it is easy to slice as thinly as you wish.

1 **Combining the ingredients.** Put the ingredients in a bowl and mix them together thoroughly. Your own hands are the best tools for this job: you can feel when the ingredients clump together too firmly and can easily break them up to combine them lightly and evenly.

2 **Adjusting the consistency.** When properly blended, the mixture should hold together, leaving the sides of the bowl clean. If not, add a little more liquid. Put the mixture into a buttered baking pan; then, after wetting your hands with cold water to keep the meat from sticking to them, shape it into a loaf.

3 **Saucing and baking.** Cover the loaf with tomato sauce *(inset)*, and bake, uncovered, in a preheated 350° to 375° F. [180° to 190° C.] oven. Baste the loaf occasionally with sauce; add water if needed. At serving time, the sauce will have been reduced and enriched with meat juices—a natural gravy for the loaf.

Improvisations with Meatballs

Meatballs can be cooked by practically any method: broiling, grilling, frying, poaching, braising or baking. The demonstration here is intended as an encouragement to experimentation. If the meatballs are to be fried, flouring them beforehand will help them to brown without sticking or crumbling, and will produce a crusty exterior surface. After frying them until they are colored on all sides, either serve them straight away or simmer them in one of any number of liquids, ranging from stock—as here—to tomato sauce or even yogurt. If you poach the meatballs without preliminary frying, do not flour them first.

Some recipes for *kefta*—Middle Eastern or North African meatballs—call for very finely chopped or ground meat. Traditionally, *kefta* are made with a pestle and mortar, but you could use a food processor to reduce the meat to a proper paste quickly and easily.

1 **Molding the meatballs.** After you have combined the ingredients—in this case, ground beef, eggs, bread crumbs and herbs—pinch off pieces of the seasoned mixture and roll them into balls between your moistened palms. Handle the meat gently so that the balls will have a light texture.

2 **Dredging with flour.** If you are coating the meatballs before frying, sift some flour onto a plate. Roll the balls lightly in the flour by moving the plate with a swiveling motion. Shake the balls gently to remove excess flour.

3 **Browning.** Heat some butter and oil in a heavy pan, slide the floured meatballs gently into the pan *(above)* and fry the meatballs until they are lightly browned on all sides. Shake the pan frequently to keep them from sticking.

4 **Adding liquid.** To poach the meatballs, discard the fat from the frying pan. Pour into the pan enough stock *(above)* or sauce to barely cover them. Bring the liquid to a boil, cover the pan and let the contents simmer gently over low heat. The meatballs will be done in about 30 minutes, but they may simmer for up to an hour if you like.

5 **Serving.** Using a slotted spoon so that the cooking liquid can drain from them, transfer the meatballs to a heated serving dish. Reduce the liquid remaining in the pan over high heat, sprinkle it with chopped fresh herbs and serve it as an accompanying sauce.

A Pudding of Veal and Vegetables

A small quantity of ground veal can be transformed into a light, moist pudding by binding it with bread crumbs and plenty of beaten eggs, then baking it in a moderate oven until the eggs are set *(recipe, page 165)*. Make the pudding either from finely chopped, leftover cooked veal or from uncooked veal that has been chopped and gently fried. In addition to eggs and bread crumbs, you can mix in other ingredients that complement the pale and delicate veal; the pudding in this demonstration includes sweet red peppers and tomatoes as well as freshly grated nutmeg. You could also use other lightly precooked, chopped vegetables— mushrooms, for example, or scallions or zucchini—and other spices or herbs.

If you cook the pudding in a mold and turn it out for serving, the dish will be both handsome and economical. Choose a smoothly shaped, curved mold and lavish butter on the inside so the pudding will not stick. If you like, line the bottom with sorrel, lettuce, chard or very young spinach leaves before you add the veal; the leaves will blend into the surface of the pudding as it cooks, adding a faint flavor as well as a decorative pattern.

1 **Preparing the mold.** Coat the mold thickly with butter and lay a pattern of leaves in it. Sorrel leaves — used here — need only be washed and trimmed beforehand; spinach leaves must be blanched in boiling water to make them limp. To coat the pudding, sprinkle dry bread crumbs into the mold.

2 **Filling the mold.** Spoon the pudding mixture into the mold, filling it to the rim, and tap the mold on a work surface so the ingredients will settle. Cover the pudding with buttered wax paper to keep it from drying. Bake the pudding in a moderate oven for 40 minutes, or until it is firm but still moist.

3 **Unmolding the pudding.** Using a cloth to protect your hands, remove the wax paper and place a warmed plate over the top of the mold. Hold plate and mold together *(above)* and invert them. Lift the mold, leaving the pudding on the plate *(right)*. To enhance the pudding, serve it with a sauce, such as puréed tomatoes enriched with cream.

Anthology of Recipes

Drawing upon the cooking traditions and literature of more than 23 countries, the Editors and consultants for this volume have selected 200 published beef and veal recipes for the Anthology that follows. The selections range from the simple to the unusual—from plain roast beef with Yorkshire pudding to spicy Moroccan ground-meat sausages grilled on skewers.

The Anthology also spans nearly 200 years and includes recipes by 132 writers, many of them distinguished exponents of the culinary art. But there are also recipes by little-known authors of out-of-print books held in private collections; a number of these recipes have never before been published in English. Whatever the sources may be, the emphasis always is on authentic dishes meticulously prepared with fresh, natural ingredients that will blend harmoniously.

Since many early recipe writers did not specify amounts of ingredients, the missing information has been judiciously added. Where appropriate, clarifying introductory notes have also been supplied; they are printed in italics. Modern terms have been substituted for archaic language; but to preserve the character of the original recipes, and to create a true anthology, the authors' texts have been changed as little as possible. Some instructions have been expanded, but in cases where recipes may seem abrupt, the reader has only to refer to the appropriate demonstrations in the front of the book to find the technique explained in words and pictures.

For ease of use, the Anthology gives beef recipes first, then veal recipes; within these sections the recipes are organized by cooking method. Recipes for standard preparations—stock, pastry and basic sauces—appear at the end of the Anthology. The serving suggestions and accompaniments in some recipes are, of course, optional.

All recipe ingredients are listed in order of use, with both the customary U.S. and the new metric measurements provided in separate columns.

The metric quantities supplied here reflect the American practice of measuring solid ingredients, such as flour or sugar, by volume rather than by weight, as European cooks do. To make the quantities simpler to measure, the figures have been rounded off to correspond to the gradations that are now standard on metric measuring spoons and cups. (One cup, for example, equals precisely 240 milliliters; in these recipes, however, a cup appears as a more readily measurable 250 milliliters.) Similarly, weight, temperature and linear metric equivalents are rounded off slightly. For these reasons, the American and metric figures are not equivalent—but using either set of figures will produce equally good results.

Beef

Roast Beef with Yorkshire Pudding and Horseradish Sauce

To ensure that the pudding and the beef are ready at the same time, place the pudding in the oven about 15 minutes before the roast has finished cooking. The pudding should remain in the oven through the resting time for the beef.

	To serve 8 to 10	
5 lb.	beef rib or sirloin tip roast	2½ kg.
	black pepper	
	Yorkshire pudding	
1 cup	flour	¼ liter
½ tsp.	salt	2 ml.
2	eggs	2
1¼ cups	milk	300 ml.
1 tbsp.	cold water	15 ml.
	Spiced horseradish sauce	
1	horseradish root, 4 inches [10 cm.] long	1
¾ cup	heavy cream	175 ml.
1 tsp.	sugar	5 ml.
½ tsp.	dry mustard	2 ml.
½ tsp.	salt	2 ml.
½ tsp.	white pepper	2 ml.
2 tsp.	white wine vinegar	10 ml.

Put the beef into a roasting pan, without adding fat. Sprinkle the beef with pepper. Roast in a hot oven, preheated to 425° F. [220° C.], for 15 minutes. Lower the heat to 375° F. [190° C.] for the rest of the cooking time, allowing 15 minutes to the pound. Baste the meat frequently with the pan juices. The beef should be served underdone, and should be transferred to a heated platter and left to rest for 15 minutes before carving.

While the beef is roasting, make the Yorkshire pudding. Sift the flour and the salt together into a mixing bowl. Add the eggs and stir. Add half the milk slowly and stir until the mixture is smooth. Add the remaining milk slowly and beat the batter well, then beat in the cold water.

About 15 minutes before the beef comes out of the oven, pour 2 tablespoons [30 ml.] of its fat into a baking pan 10 inches [25 cm.] square, and put the pan into the oven. When the fat is sizzling hot, pour in the pudding batter. Bake the batter on the top shelf of the oven for 30 minutes. The pudding should be well risen, puffy, crisp and brown on top and bottom, and should be served, cut in squares, straight from the pan in which it baked.

The horseradish root should remain in cold water for 1 hour, then be washed well and scraped into very thin shreds with a sharp knife. To make the sauce, whip the cream to stiff peaks, and fold in the horseradish, sugar, mustard, salt, pepper and vinegar. Serve the sauce cold.

MARY NORWAK
THE FARMHOUSE KITCHEN

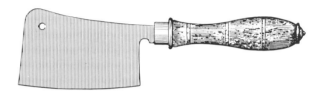

Rib Roast of Beef

If dinner is delayed, do not reheat a rib roast. Serve it warm or cool. It's still wonderful.

	To serve 10 to 12	
4 rib	standing rib beef roast	4 rib
½ cup	coarse salt	125 ml.
2 tsp.	freshly ground black pepper	10 ml.
	Horseradish sauce	
1 cup	heavy cream	¼ liter
	grated horseradish	

Bring the roast to room temperature and rub salt—coarse salt makes an attractive crust—and pepper on top of the fat but not over the flesh.

Stand the roast on its bones, fatty side up, in a shallow roasting pan and put it into an oven, preheated to 350° F. [180° C.]. Time it: calculate 17 minutes of cooking time per 1 pound [½ kg.] for a roast that is to be well done on the outside and very rare inside—so that it can be allowed to stand for 15 minutes out of the oven before it is carved. This gives the juices a chance to settle and makes carving easier.

If you are using a meat thermometer, insert it so that the point is in the center of the meat, not touching the bone. For very rare meat, the internal temperature should read 125° F. [50° C.]. Remember, the roast continues to cook after it is taken out of the oven.

Because I like to taste the beef, I do not make any kind of gravy or brown sauce. I do, however, like the English custom of accompanying rib roast with horseradish sauce—made by simply whipping the heavy cream and folding in horseradish, preferably fresh horseradish, to taste. And I always serve roast beef with potatoes.

JULIE DANNENBAUM
JULIE DANNENBAUM'S CREATIVE COOKING SCHOOL

The No-Roast Beef Roast

This method of roasting achieves perfectly rare beef, pink and juicy from end to end, with just the outer surface richly crusted, but it cannot be adapted to pieces of beef smaller than a 5-pound [2½-kg.] roast.

To serve 10

5 lb.	beef rib roast or rolled rump	2½ kg.
	salt and freshly ground black pepper	
4 tbsp.	lard or butter	60 ml.

Preheat the oven to 500° F. [260° C.] for at least 20 minutes. Then rub the meat all over with salt and pepper, and spread the lard or butter over it. Lay the meat on a rack in a roasting pan.

Place the beef in the oven. Roast for 5 minutes per pound [10 minutes per kg.]; then switch off the heat and leave the beef for 2 hours more. *Do not, under any circumstances, open the oven door during this time.*

When the 2 hours are up, open the door and, without removing the pan from the oven, touch the beef with your finger. If it feels hot, go ahead and serve it. Because some ovens do not retain their heat as well as others do, you may find the beef on the lukewarm side. If so, close the door, reheat the oven, still set to 500° F. [260° C.], and give the beef a further 10 minutes or so. This will raise the temperature of the beef without affecting its rareness.

Serve the beef on a warmed platter, accompanied by gravy made with the pan juices.

ROBERT CARRIER
THE ROBERT CARRIER COOKERY COURSE

Steak Barry Wall

To serve 4

2 lb.	beef steak, cut 1½ inches [4 cm.] thick	1 kg.
2 tsp.	butter	10 ml.
½ tsp.	dry English mustard	2 ml.
1 tsp.	Worcestershire sauce	5 ml.
1 tsp.	minced parsley	5 ml.
	salt and freshly ground black pepper	

Blend the butter with the mustard, Worcestershire sauce and the parsley. Broil the steak under a hot flame (or an electric broiler unit heated to its highest setting) for 3 to 4 minutes on each side.

Then, with a sharp knife, cut five or six crisscrossing diagonal slashes into one side of the steak. Spread on the seasoned butter, sprinkle the steak with salt and plenty of freshly ground black pepper, and broil for 1 more minute.

NARCISSE CHAMBERLAIN AND NARCISSA G. CHAMBERLAIN
THE CHAMBERLAIN SAMPLER OF AMERICAN COOKING

Beefsteak Florentine-Style

To serve 2

1	porterhouse steak, 2 inches [5 cm.] thick	1
1 tbsp.	olive oil	15 ml.
½ tsp.	salt	2 ml.
½ tsp.	pepper	2 ml.
1 tsp.	fresh lemon juice	5 ml.
½	lemon, cut into wedges	½

Place the steak in a dish with a marinade made by mixing the olive oil, salt and pepper. Let it stand for 1 hour, turning occasionally. Grill the steak over charcoal, about 8 minutes on each side. Remove the steak from the grill, return it to the dish, sprinkle the lemon juice over the steak and garnish with lemon wedges.

ADA BONI
THE TALISMAN ITALIAN COOK BOOK

Deviled Short Ribs

To serve 4

3 lb.	lean beef short ribs, each 4 to 5 inches [10 to 13 cm.] long	1½ kg.
¼ cup	finely chopped onion	50 ml.
¼ cup	strained fresh lemon juice	50 ml.
¼ cup	vegetable oil	50 ml.
3 tbsp.	prepared mustard	45 ml.
1 tsp.	finely chopped garlic	5 ml.
2 tsp.	salt	10 ml.
	freshly ground black pepper	

Combine the onion, lemon juice, oil, mustard, garlic, salt and a liberal grinding of pepper in a deep bowl and mix them well. Add the short ribs and turn them about with a spoon until they are evenly coated. Then marinate the ribs at room temperature for about 2 hours, turning them occasionally.

Preheat the oven to 400° F. [200° C.]. Arrange the ribs, fat side up, in a single layer on a rack set in a shallow roasting pan. (Discard the remaining marinade.) Roast the ribs uncovered in the middle of the oven for 20 minutes. Then reduce the heat to 350° F. [180° C.] and continue to roast for 1 hour and 15 minutes longer, or until the meat is tender and shows no resistance when pierced with the point of a small skewer or sharp knife. Arrange the ribs attractively on a heated platter and serve at once.

FOODS OF THE WORLD
AMERICAN COOKING: THE EASTERN HEARTLAND

Flank Steak with Marinade

To serve 4

2 lb.	beef flank steak, sliced diagonally into strips 1 inch [2½ cm.] wide	1 kg.
½ cup	dry red or white wine	125 ml.
⅓ cup	soy sauce	75 ml.
1	garlic clove, chopped	1
½ cup	chopped onion	125 ml.
1 tbsp.	fresh lime juice	15 ml.
2 tbsp.	brown sugar	30 ml.
1 ½ tsp.	salt	7 ml.
	pepper	

Make a marinade of the wine, soy sauce, garlic, onion, lime juice, brown sugar, salt, and pepper to taste. Pour the marinade over the meat and refrigerate for 24 hours.

Drain the meat; reserve the marinade. Grill the meat quickly over hot coals, turning the strips once. Allow 2 minutes for each side. Baste the strips often with the marinade.

MARION BROWN
MARION BROWN'S SOUTHERN COOK BOOK

Barbecued Beef

This is a variation of Texas-style barbecued beef, which traditionally is cooked over a pit filled with live coals.

To serve 6 to 8

4 lb.	beef top round	2 kg.
8 tbsp.	lard	120 ml.
1 tbsp.	salt	15 ml.
½ tsp.	cayenne pepper	2 ml.
8 tbsp.	butter	120 ml.
½ cup	boiling water	125 ml.
½ cup	tarragon vinegar	125 ml.
2 cups	dry red wine	½ liter
⅓ cup	grated onion	75 ml.
2 tbsp.	Worcestershire sauce	30 ml.

Wipe the meat thoroughly with a damp cloth and rub it well with half of the lard mixed with the salt and cayenne. Melt the remaining lard and the butter in the boiling water, add all the other ingredients and pour the liquid over the meat

which has been placed in a medium-sized mixing bowl. Let the meat stand in the liquid for 2 days in the refrigerator, well covered, turning from time to time so that both sides of the meat may absorb the marinade.

Place the meat on a rack in the broiler at 300° F. [150° C.] and broil under very low heat for 20 minutes on each side. (If you cannot regulate broiler temperature, make sure the meat is 8 inches [20 cm.] from the heat source.) Remove the meat from the broiler, put it back in the marinade for 10 minutes and then broil it under the same extremely low heat for another 20 minutes. Repeat this four times. Then place the meat in a baking pan with what remains of the marinade and finish cooking in a moderate oven, preheated to 350° F. [180° C.], until the meat is tender, basting constantly.

SHEILA HIBBEN
AMERICAN REGIONAL COOKERY

Spit-roasted Beef Tenderloin with Anchovies

Filet de Boeuf en Brochette, aux Anchois

To serve 4

2 lb.	beef tenderloin, cut into 4 slices each 1½ to 2 inches [4 to 5 cm.] thick	1 kg.
5	thin pieces lean salt pork without the rind, blanched in boiling water for 5 minutes and drained	5
4	garlic cloves, halved	4
	salt	
½ tsp.	finely chopped rosemary	2 ml.
⅛ tsp.	pepper	½ ml.
⅓ cup	olive oil	75 ml.
4	anchovy fillets, soaked in water for 10 minutes and patted dry	4

Thread the slices of salt pork and beef alternately onto a spit, and tuck a piece of garlic on either side of each slice of beef. Push the slices tightly together. Sprinkle the outside surfaces lightly with the rosemary and pepper. Tie the slices firmly together, then put the spit in front of the fire or on a barbecue. Put the oil in a small pot, add the anchovies, put the pot in a pan of simmering water and soften the anchovies over low heat. This will take 5 minutes. Pour the mixture into a small bottle and use it to baste the meat from time to time, shaking the bottle before each use.

After cooking the meat for about 20 to 30 minutes, it should be browned on the outside, pink at the center and full of flavor. Salt it before serving. If you do not like garlic, the pepper-and-rosemary mixture is sufficient seasoning.

LOUIS GINIÉS
CUISINE PROVENÇALE

"Sons of Rest" Beefsteak

The "Sons of Rest" were hangers-on in 19th Century Tucson gambling saloons. They were given money by saloon owners to play at the tables and create a busy, sociable atmosphere.

To serve 1 or 2

1	porterhouse steak, 2 inches [5 cm.] thick	1
2 tbsp.	butter, softened	30 ml.
1 to 2 tbsp.	prepared mustard, preferably English or Dijon mustard	15 to 30 ml.
	salt and pepper	
½ cup	dry sherry	125 ml.
1½ tsp.	chopped fresh parsley	7 ml.

Broil the porterhouse steak very rare. Leave it on the broiling rack and quickly cut rather deep diagonal gashes in it about 1½ inches [4 cm.] apart. Spread the steak lavishly with softened butter, pressing the butter into the incisions. Then spread the steak with the mustard of your choice. Salt and pepper to taste. Pour the sherry over the steak. Place the steak in a very hot oven, preheated to 450° F. [230° C.], for 10 to 12 minutes. Transfer the steak to a hot platter and pour the pan juices over it. Garnish with chopped parsley.

JAMES BEARD
JAMES BEARD'S AMERICAN COOKERY

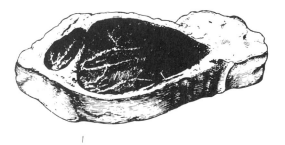

Flank Steak Orientale

To serve 6

2	beef flank steaks	2
3	garlic cloves, finely chopped	3
1 tsp.	freshly ground black pepper	5 ml.
⅔ cup	Japanese soy sauce	50 ml.
½ tsp.	Tabasco	2 ml.
⅓ cup	dry sherry (or substitute dry vermouth)	75 ml.
	salt	

Rub the steaks well with the chopped garlic and the pepper. Place them in a shallow dish and add the soy sauce, Tabasco and wine. Turn the steaks in the mixture several times. Let them stand for an hour or two at room tempera-

ture or even overnight in the refrigerator.

Broil the steaks at high temperature, close to the heat, for just 3 minutes on each side if you want them rare. Salt to taste and slice in very thin slices with a sharp knife—holding the knife so that the flat of the blade is almost parallel to the steak in order to produce wide, diagonally cut slices.

JOSÉ WILSON (EDITOR)
HOUSE AND GARDEN'S NEW COOK BOOK

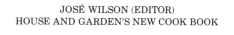

Broiled Beef with Piquant Sauce

La Chouio

To serve 4

2 to 2½ lb.	beef rib eye, boneless sirloin, strip or tenderloin steak, cut into 4 thick slices	1 kg.
	Piquant sauce	
2	shallots	2
2 tbsp.	olive oil	30 ml.
2	anchovy fillets, soaked in water for 10 minutes, patted dry and chopped	2
½ cup	red wine vinegar	125 ml.
3 or 4	garlic cloves	3 or 4
1	bay leaf	1
½ tsp.	thyme	2 ml.
1	whole clove	1
1 or 2	small red chilies, stemmed and seeded	1 or 2
	salt and pepper	
1 tbsp.	flour	15 ml.
2 cups	beef stock	½ liter
1 tbsp.	finely chopped gherkins	15 ml.
1 tbsp.	capers, rinsed in cold water, drained well and finely chopped	15 ml.

Brown the shallots in the oil in an enameled or stainless-steel saucepan. Add the anchovies, then pour the vinegar into the pan. Add the garlic, bay leaf, thyme, clove and chilies. Season with salt and pepper.

As soon as the vinegar has evaporated, add the flour and brown it. Then add the stock little by little, stirring constantly to achieve a completely smooth sauce. Stir until all the stock is added and well mixed. Leave on gentle heat for about 30 minutes.

Ten minutes before serving, add the gherkins and capers to the sauce. Cover the pan to keep the sauce warm while you broil the beef, then serve the sauce with the meat.

RENÉ JOUVEAU
LA CUISINE PROVENÇALE

Beefsteak with Potatoes

Bifteck aux Pommes de Terre

To serve 4

8	slices beef tenderloin, cut 1 inch [2½ cm.] thick	8
	ground allspice	
½ cup	olive oil	125 ml.
2 tbsp.	chopped fresh parsley	30 ml.
2 tbsp.	chopped onion	30 ml.
1 tbsp.	fresh lemon juice	15 ml.

Using a mallet, flatten each slice of beef to a thickness of about ½ inch [1 cm.]. Marinate the slices in a mixture of the allspice, olive oil, parsley, onion and lemon juice. Grill the meat under a broiler, preheated to its highest setting, for 2 or 3 minutes on each side. It is essential to serve the slices rare and very hot. Serve with potatoes stewed gently in butter and sprinkled with fines herbes.

OFFRAY AINÉ
LE CUISINIER MÉRIDIONAL

Grilled Beef with Bean Paste

Gyūniku No Misozuke-Yaki

The miso called for in this recipe is a bean paste made from fermented soybeans, and may be reddish or white in color. Both miso and pickled ginger root are obtainable from Oriental food stores. Sake is a strong, Japanese rice wine.

To serve 4

¾ lb.	beef rump or round, cut into 4 thin steaks	⅓ kg.
1 cup	red or white *miso*	¼ liter
¼ cup	sugar	50 ml.
2 tbsp.	*sake*	30 ml.
	lettuce leaves	
	pickled ginger root, sliced	

Score the edges of the steaks by making a small slit along the center of each side, then make two small cuts in both surfaces of each steak. Put the bean paste in a bowl with the sugar and *sake*, and mix until smooth.

Choose a dish large enough to hold all the steaks in one layer and spread half the bean-paste mixture on the bottom of the dish. Cover the paste with a double thickness of cheesecloth, cut to fit inside the dish. Arrange the steaks on top of the cheesecloth and cover them with a double thickness of cheesecloth. Spread the rest of the bean-paste mixture on the cheesecloth. Cover the dish tightly with aluminum foil and refrigerate the steaks for one or two days.

When you are ready to cook the steaks, lift them out. If desired, scrape the bean paste off the cheesecloth and reserve the paste for another use.

Broil the steaks on a rack set 2 inches [5 cm.] under a broiler preheated to its highest setting, or grill them over coals in a barbecue, for 2 minutes on each side or until they are lightly browned and cooked to the desired degree of doneness. Cut the steaks diagonally into bite-sized slices. Arrange them on a warmed platter and serve garnished with lettuce and pickled ginger.

ELISABETH LAMBERT ORTIZ WITH MITSUKO ENDO
THE COMPLETE BOOK OF JAPANESE COOKING

Beef Olives

Bragoli Mixwijin

Pork caul, the fatty membrane that encloses a pig's stomach, can be ordered from a butcher.

To serve 8

8	beef rump or round steaks, sliced ¼ inch [6 mm.] thick	8
8	bay leaves	8
8	pieces pork caul	8
	Pork and egg stuffing	
¼ lb.	lean salt pork without the rind, blanched in boiling water for 5 minutes, drained and finely chopped (about ½ cup [125 ml.])	125 g.
2	hard-boiled eggs, chopped	2
2 tbsp.	chopped fresh parsley	30 ml.
¼ cup	fresh bread crumbs	50 ml.
	salt and pepper	
¼ tsp.	chopped garlic (optional)	1 ml.

Trim the steaks and flatten them slightly by pounding them with a meat mallet. Mix together all the stuffing ingredients. Put 1 to 2 tablespoons [15 to 30 ml.] of stuffing on each steak, leaving a third of each steak uncovered. Roll the steaks from the covered ends and tie the beef olives securely with cotton string. Cover each beef olive with caul, putting a bay leaf between the steak and the caul fat. Thread olives crosswise onto skewers and broil them on a rack set 4 to 5 inches [10 to 13 cm.] below a preheated broiler for about 30 minutes, turning the skewers two or three times to brown the beef olives evenly.

ANNE AND HELEN CARUANA GALIZIA
RECIPES FROM MALTA

Steak Kebabs

Teriyaki

To serve 4 to 6

2 lb.	beef sirloin steak, sliced ½ inch [1 cm.] thick and cut in strips ½ inch wide and 6 inches [15 cm.] long	1 kg.
	Soy sauce marinade	
½ cup	soy sauce	125 ml.
¼ cup	sake (or substitute dry sherry)	50 ml.
1	garlic clove, crushed	1
1 tsp.	ground ginger	5 ml.
1 tsp.	sugar	5 ml.

Combine the marinade ingredients in a bowl. Add the beef strips and marinate for 1 hour. Weave the strips onto small bamboo skewers that have been soaked well in cold water to prevent them from charring. Grill over a hot charcoal fire for not more than 30 seconds a side—preferably less. The meat will be rare, juicy and delicious.

JOSÉ WILSON (EDITOR)
HOUSE AND GARDEN'S PARTY MENU COOKBOOK

Broiled Skewered Beef

Basturma Shashlik

Fresh pomegranates are available in September and October. Halve them and squeeze them to extract their juice, then strain out their seeds.

To serve 4

2 lb.	beef tenderloin or boneless sirloin, sliced 1½ inches [4 cm.] thick and cut into 1½-inch cubes	1 kg.
1	medium-sized onion, finely grated	1
¼ cup	red wine vinegar or fresh pomegranate juice	50 ml.
1 tsp.	salt	5 ml.
¼ tsp.	freshly ground black pepper	1 ml.
	melted butter (optional)	
2	medium-sized tomatoes, cut into eighths	2
8	scallions	8
	sprigs fresh coriander or parsley	
1	lemon, quartered	1

In a large bowl combine the beef, onion, vinegar or pomegranate juice, salt and pepper. Mix well. Cover and let stand at room temperature for 3 hours or in the refrigerator for 6

hours, occasionally turning the cubes of meat to keep them well moistened.

Remove the meat from the marinade and thread onto long skewers. If desired, brush the meat with melted butter and then broil it, preferably over charcoal, for 15 minutes or until the meat is done to your taste, turning frequently.

Using a fork, push the meat off the skewers onto warmed individual plates and garnish with the tomatoes, scallions, coriander or parsley, and lemon. Serve at once.

SONIA UVEZIAN
THE BEST FOODS OF RUSSIA

Skewered Broiled Beef and Vegetables

To serve 4

1 lb.	lean beef round steak, sliced 1 inch [2½ cm.] thick and cut into 1-inch cubes	½ kg.
½ lb.	fresh mushrooms, halved if large	¼ kg.
1	green or red pepper, halved, seeded, deribbed and cut into 1½-inch [4-cm.] squares	1
8	small boiling onions	8
	Soy sauce and sherry marinade	
½ cup	soy sauce	125 ml.
2 tbsp.	sugar	30 ml.
3 tbsp.	dry sherry	45 ml.
2 tsp.	sesame oil	10 ml.
1 tsp.	fresh lemon juice	5 ml.
¼ tsp.	finely chopped fresh ginger root	1 ml.
½	garlic clove, crushed	½

In a medium-sized mixing bowl, stir together the soy sauce, sugar, sherry, oil, lemon juice, ginger and garlic. Add the meat and marinate it for 30 minutes at room temperature.

Skewer the meat and vegetables, alternating the ingredients. Cook over hot coals on an hibachi or charcoal grill, or on a rack set 3 inches [8 cm.] below a preheated broiler, for 5 to 8 minutes, basting with the marinade and turning several times. Heat the remaining marinade and use it as a sauce.

SANDRA TAKAKO SANDLER
THE AMERICAN BOOK OF JAPANESE COOKING

Ale-Burgers

These patties may also be broiled about 4 inches [10 cm.] from an oven broiler preheated to its highest setting.

To serve 6

2 lb.	lean ground beef	1 kg.
½ cup	finely crumbled stale rye bread with the crust removed	125 ml.
½ cup	ale	125 ml.
1	medium-sized onion, finely chopped	1
½ tsp.	crushed caraway seeds	2 ml.
	salt and pepper	

Soak the rye bread in the ale. Blend the beef with the soaked bread and then mix in all the other ingredients. Shape the mixture into patties, and let stand for 1 hour. Broil the burgers over hot coals. Serve with ale.

JULES JEROME BOND
THE OUTDOOR COOKBOOK

Grilled Ground-Meat Sausages

Kefta on Skewers

The ras el hanout called for in this recipe is a mixture of many spices that is widely used in Moroccan cooking. A version of this exotic spice mixture can be prepared from equal pinches of ground allspice, cinnamon, ginger, nutmeg, cardamom, black pepper and cloves.

To serve 6

1½ lb.	ground beef or lamb, or a mixture of the two, including 2½ oz. [75 g.] fat	¾ kg.
1	small onion, grated	1
⅓ cup	finely chopped fresh parsley	75 ml.
1 to 2 tbsp.	finely chopped fresh coriander leaves	15 to 30 ml.
1 tsp.	finely chopped fresh mint	5 ml.
½ tsp.	finely chopped fresh marjoram (or substitute ¼ tsp. [1 ml.] dried marjoram)	2 ml.
	salt and freshly ground pepper	
½ tsp.	ground cumin	2 ml.
½ tsp.	*ras el hanout* (optional)	2 ml.

Combine all the ingredients in a large bowl and knead well. Set aside at room temperature for at least 1 hour. With wet hands, separate the meat mixture, or *kefta,* into 24 pieces and form each of these into the shape of a sausage. Put two sausages each on small bamboo skewers that have been soaked in water to prevent them from charring. Grill the sausages rapidly on both sides, 2 to 3 inches [5 to 8 cm.] from the heat of a broiler set at its highest temperature, or over charcoal, until done to taste. (Moroccans prefer them well cooked.) Serve hot, at once, with Arab bread, such as *pita.*

PAULA WOLFERT
COUSCOUS AND OTHER GOOD FOOD FROM MOROCCO

Indonesian Broiled Skewered Meatballs

Sesatee Pentool

The coconut milk called for in this recipe may be prepared by mixing the grated flesh of a quarter of a coconut with ½ cup [125 ml.] of boiling water. Let the mixture sit in a bowl for about half an hour, then strain and squeeze it through muslin or cheesecloth to obtain a creamy liquid. Trassi, a pungent Indonesian shrimp paste, and tamarind paste or jelly are available at many Oriental grocery stores.

To serve 4

1 lb.	finely ground beef	½ kg.
2	fresh red chilies, stemmed, seeded and chopped	2
1 tsp.	ground coriander	5 ml.
½ tsp.	ground cumin	2 ml.
¼ tsp.	ground turmeric	1 ml.
4	Brazil nuts, shelled and ground	4
½ tsp.	dark brown sugar	2 ml.
¼ tsp.	*trassi*	1 ml.
¼ tsp.	tamarind paste or jelly	1 ml.
4	shallots, finely chopped	4
2	garlic cloves, finely chopped	2
⅓ cup	freshly grated coconut	75 ml.
	salt	
¼ cup	peanut oil	50 ml.
2	small eggs, lightly beaten	2
½ cup	thick coconut milk	125 ml.

Combine the chilies, ground spices, nuts, sugar, *trassi* and tamarind paste or jelly in a mortar. Add the shallots, garlic, grated coconut and salt to taste, then pound the mixture with a pestle until smooth. Heat the oil in a wok or heavy skillet. Add the spice mixture and fry it quickly over medium heat until slightly crisp and golden. Using a slotted spoon, remove the spice mixture to a sieve and leave it to drain for about ½ hour, stirring occasionally. When the mixture is dry, pound it again in the mortar.

Combine three quarters of the spice mixture with the meat and the eggs. Shape into small balls about 1 inch [2½ cm.] in diameter. Thread the balls onto skewers 7 to 8 inches [18 to 20 cm.] long—about four or five balls to a skewer. Combine the rest of the spice mixture with the coconut milk and brush the skewered meatballs with this sauce. Grill the meatballs over hot coals, or broil them on a rack about 4 inches [10 cm.] below a preheated broiler, for about 8 minutes, turning and basting frequently with the sauce.

EMMA W. K. STEINMETZ
ONZE RIJSTTAFEL

Nutty Grilled Hamburgers

Polpette di Carne alla Griglia

To serve 4 to 6

1½ lb.	ground beef	¾ kg.
1	medium-sized onion, finely chopped	1
1	large garlic clove, finely chopped	1
1 cup	bread crumbs	¼ liter
⅓ cup	freshly grated Romano or Parmesan cheese	75 ml.
⅔ cup	pine nuts	150 ml.
½ cup	chopped fresh parsley	125 ml.
2	eggs	2
1½ tsp.	salt	7 ml.
1 tsp.	freshly ground black pepper	5 ml.
	oil	

Preheat the broiler.

Combine the beef, onion, garlic, bread crumbs, cheese, pine nuts, parsley, eggs, salt and pepper; blend well. Shape the mixture into thick, 2½-inch [6-cm.] rounds.

Brush the preheated broiling rack with oil and grill the meat 3 inches [8 cm.] from the heat source for about 5 minutes on each side or until the hamburgers are well browned.

ANNA MUFFOLETTO
THE ART OF SICILIAN COOKING

Beef Patties

Chuletas

To serve 4 to 6

2 lb.	ground beef	1 kg.
2 cups	chopped fresh parsley	½ liter
2 cups	chopped onion	½ liter
2	large eggs	2
1 tbsp.	salt	15 ml.
½ cup	freshly grated Parmesan cheese	¼ liter
½ tsp.	Tabasco	2 ml.
1 tsp.	freshly ground pepper	5 ml.
3 cups	sifted bread crumbs	¾ liter
	olive oil (optional)	

Mix together thoroughly all the ingredients except the bread crumbs and olive oil, and form into about 30 small balls. Sprinkle the bread crumbs over a pastry board, and pat each ball in the crumbs to make a thin patty, 3 to 4 inches [8 to 10 cm.] in diameter. Turn the patties to crumb the other side. Chill well. Then sauté the patties in olive oil, or broil them at high heat on an oiled, fine-meshed grill set 1 inch [2½ cm.] from the heat, for 2½ to 3 minutes on each side.

JAMES BEARD
JAMES BEARD'S AMERICAN COOKERY

Steak Au Poivre

To serve 6 to 8

4 lb.	boneless beef sirloin steak, cut 1½ inches [4 cm.] thick	2 kg.
	whole black peppercorns	
	salt	

Take the steak from the refrigerator an hour before you plan to serve it. With a rolling pin or with a mortar and pestle, crack enough peppercorns to make 1½ tablespoons [22 ml.] of pepper. Sprinkle both sides of the steak with the pepper, then press the pepper into the meat with the heel of your hand and let stand at room temperature. Twenty-five minutes before you plan to eat the steak, rub the inside of the skillet lightly with a piece of suet cut from the steak, sprinkle with a thin layer of salt and place over high heat until the salt begins to brown and the pan is almost but not quite smoking. Add the steak and cook for 10 minutes. Turn, with two wooden spoons so as not to puncture the meat, and cook for 10 minutes on the other side. This will give you a rare but not bloody steak.

ELEANOR GRAVES
GREAT DINNERS FROM LIFE

Tournedos with Marrow and Parsley Butter

Tournedos Bercy

Tournedos are small steaks that are cut from near the tip of the tenderloin.

	To serve 6	
6	tournedos	6
6	croutons, made from firm white bread, sliced ¾ inch [2 cm.] thick and cut into crustless circles 2½ to 3 inches [6 to 8 cm.] in diameter	6
8 tbsp.	butter	120 ml.
½ cup	dry white wine	125 ml.
½ cup	veal stock	125 ml.
	Bercy butter	
3	shallots, finely chopped	3
9 tbsp.	unsalted butter	135 ml.
½ cup	dry white wine	125 ml.
½ lb.	uncooked bone marrow, cut into small dice	¼ kg.
	salt and freshly ground pepper	
½ tbsp.	chopped fresh parsley	7 ml.
2 tsp.	fresh lemon juice	10 ml.

To make the Bercy butter, sauté the shallots in a small enameled or stainless-steel saucepan, cooking them slowly with 1 tablespoon [15 ml.] of unsalted butter without browning them. When the shallots are very soft, add the wine and boil to reduce it to 3 tablespoons [45 ml.]. Meanwhile, poach the marrow for a few minutes in a separate pan of nearly boiling salted water and drain the marrow well. While the shallot pan is still very hot, but off the heat, add the remaining unsalted butter, the marrow, the chopped parsley, a pinch of salt, a large pinch of freshly ground pepper, and the lemon juice. Mix well to produce a thick, creamed butter.

In a skillet, sauté the tournedos in 2 tablespoons [30 ml.] of butter until done. Set them aside in a warm place. In another skillet, fry the croutons in 5 tablespoons [75 ml.] of butter. Then arrange the sautéed tournedos on the croutons.

Pour the wine into the skillet used for the meat, deglaze the pan and reduce the liquid to about 2 teaspoons [10 ml.]. Add the veal stock and reduce this to about 2 tablespoons [30 ml.]. Finish the sauce, off the heat, by adding the remaining tablespoon [15 ml.] of butter and mixing it into the sauce by shaking the skillet. Pour the sauce over the tournedos. On each steak place 1 teaspoon [5 ml.] of creamed Bercy butter. The rest of the Bercy butter can be served in a sauceboat.

PAUL BOCUSE
PAUL BOCUSE'S FRENCH COOKING

Congolese Peppered Steak

Steak au Poivre Congolais

The green peppercorns called for in this recipe are soft, unripened peppercorns, obtainable wherever fine spices and herbs are sold. Do not crush them before use.

	To serve 4	
4	beef sirloin steaks, about 1 inch [2½ cm.] thick, each weighing about 5 oz. [150 g.]	4
	salt	
¼ cup	green peppercorns	50 ml.
2 tbsp.	butter	30 ml.
2 tbsp.	oil	30 ml.
¼ cup	Armagnac	50 ml.
1 cup	heavy cream	¼ liter

Salt the steaks and roll them in the peppercorns. Arrange the steaks in a skillet in which you have heated the butter and the oil. Brown them for 2 to 5 minutes on each side, according to your taste. When they are cooked, drain them and put them on a hot dish. Discard the cooking fat from the skillet and deglaze it with the Armagnac; then heat the skillet and set the Armagnac alight.

Pour the cream and any juices from the steaks into the skillet, bring to a boil and allow to reduce. Arrange the steaks on a platter, cover them with the sauce and serve as soon as possible, very hot.

RAYMOND OLIVER
LA CUISINE—SA TECHNIQUE, SES SECRETS

Rib of Beef with Tomatoes, Garlic and Spices

Costata di Bue alla Pizzaiola

	To serve 4	
4	beef rib or sirloin steaks, 1 inch [2 cm.] thick	4
1 tbsp.	olive oil	15 ml.
	salt and freshly ground pepper	
3	garlic cloves, crushed	3
2	tomatoes, peeled, seeded and sliced	2
	dried oregano	

Heat the oil in a large skillet until very hot. Arrange the slices of meat in it, and brown on both sides. Turn down the heat and cook for a few minutes until done to your taste. Drain the meat, place on a platter, season with salt and a generous pinch of pepper, and keep warm.

Add the crushed garlic to the meat juices in the skillet, and cook until golden brown. Add the sliced tomatoes, and flavor with salt and a pinch of oregano. Cook the tomatoes for 8 minutes, then return the slices of meat to the pan along with the juices they have exuded. Fry for a few seconds and serve coated with the sauce.

LUIGI CARNACINA
GREAT ITALIAN COOKING

Rib Steak Bordelaise

Entrecôte Bordelaise

Some butchers sell marrow by weight; others estimate marrow yield and sell you the bones that contain it. Let the bones come to room temperature, then scoop out the marrow.

To serve 2 to 4

2 to 2½ lb.	boned beef rib steak	1 kg.
2 tbsp.	butter	30 ml.
3	shallots	3
¾ cup	dry red wine	175 ml.
¼ tsp.	crushed black peppercorns	1 ml.
3 tbsp. plus ¾ cup	veal stock	45 ml. plus 175 ml.
1¼ tsp.	potato starch or arrowroot	6 ml.
1 tbsp.	Madeira	15 ml.
3 oz.	beef marrow, cubed, poached in water for 2 minutes and drained	100 g.

Brown the meat in butter in a sauté pan or skillet over high heat. Then transfer it to another pan with another tablespoonful of butter and set over low heat so that the meat can finish cooking. Remove all but 2 tablespoons [30 ml.] of fat from the first pan and add the shallots, wine and pepper. Reduce by two thirds. Mix the potato starch with 3 tablespoons [45 ml.] of the cold veal stock.

While reduction is going on (or beforehand, if you wish), heat the remaining veal stock in a small saucepan and add to it the potato-starch mixture. Leave over low heat, stirring, until the mixture thickens—about 5 minutes. Off the heat, add the Madeira. Strain the red wine-shallot reduction through a fine strainer into the thickened stock mixture. Bring to a boil and add the poached marrow cubes. Remove from the heat, salt if necessary, and pour the sauce over the steak when ready to serve.

RAYMOND A. SOKOLOV
GREAT RECIPES FROM THE NEW YORK TIMES

Sirloin Steak, Palermo-Style

Bistecca alla Palermitana

To serve 6

6	boneless ½ lb. [¼ kg.] sirloin steaks, ½ inch [1 cm.] thick	6
2 tbsp.	fresh bread crumbs	30 ml.
2 tbsp.	freshly grated Parmesan cheese	30 ml.
6	anchovies, soaked in water for 10 minutes, patted dry and chopped	6
1	large tomato, peeled, seeded and chopped	1
¼ cup	capers, rinsed in cold water and drained well	50 ml.
2 tbsp.	olive oil	30 ml.
	salt and freshly ground black pepper	

Combine the bread crumbs, cheese, anchovies, tomato and capers; set aside.

Pan fry the steaks in hot oil to the desired rareness. Arrange them on an ovenproof platter and sprinkle with the bread-crumb mixture. Salt and pepper them to taste. Place under a preheated broiler 1 inch [2½ cm.] from the heat for 2 to 3 minutes to crisp the topping. Serve immediately.

ANNA MUFFOLETTO
THE ART OF SICILIAN COOKING

Flank Steak with Black Butter

A well-seasoned flank steak from a choice steer is a great piece of meat—boneless, easy to handle and flavorful. But it is thin and apt to become overdone, so cook it quickly over high heat and serve it hot.

To serve 4

2 to 2¼ lb.	flank steak, trimmed of fat and membrane	1 kg.
1	garlic clove	1
1 tbsp.	oil	15 ml.
	salt and pepper	
2 tbsp.	butter	30 ml.

Rub the steak on both sides with the cut side of a garlic clove. Brush the meat with oil, and sauté it quickly on both sides in a hot heavy skillet.

Remove the steak to a warmed platter or a serving board. Season with salt and pepper. Cut the steak diagonally against the grain into thin slices. Put the butter into the pan with the pan juices and heat until it is bubbling and brown; pour over the steak and serve.

ARTHUR HAWKINS
COOK IT QUICK

Steak with Onions

Côte de Boeuf à la Marseillaise

To serve 2 or 3

2 to 2½ lb.	boneless beef rib steak, 2 inches [5 cm.] thick	1 kg.
6 tbsp.	olive oil	90 ml.
3	large onions, thinly sliced	3
3 tbsp.	red wine vinegar or Dijon-type mustard	45 ml.
	salt and pepper	
⅔ cup	beef or veal stock	150 ml.

Heat 4 tablespoons [60 ml.] of the oil in a heavy skillet and sear the steak on both sides over high heat. After about 5 minutes, when the steak is well colored, turn the heat to low and cook until done to your taste. Remove the steak to a warm serving dish and keep it hot.

Discard the fat from the pan, add the remaining oil and heat it. Add the onions and fry them until they are golden brown. Then stir in the vinegar or mustard, salt and pepper, and stock. Cook for a minute over medium heat then pour the mixture over the steak.

OFFRAY AINÉ
LE CUISINIER MÉRIDIONAL

Sautéed Steaks Stuffed with Oysters

Popular with Australians, this dish is often referred to as Carpetbagger Steaks.

To serve 4

4	beef tenderloin steaks (preferably fillets or tournedos), cut 2 inches [5 cm.] thick	4
8	live oysters, shucked	8
¼ tsp.	salt	1 ml.
	freshly ground black pepper	
2 tbsp.	butter	30 ml.
1 tbsp.	vegetable oil	15 ml.
4 tbsp.	butter, melted (optional)	60 ml.
1 tbsp.	finely chopped fresh parsley (optional)	15 ml.

Have the butcher cut a pocket in each of the steaks, or do it yourself in the following way: One at a time, lay the steaks flat on a chopping board. With a long, sharp knife, cut a horizontal slit about 2 inches [5 cm.] wide and 2½ to 3 inches [6 to 8 cm.] deep into the side of each steak, but be careful not to cut entirely through to the opposite side.

Sprinkle the oysters with the salt and a few grindings of pepper, then insert 2 oysters into each steak. Close the pock-

ets with small skewers or sew them shut, using a large needle and cotton thread. Pat the steaks completely dry with paper towels and scatter as much pepper on them as you like.

In a heavy 10- to 12-inch [25- to 30-cm.] skillet, melt the butter with the oil over high heat. Add the steaks and brown them quickly for 1 to 2 minutes on each side, turning them with tongs to avoid piercing the meat. Then reduce the heat to moderate. Sauté the steaks—turning them every minute or two, so that the pepper does not form a crust on either side—for about 8 minutes if you like rare beef, about 10 minutes if you prefer medium rare.

Serve the steaks at once from a warmed platter. If you like, just before serving, pour over them the melted butter, combined with the chopped parsley.

FOODS OF THE WORLD/PACIFIC AND SOUTHEAST ASIAN COOKING

Fried Meatballs

Keftedes Tiganites

To make 36 tiny or 24 medium-sized meatballs

1 lb.	lean beef or veal, ground	½ kg.
1	medium-sized onion	1
1	garlic clove, crushed (optional)	1
2	slices firm, white bread with the crusts removed, soaked in water and squeezed dry	2
1	egg, lightly beaten	1
3 tbsp.	chopped fresh parsley	45 ml.
2	sprigs mint, chopped	2
½ tsp.	ground allspice, cinnamon or coriander	2 ml.
1 tbsp.	dry red wine	15 ml.
2 to 3 tbsp.	water, if necessary	30 to 45 ml.
	salt and freshly ground pepper	
	flour	
	vegetable oil for deep frying	

In a large bowl, combine the meat with the onion, garlic, bread, egg, parsley, mint, spice and wine, then knead for 2 minutes. The mixture should be soft; add water if necessary. Season with salt and pepper to taste, then cover and refrigerate for at least 1 hour.

Pinch off small pieces of the mixture the size of walnuts or smaller. Roll them into balls between your palms, then dredge lightly in flour. Pour oil into a skillet to a depth of ½ inch [1 cm.] and heat the oil until it almost reaches the smoking point. Slip in the *keftedes* and fry until crisp, turning constantly with tongs. Remove with a slotted spoon and drain on paper towels.

VILMA LIACOURAS CHANTILES
THE FOOD OF GREECE

Russian Meat Patties

Bitocks à la Russe

To serve 4

1 lb.	finely ground round steak, or use half veal, half beef	½ kg.
	salt and freshly ground black pepper	
2 tbsp.	chopped scallions	30 ml.
	flour	
2 tbsp.	butter	30 ml.
¼ cup	beef stock	50 ml.
½ cup	heavy cream	125 ml.
	grated nutmeg	
2 tbsp.	chopped fresh parsley	30 ml.

Lightly blend the meat with salt and pepper to taste, and the scallions. Shape the mixture into four patties and dredge lightly with flour. Brown in the butter. Remove the patties and add the stock. Reduce by half and add the cream. Cook for 1 minute. Add nutmeg to taste and the parsley, and pour the sauce over the patties.

CRAIG CLAIBORNE
THE NEW YORK TIMES MENU COOK BOOK

Ground Beef Steaks with Rice

Steaks de Riz

This recipe originated with Jacques Manière, chef and proprietor of the restaurant Le Dodin-Bouffant, Paris.

To serve 4

½ lb.	lean ground beef	¼ kg.
½ cup	raw unprocessed long-grain rice	125 ml.
1 cup	boiling water	¼ liter
3 tbsp.	butter	45 ml.
2	eggs	2
1	potato, parboiled in its skin for 10 minutes, peeled and grated	1
1	shallot, finely chopped	1
1	large sprig parsley, finely chopped	1
	salt and pepper	

Lightly fry the rice in 1 tablespoon [15 ml.] of the butter. Add the boiling water and simmer, covered, for 20 minutes until the rice is cooked.

In a large bowl, mix the ground beef, eggs, potato, cooked rice, shallot and parsley; season with salt and pepper. Shape the mixture into four patties, about 1 inch [2½ cm.] thick.

Melt 1 tablespoon [15 ml.] of the butter in a large skillet.

Add the patties and fry them on one side over medium heat for 2 to 3 minutes. Turn them over, add the remaining butter and fry them on the other side. The cooking time depends on your taste; the meat may be served rare or medium rare.

ROBERT COURTINE
MON BOUQUET DE RECETTES

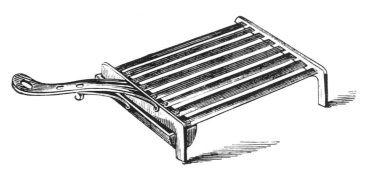

Hamburgers à la Lindström

Biff à la Lindström

To serve 4 to 6

1 lb.	lean ground beef	½ kg.
3 tbsp.	butter	45 ml.
2 tbsp.	finely chopped onion	30 ml.
4	egg yolks	4
1 tbsp.	capers, rinsed, drained and finely chopped	15 ml.
1½ tsp.	salt	7 ml.
	freshly ground black pepper	
2 tsp.	white vinegar	10 ml.
½ cup	heavy cream	125 ml.
¼ cup	finely chopped, cooked fresh beets	50 ml.
2 tbsp.	vegetable oil	30 ml.
4 to 6	fried eggs (optional)	4 to 6

In a small pan, melt 1 tablespoon [15 ml.] of the butter. When the foam subsides, add the onions and cook for 2 or 3 minutes, or until they are soft and transparent but not brown. Scrape them into a large bowl and add the meat, egg yolks, capers, salt, a few grindings of pepper and the white vinegar. Mix together and moisten with the heavy cream. Then stir in the beets. Shape the mixture into 12 to 14 round patties, about 2 to 3 inches [5 to 8 cm.] in diameter.

In a large, heavy skillet, heat the remaining butter and the oil. When the foam subsides, add the patties, three or four at a time, and cook them over moderately high heat for 5 to 6 minutes on each side, or until they are a deep brown.

In Sweden, these spicy hamburgers are frequently served with a fried egg set on top of each one, in which case the patties should be made larger and thicker.

FOODS OF THE WORLD/THE COOKING OF SCANDINAVIA

Beef and Vegetables Simmered in Soy Sauce and Sake

Sukiyaki

The final preparation of this Japanese dish is traditionally done at the dinner table. The sukiyaki can be cooked and served as described here or each diner can individually select food from the platter of ingredients and cook it in the pot of simmering liquid usually placed in the center of the table.

Shirataki are long, vermicelli-like noodles, takenoko are bamboo shoots and tofu is soybean curd. All are available in Oriental markets, as are chrysanthemum leaves. Sake is a strong, Japanese rice wine.

	To serve 4	
1 lb.	boneless lean beef, preferably tenderloin or sirloin	½ kg.
8 oz.	can *shirataki*, drained	¼ kg.
1	whole canned *takenoko*, scraped at the base, halved lengthwise and thinly sliced crosswise	1
6	scallions, including 3 inches [8 cm.] of the green tops, cut into 1½-inch [4-cm.] pieces	6
1	medium-sized onion, sliced ½ inch [1 cm.] thick	1
4 to 6	small white fresh mushrooms, cut into ¼-inch [5-mm.] slices	4 to 6
2	cakes *tofu*, cut into 1-inch [2½-cm.] cubes	2
2 oz.	Chinese chrysanthemum leaves, watercress or Chinese cabbage	75 g.
1	strip beef fat, 2 inches [5 cm.] long, folded into a square packet	1
¾ cup	Japanese soy sauce	175 ml.
3 to 6 tbsp.	sugar	45 to 90 ml.
¾ cup	sake	45 to 90 ml.

Place the beef in your freezer for about 30 minutes, or just long enough to stiffen it slightly for easier slicing. First, with a heavy, sharp knife, cut the beef against the grain into slices ⅛ inch [3 mm.] thick. Then halve the slices crosswise.

Bring 1 cup [¼ liter] of water to a boil and drop in the *shirataki;* return to a boil. Drain and cut the noodles into thirds. Run cold water over the *takenoko* slices; drain them.

Arrange the meat, *shirataki* and vegetables attractively in separate rows on a large platter.

If you are using an electric skillet, preheat it to 425° F. [220° C.]; if not, substitute a 10- to 12-inch [25- to 30-cm.] skillet on a table burner and preheat for several minutes.

Hold the folded strip of fat with chopsticks or tongs and rub it over the bottom of the hot skillet. Add six to eight slices of meat to the skillet, pour in ¼ cup [50 ml.] of soy sauce and sprinkle the meat with 3 tablespoons [45 ml.] of sugar. Cook for a minute, stir and turn the meat over. Push the meat to one side of the skillet. Add about one third of the scallions, onion, mushrooms, *tofu, shirataki,* the greens and *takenoko* in equal amounts; sprinkle them with ¼ cup of sake and cook for an additional 4 to 5 minutes.

With chopsticks or long-handled forks (such as those used for a fondue), transfer the contents of the pan to individual plates and serve. Continue cooking the remaining sukiyaki batch by batch as already described, checking the temperature of the pan from time to time. If it seems too hot and the food begins to stick, lower the heat or cool the pan more quickly by adding a drop or two of cold water to the sauce.

FOODS OF THE WORLD/THE COOKING OF JAPAN

Szechwan Shredded Beef

Both cellophane noodles and hoisin sauce can be found in Chinese grocery stores. After opening a can of hoisin sauce, transfer the contents to a glass jar. Close it tightly and store in a refrigerator; it will keep for many months.

	To serve 4	
¾ lb.	beef flank steak	⅓ kg.
1 oz.	dried cellophane noodles	50 g.
1 cup	vegetable oil	¼ liter
1 tbsp.	dry sherry	15 ml.
1 tbsp.	soy sauce	15 ml.
2 tbsp.	*hoisin* sauce	30 ml.
1 tsp.	cornstarch	5 ml.
½ cup	bamboo shoots, shredded	125 ml.
½ cup	carrots, shredded	125 ml.
½ cup	snow peas, shredded	125 ml.
1 tsp.	salt	5 ml.
1 tbsp.	shredded fresh ginger root	15 ml.
½ tsp.	chili pepper flakes	2 ml.

Using a wok or large skillet, deep fry the cellophane noodles in the oil, preheated to 350° F. [180° C.], for a few seconds. Drain on a paper towel, reserving the oil. Set them aside.

Slice the beef against the grain into very thin slices, then shred the slices. The meat will slice more easily if it is partially frozen. Combine the beef shreds, sherry, soy sauce, *hoisin* sauce and cornstarch.

Heat 2 tablespoons [30 ml.] of the reserved oil in the wok or skillet and stir fry the bamboo shoots, carrots and snow peas for 1 minute. Add salt, stir, remove the vegetables from the wok and set them aside in a bowl.

In the same wok or skillet, heat 6 more tablespoons [90 ml.] of the oil and add the ginger. Stir a few times. Add the beef mixture and stir fry for 2 minutes. Add the chili pepper flakes and mix well. (Drain off any excess oil.)

Return the cooked vegetables to the wok or skillet, and stir well, then remove the contents to a platter.

Arrange the cellophane noodles over and around the beef mixture and serve hot.

GRACE ZIA CHU
MADAME CHU'S CHINESE COOKING SCHOOL

Beef Chow Mein

To serve 4

1½ lb.	lean boneless beef, sliced ¼ inch [6 mm.] thick and cut into matchstick strips	¾ kg.
1 lb.	raw Chinese noodles	½ kg.
5 tbsp.	vegetable oil	75 ml.
1	garlic clove, crushed	1
3	scallions, cut into 1-inch [2½-cm.] segments	3
1½ cups	shredded Chinese cabbage (or substitute thinly sliced celery)	375 ml.
¼ cup	bamboo shoots	50 ml.
½ tsp.	salt	2 ml.
3	dried Chinese mushrooms, soaked in warm water for 30 minutes, then drained, stems removed and sliced into thin strips or shreds	3
2½ tbsp.	soy sauce	37 ml.
1 tsp.	sugar	5 ml.
2 tbsp.	dry sherry	30 ml.
2 tbsp.	chopped, shelled, raw fresh shrimp	30 ml.

Boil the noodles until soft. Drain and rinse under cold running water to prevent stickiness.

Heat 1 tablespoon [15 ml.] of oil in a large skillet. Add the garlic, scallions, cabbage, bamboo shoots and half the salt. Stir fry for 2 minutes over high heat. Remove and put aside.

Add 2 tablespoons [30 ml.] of oil to the same pan. When very hot, add the meat and mushrooms, and stir fry over high heat for 1 minute. Add the soy sauce and sugar, and half the sherry; then stir fry for a minute. Remove with a slotted spoon and put aside.

Add the remaining oil to the pan, and then the noodles and the shrimp to be stir fried with the gravy and oil left in the pan from previous fryings. When the noodles are heated through and browned all over with gravy and oil (about 1½ minutes), add the remaining salt, half the meat and half the cooked vegetables that were put aside. After a minute of slow stir frying, dish onto a warmed serving platter.

Now return the remainder of the vegetables and meat to the same pan together with the rest of the sherry. After a few

sizzling turns over high heat (about 15 seconds), spoon the mixed contents of the pan as garnish over the noodles and serve. To connoisseurs of chow mein, the gravy-flavored noodles are even more delicious than the meat.

KENNETH LO
CHINESE FOOD

Spicy Beef with Rice Noodles

Kan Pien Niu Jou Szu

Rice noodles and cellophane noodles are obtainable at Oriental markets.

To serve 4

1 lb.	beef sirloin or flank steak	½ kg.
1 oz.	rice noodles or cellophane noodles	50 g.
2 cups	oil for deep frying	½ liter
2 cups	julienne celery	½ liter
½ cup	julienne carrot	125 ml.
½ cup	julienne fresh hot chilies	125 ml.
1 tsp.	finely chopped fresh ginger root	5 ml.
1 tsp.	crushed dried red pepper	5 ml.
1 tsp.	sesame-seed oil	5 ml.

Soy sauce and sugar marinade

2 tsp.	sugar	10 ml.
3 tbsp.	soy sauce	45 ml.
1 tbsp.	cold water	15 ml.

Slice the steak with the grain of the beef to a thickness of about ⅛ inch [3 mm.]. Cut again with the grain into julienne 2 inches long [5 cm.]. In a mixing bowl combine the beef with the mixed marinade ingredients. Mix well with your hands and set aside for 30 minutes.

Loosen the dried noodles, then deep fry them in 2 cups [½ liter] of very hot—about 400° F. [200° C.]—oil for 5 seconds. Crush the noodles into smaller pieces and lay them in one thin layer on a platter. Reserve the oil.

Heat a wok and add 2 tablespoons [30 ml.] of the reserved oil. Stir fry the celery, carrots and hot chilies for 2 minutes. Remove the vegetables. Reheat the wok, add 3 tablespoons [45 ml.] of oil, and add the crushed dried red pepper, then the beef and ginger. Increase the quantity of dried pepper if you like a fiery dish. Stir fry over high heat for about 5 minutes or until the meat is dry and no liquid is left. Lower the heat and stir for another 2 to 3 minutes. Add the cooked vegetables. Stir together for 1 minute and add sesame oil. Mix well, then pour over the fried noodles.

FLORENCE LIN
FLORENCE LIN'S CHINESE REGIONAL COOKBOOK

Glazed Beef with Tomato

Fan Chia Hua Niu

Translations of food names from Chinese to English invariably sound strange to Americans. This dish, for instance, appears on most restaurant menus as Slippery Beef. An unusual cooking procedure gives the beef a unique coating and texture: after marinating in an egg white, cornstarch and soy-sauce mixture, the beef slices are blanched, then cooled quickly and drained well before the final stir frying with tomatoes. This is a typical Cantonese dish that has many variations. Pork or chicken may be used instead of beef; other vegetables, such as onions, broccoli or cauliflower may be used instead of tomatoes.

To serve 4

1 lb.	beef flank steak (or substitute sirloin tip, cut 1 inch [2½ cm.] thick)	½ kg.
1	egg white, lightly beaten	1
3 tbsp.	cornstarch	45 ml.
2 tbsp.	soy sauce	30 ml.
3	medium-sized tomatoes	3
4	thin slices fresh ginger root	4
3 tbsp.	peanut oil	45 ml.

Soy-glaze sauce

1 tbsp.	soy sauce	15 ml.
1 tbsp.	oyster sauce	15 ml.
1 tsp.	sugar	5 ml.

Cut the beef diagonally and across the grain into slices ¼ inch [6 mm.] thick, and then cut the slices into pieces 1½ inches [4 cm.] long to make about 2 cups [½ liter]. Place the beef in a bowl. Add the egg white, cornstarch and soy sauce. Mix well with your hands and set aside for 30 minutes.

Dip the tomatoes in boiling water for 10 seconds. Peel and cut each tomato into six to eight wedges. Remove the seeds and set the tomatoes aside on a plate.

In a large pot bring 1 quart [1 liter] of water to a rolling boil. Add the marinated beef, stirring gently to separate the pieces. Turn off the heat and drain the meat immediately. Cool the meat in 1 quart [1 liter] of cold water. Drain well again. The meat can sit for several hours at this stage.

Heat a wok over medium heat until very hot. Add the oil, tomatoes and ginger, and stir fry for 1 minute. Turn the heat to high and add the drained beef. Stir for 30 seconds. Add the mixed sauce ingredients to the beef. Keep over high heat and stir until the sauce coats everything well, about 30 seconds more. Serve immediately.

FLORENCE LIN
FLORENCE LIN'S CHINESE REGIONAL COOKBOOK

Stir-fried Beef and Peppers

To serve 4

½ lb.	beef rump, sliced ½ inch [1 cm.] thick and cut into ½-inch cubes	¼ kg.
2 tbsp.	soy sauce	30 ml.
1 tbsp.	dry sherry	15 ml.
½ tsp.	sugar	2 ml.
2	green peppers, halved, seeded, deribbed and cut into 1-inch [2½-cm.] squares	2
3 tbsp.	oil	45 ml.
½ tsp.	salt	2 ml.

Combine 1 tablespoon [15 ml.] of soy sauce with the sherry and sugar. Add to the beef and toss. Let stand for 15 minutes, turning occasionally. Heat 1½ tablespoons [22 ml.] of the oil in a large skillet or wok. Add the peppers and stir fry until slightly softened. Remove them from the pan. Heat the remaining oil. Add the beef and stir fry until the meat begins to brown. Return the peppers to the pan. Sprinkle with the salt and the remaining soy sauce. Stir fry until done (about 2 minutes more). Serve at once.

GLORIA BLEY MILLER
THE THOUSAND RECIPE CHINESE COOKBOOK

Beef Rolls Stuffed with Scallions

Gyūniku No Negimaki

Mirin is a sweet, Japanese rice wine. A tempura pan is a shallow frying pan, fitted with a rack for draining the fried food, obtainable at kitchenware stores.

If you choose to sauté these rolls instead of deep frying them—the flavor is surprisingly different—omit the flour coating. Sauté the rolls in 2 tablespoons [30 ml.] of oil in a skillet over fairly high heat, turning them frequently so that they brown on all sides.

To serve 4

¾ lb.	beef top or bottom round	⅓ kg.
2 tbsp.	soy sauce	30 ml.
1 tbsp.	mirin	15 ml.
1 tsp.	finely grated fresh ginger root	5 ml.
3	scallions	3
	flour	
	vegetable oil	
½	lemon, cut into 4 wedges	½

Cut the beef across the grain into very thin slices about ⅛ inch [3 mm.] thick. This is easier to do if the beef has been partially frozen. Place the beef slices in a dish. Combine the soy sauce, *mirin* and ginger, and pour over the beef, mixing well. Marinate for 30 minutes at room temperature.

Cut the scallions into pieces as long as the width of the beef slices. Divide the scallions lengthwise into halves or quarters so that there will be some white and some green to stuff each roll.

Lift the beef slices out of the marinade, lay a piece of scallion on each beef slice and roll up, first dabbing a little flour on the end of each beef slice to hold the roll together. Coat the rolls with flour, shaking to remove the excess.

Heat 2 to 3 inches [5 to 8 cm.] of oil in a tempura pan or a saucepan to 340° F. [175° C.], measured on a deep-frying thermometer, or until bubbles form on wooden chopsticks stirred in the oil. Fry the rolls, a few at a time, for about 2 minutes, turning once or twice. Drain them on the rack of the tempura pan or on paper towels. Garnish with the lemon wedges. Serve immediately, as hot as possible. Let diners squeeze the lemon juice over the beef rolls.

ELISABETH LAMBERT ORTIZ WITH MITSUKO ENDO
THE COMPLETE BOOK OF JAPANESE COOKING

Mushroom-Smothered Swiss Steak

To serve 6

3 to 3½ lb.	beef blade, arm or round steak, cut about 2 inches [5 cm.] thick	1½ kg.
2 tbsp.	butter or rendered bacon fat	30 ml.
1	medium-sized yellow onion, chopped	1
¾ lb.	fresh mushrooms, thinly sliced	⅓ kg.
⅓ cup	flour	75 ml.
1 cup	beef stock	¼ liter
1 cup	milk	¼ liter
½ tsp.	salt	2 ml.
⅛ tsp.	pepper	½ ml.

In a large, heavy skillet over moderately high heat, brown the steak on both sides in the butter or bacon fat. Transfer to a roasting pan that is only slightly larger than the steak.

In the drippings in the skillet, sauté the onion and mushrooms over moderate heat for about 5 to 8 minutes, until limp and lightly browned. Blend in the flour, add the stock, milk, salt and pepper, and heat, stirring constantly, until thickened and smooth—about 3 minutes.

Pour this mushroom sauce over the steak. Cover the roasting pan snugly with aluminum foil and bake in a moderate oven, preheated to 350° F. [180° C.], for about 1½ hours, or until the steak is fork-tender.

JEAN ANDERSON
THE GRASS ROOTS COOKBOOK

Christmas Stew

L'Estouffat de Noël

To serve 18 to 20

6 to 7 lb.	beef bottom round or rump roast, firmly tied	3 kg.
1½ lb.	fresh pork rind, cut into 1½-inch [4-cm.] squares	¾ kg.
7 or 8	shallots	7 or 8
2	large onions, halved or quartered	2
1 or 2	carrots	1 or 2
1	bouquet garni	1
	salt and pepper	
1 cup	Armagnac	¼ liter
1 cup	dry red wine	¼ liter

Put the pork rind into a fireproof earthenware casserole or *daubière*. Add the beef and surround it with the vegetables and the bouquet garni. Season well with salt and pepper. Pour in the Armagnac and add the red wine. Cover the pot with a sheet of parchment paper, so that the steam cannot escape, and then put on the earthenware lid.

Place the casserole over very low heat for approximately 1 to 1½ hours; then let it cook slowly in a cool oven—250° F. [130° C.]—for 24 hours. Shake the pot gently from time to time. (Traditionally, the stew is cooked in the fireplace, simmering slowly in a bed of hot ashes.)

Before serving, put the meat on a platter. Strain the cooking liquid, discard the bouquet garni and thoroughly degrease the sauce. Serve the beef with the rinds around it.

GASTON DERYS
L'ART D'ÊTRE GOURMAND

Beef with Green Peas

To serve 5 or 6

3 lb.	lean beef rump or round roast	1½ kg.
	salt and pepper	
10 tbsp.	butter	150 ml.
3 lb.	fresh green peas, shelled (about 3 cups [¾ liter])	1½ kg.

Season the meat with salt and pepper. In a skillet over high heat, sear the meat on all sides in 4 tablespoons [60 ml.] of the butter. Transfer the meat to a casserole large enough to hold it with only about ½-inch [1-cm.] space all round. Melt the rest of the butter in the skillet. Fill the space in the casserole with the green peas and pour over the butter from the skillet. Add no moisture at all. Cover tightly and cook in an oven, preheated to 275° F. [140° C.], for 2½ hours.

HAROLD WILSHAW
COOKBOOK FOR THE NEEDY GREEDY

Pot Roast of Beef with Almonds and Bacon

Carne Claveatada

Literally translated as "broad chilies," the dried ancho chilies called for in this recipe are available where Latin American foods are sold. The chilies, reddish brown and with a pungent, musky flavor, are widely used in Mexican cooking.

To serve 6

3 lb.	beef brisket, trimmed of excess fat	1½ kg.
¼ lb.	bacon or ham	125 g.
1½ tbsp.	slivered, blanched almonds	22 ml.
3	large dried *ancho* chilies	3
3	whole cloves	3
½ inch	stick cinnamon	1 cm.
⅛ tsp.	dried thyme	½ ml.
⅛ tsp.	dried marjoram	½ ml.
⅛ tsp.	dried oregano	½ ml.
4	peppercorns	4
3	garlic cloves	3
2 tsp.	salt	5 ml.
1½ tbsp.	vinegar	22 ml.
¾ cup	water	175 ml.
3 tbsp.	lard or rendered bacon fat	45 ml.
8	new potatoes, unpeeled	8

Preheat the oven to 325° F. [170° C.]. Cut the bacon or ham into small pieces. Gash the beef all over with a knife point, and insert the bacon or ham and the almonds into the gashes. Set the meat aside while the sauce is prepared.

Toast the chilies lightly for 3 to 4 minutes on a griddle or in a heavy skillet, turning them from time to time so that they do not burn. Slit them open and remove the seeds.

Put the chilies into a bowl of hot water and leave them to soak for about 20 minutes. Transfer them with a slotted spoon to the jar of an electric blender. Add the rest of the ingredients (except the lard, potatoes and meat) and blend to a smooth purée. If you do not have a blender, pound the ingredients to a paste in a mortar.

Melt the lard in a heavy casserole and, when the lard is very hot, brown the meat well all over. Remove the meat and set it aside. Drain off the fat, leaving 3 tablespoons [45 ml.]. Add the chili mixture and let it simmer briskly for about 5 minutes, stirring it all the time. Return the meat to the casserole and baste it with the sauce. Cover with a tightly fitting lid and cook in the oven for 2 hours.

Meanwhile, put the potatoes into a saucepan, cover them with boiling water, and boil for 5 minutes. Drain the potatoes and set aside; when cool enough to handle, skin them.

Remove the casserole from the oven, turn the meat over and baste it well with the sauce. Scrape the sauce from the sides and bottom of the casserole; add a little water if the sauce has thickened too much. Put the potatoes into the sauce around the meat, replace the lid of the casserole and let the meat cook until it is very tender but not falling apart—test after about 1 hour and 10 minutes.

Slice the meat fairly thick and arrange it on a warmed platter with the potatoes around it. Pour the sauce over it.

DIANA KENNEDY
THE CUISINES OF MEXICO

Beef à la Mode, the French Way

This recipe is from a book published anonymously in 1747, but generally attributed to the English cookery writer, Hannah Glasse. The technique for larding a beef roast is demonstrated on pages 56-57.

To serve 6

4 lb.	beef bottom round roast	2 kg.
2 tsp.	salt	10 ml.
1 tsp.	ground pepper	5 ml.
1 tsp.	ground mace	5 ml.
1 tsp.	grated nutmeg	5 ml.
½ lb.	fresh pork fat, cut into long thin strips	¼ kg.
4 to 5 tbsp.	vinegar	60 to 75 ml.
2 or 3	large onions	2 or 3
1	large piece lemon peel	1
1	bouquet garni	1
1	piece fresh pork rind, large enough to cover the meat	1
	fresh truffles, morels and mushrooms (optional)	

Mix together the salt, pepper, mace and nutmeg. Dip the strips of pork fat into the vinegar, roll in the spice mixture and then lard the beef with the strips. Put the meat into a heavy casserole with the onions, the lemon peel, bouquet garni and the remaining vinegar. Cover the pot tightly and put a wet cloth around the edge of the cover so that no steam can get out. Set the pot over very low heat. When you think one side is done enough, in about 3 hours, turn the meat and cover it with the pork rind. Cover the pot again as before and, in another 3 hours, when the meat is quite tender, take it out and lay it on a platter. Take off all the fat from the gravy and pour the gravy over the meat.

In doing your beef this way you must take great care that your heat is very, very low. If you would have the sauce very rich, boil truffles and morels in good gravy, till they are very tender, and add mushrooms. Mix all together with the gravy of the meat and pour it over your beef.

THE ART OF COOKERY MADE PLAIN AND EASY

Beef à la Mode

To serve 7 or 8

5 to 7 lb.	beef bottom round in 1 piece	2½ to 3 kg.
3	onions, sliced and sautéed in 4 tablespoons [60 ml.] butter	3
5 oz.	fresh pork fat	150 g.
⅔ cup	wine vinegar	150 ml.
2 tsp.	finely pounded, mixed black pepper, allspice and cloves	10 ml.
2 tsp.	finely chopped, mixed fresh herbs, including parsley	10 ml.
2	large carrots, chopped	2
1	turnip, chopped	1
1	celery stalk, separated into ribs, cored, stringed and chopped	1
1 quart	water	1 liter
⅔ cup	port	175 ml.

Fry the onions to a pale brown, and prepare the beef for stewing in the following manner: choose a fine piece of beef, cut the pork fat into long strips, about 1 inch [2½ cm.] in thickness, dip them into the vinegar, and then into a little of the spices mixed with the same quantity of herbs. With a sharp knife, make holes in the beef deep enough to introduce the strips of pork fat; then rub the beef all over with the remainder of the seasoning and herbs. Bind up the beef in a nice shape with cotton string.

Have ready a well-tinned copper stewpan (it should not be much larger than the piece of meat you are cooking), into which put the beef with the fried onions and chopped vegetables, vinegar and water. Let the beef simmer *very gently* for at least 5 hours—longer, should the meat not be extremely tender—turning it once or twice. Great care must be taken that this does not boil fast or the meat will be tough and tasteless; the liquid should only just bubble.

When ready to serve, take out the beef, remove the string and put the beef in a hot dish. Skim off every particle of fat from the gravy and add to it the port wine. Let it just boil. Pour the gravy over the beef and it is ready to serve.

MRS. ISABELLA BEETON
THE BOOK OF HOUSEHOLD MANAGEMENT

Hearty Beef Stew

Instead of using meat cut into chunks, I much prefer cooking a braising roast in one piece and slicing it as needed. Hearty Beef Stew improves measurably if prepared a day or two in advance. The fat will congeal on the surface, and can be removed easily. Also the meat can be cut into neater slices once it is chilled.

Contrary to tradition, the meat for this stew is not browned in hot fat. Nevertheless, it achieves a dark color during the long, slow cooking in red wine.

To serve 8

4 lb.	beef arm or rump roast	2 kg.
¼ cup	oil	50 ml.
1	medium-sized onion, chopped	1
1	rib celery, sliced	1
1 tbsp.	currant jelly or plum jam	15 ml.
2 tbsp.	puréed tomato	30 ml.
3 tbsp.	flour	45 ml.
1 to 2 cups	beef stock	¼ to ½ liter
4 to 5 cups	dry red wine	1 to 1¼ liters
¼ tsp.	powdered thyme	1 ml.
4	garlic cloves, mashed	4
	salt and pepper	
	bouquet garni, made of 6 sprigs parsley tied around 2 bay leaves	
4	medium-sized potatoes, quartered	4
5	carrots, cut into chunks	5
½	head cauliflower	½

Pour the oil into a large, heavy casserole and put the casserole over medium heat. Add the onion and celery, cover and simmer for 3 minutes. Add the jelly or jam and the puréed tomato, and stir until they melt. Add the flour, stir, then simmer for 1 minute. Add 1 cup [¼ liter] of the beef stock and 4 cups [1 liter] of the wine. Bring this sauce to a simmer while adding the thyme, mashed garlic, salt and pepper.

Add the meat to the casserole. Tuck in the bouquet garni. The meat should be almost completely covered by the sauce; if not, add more wine or stock, or both. Cover and simmer gently, turning the meat from time to time. The cooking time will depend on the quality and thickness of the meat; 2 to 3 hours should be about right. When pierced with a small, sharp knife, the meat should be tender.

When the meat is tender, add the potatoes and carrots, then simmer for 20 minutes. Break the cauliflower into florets and add them to the stew. Continue cooking until all the vegetables are soft, but not mushy.

To serve, remove the meat from the stew and cut away any strings. Cut the beef into thin slices and return them to the pot to reheat. Discard the bouquet garni. Serve directly from the casserole, or arrange the meat and vegetables in an attractive pattern on a large, warmed platter. Spoon a little of the sauce over the meat, and serve the rest separately.

CAROL CUTLER
THE SIX-MINUTE SOUFFLÉ AND OTHER CULINARY DELIGHTS

Rhineland Sauerbraten

Rheinischer Sauerbraten

Sauerbraten—beef marinated in spiced vinegar and served with a sweet-and-sour gravy—is indigenous to every region of Germany. But versions differ in the composition and seasoning of the gravy. In this Rhineland recipe the gravy is enriched with raisins and thickened with crumbs of *Lebkuchen*—German Christmas cookies made from honey, treacle and spices. The apple syrup that sweetens the gravy is a speciality of the Rhineland.

	To serve 6	
2 lb.	beef bottom round, in 1 piece	1 kg.
5 tbsp.	lard	75 ml.
1 cup	raisins, soaked in warm water for 20 minutes and drained	¼ liter
	salt and pepper	
1 cup	*Lebkuchen* or gingerbread crumbs	¼ liter
1 tbsp.	apple syrup (or substitute dark corn syrup)	15 ml.
1 cup	sour cream	¼ liter
Spiced vinegar marinade		
2 cups	water	½ liter
1 cup	wine vinegar	¼ liter
1 tsp.	salt	5 ml.
2	onions	2
1	carrot	1
5	peppercorns	5
2	whole cloves	2
1	bay leaf	1
2	juniper berries	2

Put all the marinade ingredients into a large pan. Bring to a boil, then lower the heat and simmer for 15 minutes; set the marinade aside to cool. Place the meat in a glazed earthenware pot, pour in the marinade and leave the pot in a cool place or the refrigerator for two to three days, turning the meat occasionally.

Drain the meat, pat it dry with paper towels and brown it in the lard in a large, heavy fireproof casserole. Strain the marinade—discarding the vegetables and seasonings—and pour it over the beef. Cook the beef in an oven, preheated to 350° F. [180° C.], for about 1½ hours, basting regularly. Add the raisins about 15 minutes before the end of cooking. When the meat is well done and very tender, transfer it to a warmed platter.

Degrease the sauce remaining in the casserole and season it with salt and pepper. Over moderate heat, thicken the sauce with the *Lebkuchen* or gingerbread crumbs, then mix in the apple syrup or dark corn syrup and the sour cream. Slice the sauerbraten and serve it in its sauce with potato dumplings or potato pancakes and unsweetened applesauce.

ROLAND GÖÖCK
DIE 100 BERÜHMTESTEN REZEPTE DER WELT

Rhone Beef Stew

Boeuf à l'estouffade des Mariniers du Rhone

This dish is traditionally cooked in a casserole hermetically sealed with flour paste to prevent evaporation during the long hours of cooking, but a close covering of aluminum foil under the lid works just as well.

	To serve 8	
4 lb.	boneless beef rump or round	2 kg.
¼ cup	olive oil	50 ml.
2 cups	dry red or white wine	½ liter
10 to 12	anchovies	10 to 12
¾ cup	chopped sour pickles	175 ml.
3 tbsp.	capers, rinsed and drained well	45 ml.
4	garlic cloves, sliced	4
¼ tsp.	thyme	1 ml.
2 cups	canned tomatoes	½ liter
1	rib celery, broken in half	1
2	bay leaves	2
	pepper	
	salt, if necessary	

Place the meat in an enameled cast-iron casserole. Pour the olive oil and ½ cup [125 ml.] of wine into a blender. Add the anchovies, pickles, capers, garlic, thyme and tomatoes. (For stronger flavor add ¼ cup [50 ml.] more pickle and an extra garlic clove.) Blend to a purée and pour this over the meat, adding more wine until the sauce almost covers the meat. Put the bay leaves between the pieces of celery and tie the celery to make a small bundle. Tuck this into the marinade. Cover and marinate the meat in a cool spot for at least 12 hours. Turn the meat occasionally.

Preheat the oven to 250° F. [120° C.]. Put the casserole over medium heat and slowly bring the marinade just to a boil. Sprinkle with pepper. When the marinade is warm, taste for salt and correct if necessary. (Remember the anchovies and pickles are salty.) Place a sheet of aluminum foil over the casserole, then cover the pot with its lid. Place the casserole in the oven and cook for about 5 hours or until the meat is fork-tender. Turn the meat once or twice while it is cooking. The meat can be cooked faster, say for 3 hours in a 350° F. [180° C.] oven, but the slower cooking produces a better blend of flavors. Besides, at 250° F. [120° C.] the simmering stew needs almost no attention.

Transfer the cooked meat to a carving board and slice. Remove the celery bundle from the sauce. Arrange the meat slices in the center of a warmed platter and spoon the hot sauce liberally over the meat.

As an alternate stewing method, allow the stew to stand for one or two days. The flavor will improve with time. Cool the stew, then refrigerate. When the dish has chilled, remove any fat that may have congealed on the surface. Cut the meat into slices while it is cold; it will slice more neatly. Then return the meat to the casserole and reheat slowly in a 325° F. [160° C.] oven for 30 to 40 minutes.

CAROL CUTLER
THE SIX-MINUTE SOUFFLÉ AND OTHER CULINARY DELIGHTS

Old-Fashioned Beef Stew

Boeuf-Mode à l'Ancienne

The technique for larding is demonstrated on pages 56-57.

To serve 6 to 8

6 or 7 lb.	beef round or rump	3 kg.
4 or 5	long, thick strips fresh pork fat	4 or 5
2 tbsp.	chopped fresh parsley and garlic, mixed with pepper	30 ml.
¼ lb.	lean salt pork with the rind removed, blanched in boiling water for 5 minutes and drained	125 g.
1¼ cups	beef stock or leftover beef roasting juice	300 ml.
2 or 3	calf's feet, boned and blanched	2 or 3
24	small carrots, blanched	24
24	small onions, browned in butter or oil	24
	White wine marinade	
2	onions, quartered	2
2	carrots, quartered	2
3	garlic cloves, crushed	3
2	sprigs thyme	2
1	bay leaf	1
4	sprigs parsley	4
	salt and pepper	
1 tsp.	mixed spices	5 ml.
1½ cups	dry white wine	375 ml.

Lard the beef all along its length and internally with the strips of fresh pork fat, previously rolled in the parsley and garlic mixture. Put the larded piece of meat into a bowl with

the marinade ingredients and put the bowl in a cool place to marinate for 5 to 6 hours.

Line the bottom of a heavy casserole with the slices of salt pork. Place the meat on top and surround it with the vegetables from the marinade. Cover and leave to sweat over a low heat, shaking the casserole from time to time and turning the meat to color it on all sides. When the juices have evaporated, moisten with the marinade and leave this to reduce by half over low heat.

Add 1 cup [¼ liter] of the stock or meat juices. Put in the calf's feet. Cover and cook slowly in an oven, preheated to 300° F. [150° C.], for 5 to 6 hours, turning the meat from time to time. Meanwhile, cook the carrots and small browned onions in a saucepan with the remaining stock or beef juices.

Fifteen minutes before serving, strain the cooking juices from the casserole into a saucepan. Discard the quartered vegetables. Simmer the cooking juices and skim well. Add the onions and the carrots to the juices together with the meat from the calf's feet, cut into pieces. Simmer this sauce for a few minutes. Serve the beef on a warmed platter, surrounded by the vegetable garnish and coated with the sauce.

J. B. REBOUL
LA CUISINIÈRE PROVENÇALE

Beef Certosina-Style

Beef alla Certosina

To serve 6

2½ lb.	beef eye of round in 1 piece	1 kg.
1 tbsp.	olive oil	15 ml.
1 tbsp.	butter	15 ml.
1	slice bacon, chopped	1
	salt and pepper to taste	
⅛ tsp.	grated nutmeg	½ ml.
3 or 4	anchovy fillets, soaked in water for 10 minutes, patted dry and finely chopped	3 or 4
2 tsp.	chopped fresh parsley	10 ml.
1 cup	beef stock or water	¼ liter

Put the meat in a large saucepan with the oil, butter, bacon, salt, pepper and nutmeg, and brown the meat slowly but thoroughly. When it is well browned, add the anchovies, parsley and stock or water. Reduce the heat, cover the pan and cook slowly for about 1¼ hours, or until the meat is tender. Slice the meat and serve it covered with its gravy. Add a little water to the gravy if necessary.

ADA BONI
THE TALISMAN ITALIAN COOK BOOK

Oven Beef Brisket

Fresh brisket, so often boiled and served with horseradish sauce, is much more delicious cooked this way. It shrinks considerably less, too. Long, slow baking is the secret.

To serve 6 to 8

3 lbs.	beef brisket	1½ kg.
	salt and pepper	
1	small onion, chopped	1
1	rib celery, chopped	1
½	bay leaf	½

Hot cream mustard

3 tbsp.	cold water	45 ml.
1 tbsp.	dry mustard	15 ml.
½ cup	sour cream	125 ml.
1 tsp.	vinegar	5 ml.
	salt	

Sprinkle the meat with salt and pepper to taste. Put the onion and celery on the bottom of a heavy 2-quart [2-liter] casserole. Lay the brisket on top and add the bay leaf. Cover and bake in an oven, preheated to 350° F. [180° C.], for 3½ hours until the meat is meltingly tender.

Meanwhile, make the hot cream mustard. In a small bowl blend the cold water with the dry mustard until the mixture is the consistency of heavy cream. Let it stand 15 to 20 minutes. Mix in the sour cream and vinegar. Salt to taste.

Slice the meat thin and serve with steamed whole potatoes and hot cream mustard.

RUTH CONRAD BATEMAN
I LOVE TO COOK BOOK

Black Pot Roast

To serve 6 to 8

4 lb.	boneless beef rump, in 1 piece	2 kg.
3 or 4	garlic cloves, slivered	3 or 4
	salt and pepper	
1 cup	cider vinegar	¼ liter
2 tbsp.	lard	30 ml.
2 cups	strong black coffee	½ liter
2 cups	hot water	½ liter
¼ cup	flour, blended with 4 tbsp. [60 ml.] butter	50 ml.

Pierce deep gashes into the meat on all sides and insert slivers of garlic. Rub the meat thoroughly with salt and pep-

per. Tie the meat, if necessary, into a firm round shape.

Place the meat in a deep bowl just large enough to hold it. Pour in the vinegar. Cover and let the meat stand 24 hours, turning it several times. Before cooking remove the meat from the bowl and pat it dry with paper towels.

Heat the lard in an iron pot. Brown the meat on all sides over high heat—really brown it. Add the coffee and hot water. Cover the pot and cook, barely simmering, for 4 to 6 hours, or until the meat is very tender; or, roast, covered, for 4 hours at 275° F. [140° C.]. The slower the oven and the longer the cooking, the more succulent the meat will be.

When done, remove the meat to a heated platter. Skim off all grease from the remaining pan juices, and thicken them with the flour-and-butter mixture. Cook, stirring constantly, until this gravy is smooth and of the desired consistency.

MORTON GILL CLARK
THE WIDE, WIDE WORLD OF TEXAS COOKING

Braised Beef with Marrow

Boeuf à la Bordelaise

To serve 4 to 6

1½ lb.	boneless beef rump, round or chuck, trimmed of excess fat	¾ kg.
1 tsp.	flour	5 ml.
2 tbsp.	wine vinegar	30 ml.
½ cup	dry red wine	125 ml.
2 tbsp.	heavy cream	30 ml.
2 oz.	beef marrow, poached	75 g.

Carrot marinade

½ cup	olive oil	125 ml.
2	sprigs parsley	2
1	garlic clove, crushed	1
2	shallots, sliced	2
1	onion, sliced	1
1 tsp.	crumbled dried thyme	5 ml.
1	bay leaf, crumbled	1
1	carrot, sliced into rounds	1

A day in advance, begin to marinate the meat. First, rub the piece with 2 tablespoons [30 ml.] of the oil and place it in a bowl. Add the parsley, garlic, shallots, onion, thyme, bay leaf and carrot. Sprinkle these ingredients with the remaining oil and set in a cool place or refrigerator overnight.

Next day, remove the meat from the marinade, place the meat in a roasting pan, cover it and set it in an oven, preheated to 300° F. [150° C.]; or place the meat in a fireproof casserole and set it over very low heat. Cook, moistening the meat frequently with oil from the marinade, for about 1½ hours, or until the juices that run out when the meat is pierced are pink. Leave the meat in the pan, but pour off the cooking juices or remove them with a bulb baster. Strain the juices through a fine sieve.

In a saucepan make a roux with the flour and 1 tablespoon [15 ml.] of the strained cooking juices. Add the wine vinegar, simmer the sauce for 2 to 3 minutes, and pour it over the meat. Cook the meat and sauce together in the oven or over low heat for a further 2 minutes. Remove the roast to a heated serving platter. Degrease the sauce and deglaze the pan with the red wine. Mash the bone marrow with a fork and add it to the sauce with the cream. Serve the sauce separately, boiling hot.

JEAN E. PROGNEAUX
LES SPECIALITÉS ET RECETTES GASTRONOMIQUES BORDELAISES ET GIRONDINES

Red Deer of Beef

The techniques for larding beef are shown on pages 56-57.

This recipe of Martha Washington's tastes as good today as it must have in the Presidential dining room. It is quite similar to the German sauerbraten.

	To serve 6	
3 lb.	beef top round in 1 piece, larded	1½ kg.
1 tsp.	salt	5 ml.
½ tsp.	grated nutmeg	2 ml.
¼ tsp.	ground ginger	1 ml.
2 cups	dry red wine	½ liter
½ cup	vinegar	125 ml.
1	bay leaf	1
½ tsp.	peppercorns	2 ml.
½ cup	water	125 ml.
2 tbsp.	butter	30 ml.
½ tsp.	sugar	2 ml.
2 tbsp.	flour, mixed with 3 to 4 tbsp. [45 to 60 ml.] water	30 ml.

Rub the beef with the salt, nutmeg and ginger. Place the meat in a bowl and cover with the wine and vinegar. Add the bay leaf, peppercorns and water. Cover the bowl, refrigerate and let the beef stand two days, turning it twice a day.

Before cooking, wipe the meat dry. Melt the butter in a

Dutch oven and brown the meat quickly. Reduce the heat and add 2 cups [½ liter] of the liquid in which the meat has soaked. Cover and cook slowly for 3 to 4 hours, or until the meat is tender, turning frequently. Transfer the meat to a warmed platter. Add the sugar to the gravy and thicken it with the flour-and-water mixture.

POPPY CANNON & PATRICIA BROOKS
THE PRESIDENTS' COOKBOOK

Steak with Bordeaux

Sigir Yahnesi

	To serve 6	
2 lb.	beef rump or round steak	1 kg.
⅔ cup	red Bordeaux	150 ml.
1	shallot, finely chopped	1
1	garlic clove, crushed	1
1 tsp.	ground allspice	5 ml.
1 to 2 tbsp.	fresh lime juice	15 to 30 ml.
	salt and pepper	
1 tsp.	finely cut fresh chives	5 ml.
1 tsp.	finely chopped fresh parsley	5 ml.
1 tsp.	dried sage	5 ml.
3 tbsp.	olive oil	45 ml.
12	small boiling onions	12
⅓ cup	flour	75 ml.
3 cups	beef stock	¾ liter
3	young carrots	3
3	slices salami	3

Trim and bone the meat. Wipe it over with a vinegar-soaked cloth. Put the Bordeaux, shallot, garlic, allspice, lime juice, salt, pepper and herbs in a bowl. Mix well and add the meat. Marinate at room temperature for 5 hours, basting often. Remove the meat and drain well; do not wipe dry.

Heat the olive oil and fry the meat for 10 minutes, 5 minutes on each side, until it is a pale brown color. Add the onions and cook for 5 minutes more. Remove the meat and onions, and keep them hot.

Add the flour to the oil remaining in the pan and cook until deep brown, stirring from time to time. Add the stock and the liquor in which the meat marinated and bring to a boil, stirring the sauce frequently to prevent lumpiness. Add the meat, the onions and the carrots. Cover with slices of salami and simmer for 2½ hours, covered, shaking the pan occasionally to prevent burning. Serve hot.

IRFAN ORGA
COOKING THE MIDDLE EAST WAY

Meatballs in Beer

Frikadeller Med Øl

To serve 4 to 6

1 lb.	ground beef chuck	½ kg.
1 lb.	ground pork	½ kg.
1	onion, finely chopped	1
5 tbsp.	butter	75 ml.
1 tsp.	salt	5 ml.
¼ tsp.	pepper	1 ml.
	grated nutmeg	
4	slices stale bread	4
1	egg, lightly beaten	1
	flour	
1½ cups	beer	375 ml.
2 tbsp.	fresh lemon juice	30 ml.

Brown the onion in 2 tablespoons [30 ml.] of the butter. Add salt, pepper and a pinch of nutmeg, and transfer the onions to a bowl. Reduce the bread slices to fine crumbs and mix them with the beef and pork. Add to the onions. Add the egg, mix well and form into walnut-sized balls. Roll them in a small amount of flour.

Brown the meatballs in the remaining butter. When well browned, add the beer and lemon juice. Bring to a boil, reduce the heat, cover the pan and let simmer for 30 minutes.

Serve the meatballs with buttered noodles sprinkled with toasted bread crumbs.

INGEBORG DAHL JENSEN
WONDERFUL, WONDERFUL DANISH COOKING

Leek Meatballs

To serve 4

1 lb.	ground beef	½ kg.
8 to 10	leeks (about 2 lb. [1 kg.]), including 1 inch [2½ cm.] of the green leaves	8 to 10
	salt	
1 cup	fresh bread crumbs	¼ liter
	freshly ground pepper	
2	eggs, lightly beaten	2
2 to 3 tbsp.	oil	30 to 45 ml.
2 to 3 tbsp.	fresh lemon juice	30 to 45 ml.
3 tbsp.	butter	45 ml.
1 cup	water	¼ liter

Cook the leeks in boiling, salted water until tender—about 15 to 20 minutes. Drain thoroughly and chop them very fine.

Mix with the meat and bread crumbs, season well, and stir in the eggs to bind the mixture.

Heat the oil in a heavy frying pan. Shape the mixture into walnut-sized balls, and fry until the meatballs are lightly browned. Remove and drain them. Put the lemon juice, butter and water into a saucepan, season well and bring to a boil. Drop in the meatballs, cover and simmer for 15 minutes, shaking the pan occasionally and adding a little more water and lemon juice if the liquid is being absorbed too quickly. When done, serve with rice or buttered noodles, and a crisp green vegetable.

PAMELA WESTLAND
A TASTE OF THE COUNTRY

Moroccan Meatball, Tomato and Egg Stew

Kefta Mkaouara

This kind of Moroccan stew is called a tagine after the shallow earthenware braising vessel with a conical cover in which it is traditionally prepared. Kefta is finely ground meat (beef or lamb), liberally spiced.

To serve 5 or 6

1 lb.	beef or lamb, finely ground	½ kg.
2 tbsp.	chopped fresh parsley	30 ml.
1 tbsp.	chopped coriander leaves (or substitute ½ tbsp. [7 ml.] ground coriander)	15 ml.
½ tsp.	ground cumin seed	2 ml.
1	small onion, grated	1
¼ tsp.	cayenne pepper	1 ml.
	salt	
2 tbsp.	vegetable oil	30 ml.

Spicy tomato sauce

2	medium-sized onions, chopped	2
1	small bunch fresh parsley, chopped	1
2 to 2½ lb.	ripe tomatoes, peeled, seeded and chopped	1 kg.
1 tsp.	ground cumin	5 ml.
1 tsp.	freshly ground black pepper	5 ml.
2	garlic cloves, chopped	2
½ tsp.	ground cinnamon	2 ml.
¼ tsp.	cayenne pepper	1 ml.
6	eggs	6

In a large bowl, combine all the *kefta* ingredients except the oil. Wet your hands to prevent the mixture from sticking and form 1-inch [2½-cm.] balls. Heat the oil in a frying pan and brown the meatballs on all sides. Remove them from the pan and set them aside, covered.

Add all the sauce ingredients except the eggs to the frying pan. Cook, uncovered, for 30 minutes, or until the sauce has reduced to a thick gravy. Return the meatballs to the sauce and cook together for 10 minutes. Carefully break the eggs into the sauce and poach them until set. Serve this dish immediately, directly from the pan.

PAULA WOLFERT
COUSCOUS AND OTHER GOOD FOOD FROM MOROCCO

Beef and Onions in Beer
Carbonnade du Nord

To serve 4 to 6

2 lb.	lean beef shoulder or round, cut into ¼-inch [6-mm.] slices, edges slashed	1 kg.
4	medium-sized onions, halved lengthwise and thinly sliced	4
⅓ cup	olive oil or lard	75 ml.
	salt	
2 tsp.	brown sugar	10 ml.
3 tbsp.	flour	45 ml.
2 cups	beer	½ liter
1 cup	beef or veal stock, or pot-au-feu broth	¼ liter
2	bay leaves	2
2 tsp.	finely crumbled, mixed dried herbs (thyme, oregano, savory, marjoram)	10 ml.
	pepper	

Cook the onions in approximately 3 tablespoons [45 ml.] of oil or lard in a skillet over low heat, stirring or tossing the slices regularly until softened and lightly caramelized. If necessary, turn up the heat slightly in order to color the onions. Empty them into a sieve over a mixing bowl or over the ovenproof casserole that will serve for cooking the dish. Be certain that no fragment of onion remains in the skillet.

Pour the drained fat back into the skillet, adding a bit more oil if necessary, and, over fairly high heat, brown the salted slices of steak. This will have to be done in two or three shifts. Remove those that are done to the sieve with the onions. From time to time pour back into the skillet the fat and juices that drain from the onions and seared meat.

When all the steaks have been browned, turn the heat to low, add the sugar to the skillet and stir around. Then add the flour and cook, stirring, for a few moments. Deglaze with the beer; add it slowly and stir the while, scraping well to loosen all caramelized adherences. Stir in the stock, bring to a boil and remove the pan from the heat. Taste for salt.

Arrange the slices of meat in the casserole in layers, alternating with the onions (three layers of meat slices and

two of onions). Place a bay leaf and a sprinkling of herbs on each layer of onions. Pour over the liquid—the ingredients should be well immersed; add a bit more beer or some water or stock, if necessary. Bring to a boil on top of the stove and cook, tightly covered, in a preheated 325° F. [160° C.] oven for about 3 hours, testing for tenderness after 2½ hours.

Before serving, carefully lift all the fat from the surface of the cooking liquid, first with a tablespoon, then with absorbent paper. Season with pepper at the table and accompany with steamed potatoes or fresh egg noodles.

RICHARD OLNEY
SIMPLE FRENCH FOOD

Meatballs with Egg-Lemon Sauce
Youverlakie me Avgolemono

To serve 4

1 lb.	lean ground beef	½ kg.
⅓ cup	chopped onion	75 ml.
1 tsp.	finely chopped fresh mint	5 ml.
1 tbsp.	chopped fresh parsley	15 ml.
2 tbsp.	raw unprocessed rice	30 ml.
	salt and pepper	
1½ cups	beef stock	375 ml.
1 cup	water	¼ liter
2	egg yolks	2
1 to 2 tbsp.	fresh lemon juice	15 to 30 ml.

Mix together the beef, onion, mint, parsley and rice. Season with salt and pepper, and add ¼ cup [50 ml.] of the beef stock. Mix well and form into walnut-sized balls. In a large pot, bring the remaining stock and the water to a boil and drop the meatballs into it. Lower the heat and simmer for 45 minutes. In a bowl, beat the egg yolks and add the lemon juice. Still beating, slowly add a few tablespoons of the hot stock to the egg yolks. Then stir the egg-yolk mixture into the stock and meatballs in the pot. Cover, remove from the heat and let stand 5 minutes.

MAMMA PAPPAS
LOUIS PAPPAS' FAMOUS GREEK RECIPES

Beef Stew, Burgundy-Style

Sauté de Boeuf à la Bourguignonne

For instructions on larding see pages 56-57.

To serve 6

3 lb.	boneless beef round	1½ kg.
3 oz.	fresh pork fat, cut into strips about 1 inch [2½ cm.] long and ¼ inch [6 mm.] square	100 g.
2 tbsp.	finely chopped fresh parsley	30 ml.
1 tsp.	dried thyme (or substitute mixed herbs)	5 ml.
½ lb.	lean salt pork with the rind removed, sliced ½ inch [1 cm.] thick, cut crosswise into ½-inch sections, blanched in boiling water for 5 minutes and drained	¼ kg.
2 tbsp.	olive or vegetable oil	30 ml.
3 or 4	medium-sized carrots, cut crosswise into 1- to 2-inch [2½- to 5-cm.] lengths	3 or 4
3	large onions, each cut into 4 to 6 pieces	3
	salt	
3 tbsp.	flour	45 ml.
¼ cup	Cognac	50 ml.
1	bouquet garni	1
2	garlic cloves, crushed	2
1 cup	boiling veal stock, pot-au-feu broth, or water	¼ liter
½ lb.	firm, fresh button mushrooms	¼ kg.
	pepper	
6 tbsp.	butter	90 ml.
30	small boiling onions	30

Red wine marinade

2 tbsp.	olive oil	30 ml.
½ tsp.	dried thyme (or substitute mixed herbs)	2 ml.
3 cups	red Burgundy wine	¾ liter

Cut the section of beef in half crosswise, then divide each section into six pieces, respecting the muscle structure; each piece should remain intact within its membrane. Roll the fresh pork fat in the parsley mixed with the thyme or mixed herbs. Using a small, sharp knife, pierce each piece of meat, with the grain, in one or two places and force a strip of fat into each slit. Put the meat in the marinade for about 3 hours. Turn the pieces two or three times during this period.

In a skillet over medium heat, cook the salt-pork pieces in the oil, turning the pieces until they are golden and the surfaces are slightly crisp. Put the pieces aside, lower the heat and cook the carrots and onions in the same oil, stirring regularly, for 20 to 30 minutes. The onions should be only lightly browned. With a perforated skimming spoon, remove the vegetables from the pan, drain them of all fat and make certain to leave no fragments of onion behind—they would inevitably burn and leave a bitter taste in the sauce.

While the vegetables are cooking, remove the pieces of meat from the marinade, drain them well in a colander or large sieve, collecting the liquid, and wipe them with a paper towel until dry. Raise the heat and, still in the same oil, brown the meat on all sides, adding more oil if necessary, and salting the pieces only after they have been turned once. Reduce the heat to medium, drain off any excess oil, sprinkle the flour over the meat and turn the pieces two or three times over a period of 5 or 6 minutes until the flour is lightly browned. Return the onions and carrots to the pan, stir everything together, and pour in the Cognac and the reserved marinade. Stir and scrape the bottom of the pan with a wooden spoon to loosen all the caramelized deposits.

Transfer the pieces of meat to a fireproof casserole, and pour in the liquid and vegetables. Add the bouquet garni, the garlic and enough boiling stock (or water) to cover. Bring the liquid back to a boil, cover, and cook—with the surface hardly bubbling—preferably in the oven at 300° F. [150° C.] for 2½ to 3 hours, or until the meat is tender but still firm. Skim the surface fat two or three times during this period and gently move the pieces of meat about in their sauce to ensure that nothing sticks to the bottom of the casserole.

Toss the mushrooms, salted and peppered, in half the butter, over high heat for a couple of minutes, or until they are lightly colored and their superficial moisture has evaporated. Season the pickling onions and cook them whole over low heat in the remaining butter, in a pan just the right size to hold them in one layer. Toss or turn the onions from time to time until they are yellow and tender, but not browned.

With a spoon, remove the pieces of meat and carrot from the sauce, discard the bouquet garni and pass everything else through a fine sieve. Return the meat and the carrots to the casserole, add the reserved salt pork, the glazed onions and the sautéed mushrooms. Keep the casserole covered while finishing the sauce.

Bring the sauce to a boil and, keeping the saucepan to the side of the heat, simmer and skim regularly for 30 minutes. If at this point the sauce seems too thin, reduce it for a couple of minutes over high heat, stirring until it reaches the desired consistency. Pour the sauce over the garnished meat, slowly reheat and simmer gently for about 20 minutes. Serve the meat in its casserole accompanied by freshly steamed potatoes in a separate dish.

RICHARD OLNEY
THE FRENCH MENU COOKBOOK

Curried Beef

Madoo Vindaloo

To make ghee (the Indian version of clarified butter), start with at least one third more butter than the amount specified in the recipe. Melt the butter over low heat without browning it, then bring the butter to a boil. When it foams, reduce the heat to very low. Simmer uncovered for 45 minutes. Strain the clear liquid ghee through a sieve lined with 4 layers of dampened cheesecloth. Discard the milk solids.

To serve 4

1 lb.	beef stew meat, cut into fairly large pieces	½ kg.
½ tbsp.	ground coriander	7 ml.
½ tsp.	ground cumin	2 ml.
½ tsp.	ground mustard	2 ml.
½ tsp.	pulverized dried chili or cayenne pepper	2 ml.
1 tsp.	ground turmeric	5 ml.
¼ tsp.	ground black pepper	1 ml.
¼ tsp.	ground ginger	1 ml.
	wine vinegar	
1	large onion, thinly sliced	1
2	garlic cloves, thinly sliced	2
2	fresh or pickled green chilies, finely chopped	2
4 tbsp.	*ghee* or other fat	60 ml.
	salt and lemon juice to taste	

Mix the spices with vinegar to make a paste. Lightly fry the onion, garlic and chopped chilies in the *ghee* for 3 or 4 minutes. Add the paste and cook for 3 or 4 minutes longer. Then add the meat and, with the pan covered, let it cook in its own juice for 1 to 1½ hours. As necessary, add just enough water to keep the meat from sticking. This will form a thick, rich gravy. Add salt and lemon juice to taste.

E. P. VEERASAWMY
INDIAN COOKERY

Beef Casserole, Belgian-Style

To serve 4

1½ lb.	beef round, sliced 1 inch [2½ cm.] thick and cut into 1-inch cubes	¾ kg.
4 tbsp.	butter	60 ml.
2 cups	beef stock	½ liter
1¼ cups	dried apricots	300 ml.
1 tsp.	sugar	5 ml.
4 or 5	leeks, white parts only	4 or 5
	salt and pepper	
1 tsp.	grated lemon peel	5 ml.

In a fireproof casserole set over fairly high heat, brown the beef briskly in the butter. Add the stock, apricots and sugar,

reduce the heat to low and leave to simmer for 15 minutes.

Blanch the leeks by putting them into cold water and gradually bringing them to a boil; then drain them. Add the leeks to the casserole, and season to taste. Cover and simmer gently for 2 hours until the beef is fork-tender. Check the seasoning, add the lemon peel, stir, and simmer for 5 minutes. Serve with mashed potatoes and buttered lima beans.

NINA FROUD
THE WORLD BOOK OF MEAT DISHES

Beef Short Ribs with Spiced Lemon and Caper Sauce

Westfälischer Pfefferpotthast

To serve 4

2 lb.	beef short ribs, cut into 2-inch [5-cm.] pieces	1 kg.
	salt and freshly ground black pepper	
2 tbsp.	lard	30 ml.
6	medium-sized onions, finely sliced	6
1	small bay leaf	1
¼ tsp.	ground cloves	1 ml.
1 quart	cold water	1 liter
3 tbsp.	fresh rye bread crumbs	45 ml.
2 tsp.	capers, rinsed in cold water and drained well	10 ml.
2 tbsp.	fresh lemon juice	30 ml.
½ tsp.	finely grated lemon peel	2 ml.

Sprinkle the short ribs with salt and pepper. In a 3- to 4-quart [3- to 4-liter] saucepan or Dutch oven, heat the lard over high heat until it begins to splutter. Add the short ribs and brown them on all sides, regulating the heat so that the ribs brown quickly and evenly without burning.

Remove the meat to a platter. Reduce the heat. Add the onions to the fat remaining in the pan and cook, stirring occasionally, for about 5 minutes, until they are soft and transparent but not brown. Add the bay leaf and cloves, and pour in the water. Bring to a boil over high heat, scraping in any brown bits clinging to the bottom and sides of the pan.

Return the ribs to the pan, cover and reduce the heat to its lowest point. Simmer for about 1½ hours, or until the meat shows no resistance when pierced with the tip of a small, sharp knife. Then transfer the short ribs to a deep heated serving dish and cover with foil to keep them warm.

Discard the bay leaf, and skim off the fat from the liquid remaining in the pan. Stir in the bread crumbs, capers, lemon juice and lemon peel, and bring to a boil over high heat. Reduce the heat; simmer uncovered for a minute or two. Taste for seasoning; the sauce should be quite peppery; add more pepper to taste if necessary. Then pour the sauce over the meat and serve at once.

FOODS OF THE WORLD/THE COOKING OF GERMANY

Provençal Braised Beef

Daube à la Provençale

To serve 8 to 10

3½ lb.	beef without bones (round, shank, chuck, or a mixture)	1½ kg.
½ cup	Cognac	125 ml.
3 tbsp.	olive oil	45 ml.
3 cups	dry white wine	¾ liter
½ lb.	lean salt pork (or substitute bacon)	¼ kg.
5 oz.	pork rind	150 g.
2	medium-sized carrots, thinly sliced	2
4	medium-sized tomatoes (about 1 lb. [½ kg.]), peeled, seeded and coarsely chopped	4
4	garlic cloves, finely chopped	4
2	medium-sized onions, finely chopped	2
½ lb.	mushrooms, finely chopped	¼ kg.
½ cup	pitted black olives (unpitted if they are tiny Niçoise olives)	125 ml.
2 tsp.	mixed thyme, oregano and savory	10 ml.
	salt	
2	bouquets garnis, each made of 3 sprigs parsley, 1 bay leaf, 1 strip dried orange peel	2
1 cup	leftover juice from roasted or braised beef or veal, veal stock, pot-au-feu broth or water	¼ liter
	flour-and-water paste	

Seasoned lardons

¼ lb.	fresh pork fat	125 g.
2	garlic cloves	2
3 tbsp.	chopped fresh parsley	45 ml.

Cut the meat into fairly large pieces of more or less regular shape, respecting as nearly as possible the natural muscle structure. You should have 15 or 16 pieces.

To lard the meat, remove the rind from the pork fat and save it. Cut the fat into strips approximately ¼ inch [6 mm.] square and 1 to 1½ inches [2½ to 3½ cm.] long. In a mortar, reduce the garlic to a paste, add the chopped parsley, mix well, then add the strips of pork fat and stir well together.

With a small, sharp knife, pierce each piece of meat completely through, with the grain, being careful not to make a wide and messy gash. Gently force a strip of pork fat, well coated with the garlic-and-parsley mixture, into the center of each piece of meat. Place the pieces in a bowl. Sprinkle the Cognac and the olive oil over the pieces, turning them

around until all sides are moistened. Pour the white wine over and leave to marinate for 2 to 3 hours.

Remove the rind from the salt pork and cut all the pork rind you have—including the rind reserved earlier—into small pieces, approximately ½ inch [1 cm.] square. Parboil them for 5 or 6 minutes and drain them. Cut the salt pork into ½-inch strips across the grain and parboil them for 2 or 3 minutes. In a bowl, mix together the carrots, tomatoes, garlic, olives, onions, mushrooms, mixed herbs and salt. Add to them the salt-pork strips.

Choose a cooking utensil (preferably of earthenware, but enameled ironware or heavy copper will do) of approximately 4-quart [4-liter] capacity to hold the ingredients exactly. The lid should fit as tightly as possible.

The different ingredients must now be arranged in layers—whether two, three or more layers will be necessary depends on the proportionate height and width of the cooking vessel. Begin by sprinkling the bottom with pork-rind pieces, remove the meat pieces from the marinade and arrange them in a layer atop the rind, close together but not packed in. Then add a layer of the pork-strips mixture. Place the bouquets garnis on this bed and begin again with rind, beef, etc. Pour in the marinade and add sufficient meat juice (or water) barely to cover.

If the lid to your chosen *daubière* should not fit tightly, tear a long strip of cloth about 1 inch [2½ cm.] wide, dip it into a thin flour-and-water paste and squeeze out the excess liquid. Place the lid upside down and wrap the cloth around the outside of the fitting ridge. Then turn the lid right side up and carefully cover the *daubière*.

Place the *daubière* in a medium oven, 325° to 350° F. [160° to 180° C.]. After about 45 minutes, it should be approaching the boiling point—you will hear it beginning to bubble. Reduce the temperature to 250° to 275° F. [120° to 140° C.] and forget about it for a good 5 hours.

Break the seal, if you have used one on the *daubière*, lift off the lid and skim off most of the fat floating on the surface. Discard the bouquets garnis. At this point the dish may be served immediately or put aside to be reheated the next day.

RICHARD OLNEY
THE FRENCH MENU COOKBOOK

Beef Goulash

Bográcsgulyás

To serve 8

2½ lb.	lean beef chuck or round, trimmed of fat, sliced ¾ inch [2 cm.] thick and cut into ¾-inch cubes	1 kg.
2 tbsp.	lard	30 ml.
2	medium-sized onions, coarsely chopped	2
½ lb.	beef heart, sliced ¾ inch [2 cm.] thick and cut into ¾-inch cubes (optional)	¼ kg.
1	garlic clove	1
	caraway seeds	
	salt	
2 tbsp.	Hungarian paprika	30 ml.
2½ quarts	warm water	2½ liters
1	medium-sized ripe tomato, peeled, sliced 1 inch [2½ cm.] thick and cut into 1-inch pieces	1
2	Italian peppers, cored and sliced into rings	2
4	medium-sized potatoes, peeled, sliced ¾ inch [2 cm.] thick and cut into ¾-inch cubes	4

Little dumplings

1	egg	1
3 tbsp.	flour	45 ml.
¼ tsp.	salt	1 ml.

Melt the lard in a heavy 6- to 8-quart [6- to 8-liter] casserole. Sauté the onions in the lard. The heat should be low in order not to brown the onions. When the onions become glossy, add the beef and the beef heart, if you are using it. Stir so that during this part of the process, which should last for about 10 minutes, the meat will sauté with the onions.

Meanwhile, chop the garlic, and use the flat side of a heavy knife to crush it, along with a pinch of caraway seeds and a little salt.

Take the casserole off the heat. With a wooden spoon rapidly stir in the paprika and the garlic mixture. Immediately after the paprika is absorbed, add the warm water. (Cold water toughens meat if you add it while the meat is frying.) Cover the casserole, replace it over low heat and cook for about 1 hour.

After the meat has been braised for about 1 hour (cooking time may vary; the meat should feel almost completely tender when pierced with a fork), add the tomato and peppers and enough water to achieve a soupy consistency. Add a little salt. Simmer slowly for another 30 minutes. Add the potatoes and cook the goulash, still covered, until it is done. Adjust the salt.

To make the dumplings, mix the egg with the flour and salt. Spoon the mixture into the goulash, ¼ teaspoon [1 ml.] at a time, 2 to 3 minutes before serving. Keep the casserole covered to cook the dumplings through.

Serve the goulash and dumplings steaming hot in large, extra-deep bowls. The meat should be tender, but not to the point that it is falling apart.

GEORGE LANG
THE CUISINE OF HUNGARY

Beef Slices, Semarang-Style

Lapis Daging Semarang

To serve 3 or 4

1 lb.	beef rump (chuck or round will do but take a little more cooking), sliced into thin scallops	½ kg.
1 tbsp.	butter or coconut oil *(copha)*	15 ml.
1	large onion, thinly sliced lengthwise	1
1	large tomato, peeled and chopped	1
2 inches	stick cinnamon (optional)	5 cm.
2	whole cloves (optional)	2

Peppery marinade

1	large onion, finely chopped	1
3	garlic cloves, finely chopped	3
10	peppercorns, crushed	10
3 tbsp.	dark soy sauce	45 ml.
3 tbsp.	brown sugar (optional)	45 ml.
	grated nutmeg (optional)	

Pound the beef slices with a meat mallet until they are very thin. To make the marinade, mash the onion and garlic to a fine paste. Combine this with the pepper and soy sauce and, if you are using them, the sugar and a pinch of nutmeg. Marinate the meat in this sauce for 30 minutes to 1 hour.

Heat the butter or oil in a wok or a large skillet, add the sliced onion and fry it until soft. Add the beef slices and marinade, and stir fry for 1 minute. Then add the tomato and a little water. Stir and allow to cook uncovered until the meat is tender, the tomato soft and there is not too much gravy—about 5 minutes.

To cook this dish to Sumatran taste, do not add sugar to the marinade, but add stick cinnamon and whole cloves during the final cooking and remove them before serving.

ROSEMARY BRISSENDEN
SOUTH EAST ASIAN FOOD

Beef with Onions

Sovanli Yahni

To serve 4 to 6

2 lb.	beef stew meat, sliced 1 inch [2½ cm.] thick, cut into 1-inch cubes	1 kg.
3 tbsp.	butter	45 ml.
2	tomatoes, peeled, seeded and chopped	2
10 to 12	white boiling onions	10 to 12
2	garlic cloves (optional)	2
½ tsp.	ground allspice	2 ml.
2 tbsp.	vinegar	30 ml.
	salt and pepper	
1 cup	tomato juice	¼ liter

In a covered saucepan cook the meat in the butter over low heat for 1 hour. Shake the saucepan from time to time to prevent scorching. Add all of the other ingredients. Cover and continue to cook over low heat for 1 hour more or until the meat is tender.

This dish should not be dry, but must have its own sauce. If necessary, a little warm water may be added. Serve warm with boiled Brussels sprouts or noodles.

NESET EREN
THE ART OF TURKISH COOKING

Swiss Steak

To serve 4

2 to 2½ lb.	beef round or chuck steak, sliced 1 to 1½ inches [2½ to 4 cm.] thick and trimmed of fat	1 kg.
½ cup	flour	125 ml.
3 tbsp.	chopped beef suet or trimmed beef fat	45 ml.
1	onion, finely chopped	1
1	garlic clove	1
	finely chopped fresh thyme, marjoram and either rosemary or savory	
½ cup	tomato juice or water	125 ml.
	salt and pepper	

Cut the meat into serving-size pieces or not, as you wish. Pound the flour into the meat until the meat will hold no more flour. Render the suet or beef fat in a heavy pan. Add the meat and brown it slowly on both sides (allowing about 30 minutes in all). Remove the meat from the pan, discard the fat, and add to the pan the onion, garlic and a sprinkling of herbs to taste. Add the tomato juice or water and stir to deglaze the pan, seasoning with salt and pepper. Season the

meat and return it to the pan. Cover the pan and cook very slowly for about 1¼ to 1¾ hours, or until the meat is tender.

CATHERINE C. LAUGHTON (EDITOR)
MARY CULLEN'S NORTHWEST COOK BOOK

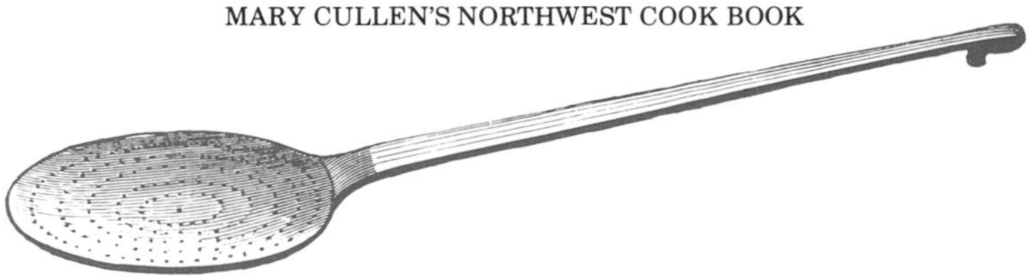

Flank Steak with Meat Stuffing, Shaker-Style

To serve 6 to 8

2 to 2½ lb.	beef flank steak, thoroughly trimmed of fat and membrane	1 kg.
8 tbsp.	butter	120 ml.
4 or 5	slices firm, white bread, cut into ¼-inch [6-mm.] cubes (about 2 cups [½ liter])	4 or 5
1 cup	finely chopped onions	¼ liter
1 cup	finely chopped celery	¼ liter
¼ lb.	lean ground beef	125 g.
¼ lb.	lean ground veal	125 g.
¼ lb.	lean ground pork	125 g.
1	egg	1
¼ cup	finely chopped fresh parsley	50 ml.
¼ tsp.	dried rosemary	1 ml.
½ tsp.	dried basil	2 ml.
½ tsp.	dried savory	2 ml.
¼ tsp.	ground sage	1 ml.
1½ tsp.	salt	7 ml.
¼ tsp.	freshly ground black pepper	1 ml.
2 tbsp.	vegetable oil	30 ml.
2	ribs celery, trimmed and cut crosswise into slices ¼ inch [6 mm.] thick	2
1	medium-sized carrot, scraped and coarsely chopped	1
1 cup	beef stock, fresh or canned (or substitute 1 cup water or a combination of the two)	¼ liter

Have the butcher cut a pocket in the steak, or do it yourself in the following manner: With a long, very sharp knife, slit the steak horizontally along one long side, cutting through the meat to within about ½ inch [1 cm.] of the other long side and to within about 1 inch [2½ cm.] of each short end.

Preheat the oven to 350° F. [180° C.]. In a heavy 8- to 10-inch skillet, melt 4 tablespoons [60 ml.] of the butter over moderate heat. Add the bread cubes and, stirring frequently, fry them until they are crisp and golden brown. With a slotted spoon, transfer the cubes to a deep bowl.

Melt 2 more tablespoons [30 ml.] of butter in the skillet, add the chopped onions and chopped celery, and stir for about 5 minutes, until they are soft but not brown. With a rubber spatula, scrape the onions and celery over the bread cubes. Add to the bowl the ground beef, veal, pork, egg, parsley, rosemary, basil, savory, sage, salt and pepper. Knead vigorously with both hands, then beat with a wooden spoon until all the ingredients are well blended.

Holding the steak upright on its long, closed side, pack the stuffing tightly into the pocket, a handful at a time. Then lay the steak flat and close the open side by sewing it with a large needle and white cotton thread.

Melt the remaining 2 tablespoons of butter with the oil in a heavy casserole large enough to hold the steak comfortably. Brown the steak in the hot fat, regulating the heat so that the meat colors richly and evenly on both sides without burning. Transfer the steak to a plate and add the sliced celery, sliced onion and carrot to the fat remaining in the casserole. Stirring frequently, cook for 8 to 10 minutes, or until the vegetables are soft and delicately browned.

Pour in the stock or water, or stock-and-water combination, and bring to a boil over high heat, scraping in the brown particles clinging to the bottom and sides of the pan. Return the steak to the casserole and braise in the middle of the oven for 1 hour, or until the steak shows no resistance when pierced deeply with the point of a small sharp knife. Place the steak on a heated platter. Remove the thread.

Skim off the surface fat and strain the cooking liquid through a fine sieve into a sauceboat or bowl, pressing down hard on the vegetables with the back of a spoon to extract all their juices before discarding the pulp. Taste for seasoning, and serve the gravy separately with the steak.

FOODS OF THE WORLD
AMERICAN COOKING: THE EASTERN HEARTLAND

Beef Rolls

Rouladen

To serve 4 to 6

2 lb.	beef round or flank steak	1 kg.
4	slices bacon, diced	4
3	dill pickles, halved lengthwise	3
1 tsp.	prepared mustard	5 ml.
	marjoram	
2 to 3 tbsp.	flour	30 to 45 ml.
2 tbsp.	fat	30 ml.
2 cups	beef stock	½ liter

The meat should be cut into four to six rectangular portions. Pound each with a meat mallet or the edge of a plate until

the portion is quite thin and all the tissues have been broken down. Place a bacon slice, pickle slice and a dab of mustard on each portion. Sprinkle with marjoram. Roll up, dredging the outside of each roll with a little of the flour. Secure the rolls with wooden picks where the meat overlaps, keeping the picks parallel with the length of the rolls.

Sauté the *rouladen* in hot fat in a skillet until well browned on all sides. Transfer to a heavy casserole. Add the remaining flour to the pan drippings, cook a few seconds, then slowly add the beef stock. Simmer until thickened. Pour over the meat in the casserole. Cover tightly, simmer for 1½ hours or until tender. *Rouladen* are excellent when cooked ahead and reheated in their gravy.

Sometimes the dill pickle is omitted and, instead, sauerkraut is piled inside each of the *rouladen*. About 1 cup [¼ liter] sauerkraut will be needed.

BETTY WASON
THE ART OF GERMAN COOKING

Spiced Beef and Beets

To serve 4 to 6

2 to 2½ lb.	lean beef stew meat, sliced 1 inch [2½ cm.] thick and cut into 1-inch cubes	1 kg.
2 tbsp.	lard	30 ml.
1	large onion, thinly sliced	1
1 cup	dry red wine	¼ liter
¼ cup	red wine vinegar	50 ml.
8	juniper berries, crushed	8
8	whole allspice, crushed	8
2 tsp.	brown sugar	10 ml.
8	small beets, peeled and halved	8
	salt and pepper	
2 tbsp.	sour cream	30 ml.
2 tsp.	dry mustard	10 ml.
2 tbsp.	grated horseradish	30 ml.

Melt the lard over high heat in a heavy fireproof casserole. Add the beef and brown the cubes all over, remove and set them aside. Lower the heat, stir in the onions and cook them until they are soft. Pour in the wine and vinegar, raise the heat again and bring to a boil. Stir in the spices and sugar, and add the beef and the beets. Season with salt and pepper. Cover the casserole and put in an oven, preheated to 325° F. [170° C.]. Bake for 1½ hours.

Blend together the sour cream, mustard and horseradish and stir them into the casserole just before serving.

GAIL DUFF
FRESH ALL THE YEAR

Beef with Almonds and Olives

Carne Machada à la Anduluza

To serve 4 to 6

2 lb.	beef round or chuck roast, cut 1 inch [2½ cm.] thick	1 kg.
½ cup	slivered, blanched almonds	125 ml.
½ cup	green olives, pitted and chopped	125 ml.
	salt	
1 tsp.	ground cinnamon	5 ml.
	olive oil	
1	onion, quartered	1
1	tomato, peeled and quartered	1
1	garlic clove	1
½ cup	dry red wine	125 ml.
	beef or veal stock	
	pepper	

Make cuts on one side of the meat and fill them with a mixture of the almonds, olives, salt and cinnamon. Roll the meat, tie it up and brown it in hot oil in a heavy casserole. When it looks golden brown all over, put in the onion, the tomato and garlic. Add the wine and about an equal amount of stock to cover. Season well, cover the casserole and cook on very low heat till the meat is tender—about 2 to 3 hours.

To serve, slice the meat and strain the sauce over it.

ANNA MACMIADHACHÁIN
SPANISH REGIONAL COOKERY

Steak with Caper Sauce

To serve 4

2 lb.	beef round steak, cut ½ inch [1 cm.] thick	1 kg.
	salt and pepper	
	flour	
4 tbsp.	butter	60 ml.
2	medium-sized onions, chopped	2
¼ cup	capers, rinsed in cold water and drained well	50 ml.
2 to 3 tbsp.	sharp-flavored prepared mustard	30 to 45 ml.
1 cup	water	¼ liter
1 cup	sour cream at room temperature	¼ liter

Pound the steak with a meat mallet until it is ¼ inch [6 mm.] thick. Season with salt and pepper. Dredge it in flour. Melt 2 tablespoons [30 ml.] of butter in a large skillet. Add the steak; brown it on both sides. Remove to a plate.

Add the remaining butter to the fat and fry the onions in it until tender but not browned. Add the capers, mustard, water and the steak. Cook very slowly, covered, for 30 minutes, adding more water if the liquid evaporates to a shallow layer. Remove the steak to a warm platter and keep it warm. Stir the sour cream into the pan gravy and leave on the stove long enough to heat through. Spoon the sauce over the steak.

KAY SHAW NELSON
THE EASTERN EUROPEAN COOKBOOK

Beef Stew with Prunes and Pine Nuts

Estofado con Ciruelas y Piñones

To serve 4

2 lb.	beef stew meat, sliced 2 inches [5 cm.] thick and cut into 2-inch cubes	1 kg.
⅓ to ½ cup	olive oil	75 to 125 ml.
1	medium-sized onion, thickly sliced	1
2	garlic cloves	2
1	large tomato, unpeeled, cut into 8 pieces	1
2 tbsp.	Cognac	30 ml.
½ cup	dry white wine	125 ml.
	salt to taste	
½ tsp.	paprika	2 ml.
⅛ tsp.	ground cinnamon	½ ml.
1	sprig fresh thyme (or substitute ½ tsp. [2 ml.] dried thyme)	1
½	bay leaf	½
1½ tbsp.	flour	22 ml.
1 cup	boiling water	¼ liter
½ lb.	dried prunes	¼ kg.
½ cup	pine nuts	125 ml.

Heat 3 tablespoons [45 ml.] of olive oil over high heat in a heavy metal casserole. When the oil is on the verge of smoking, brown the meat rapidly in small batches so you do not crowd the pan. As the meat browns, remove it to a bowl. (If you do not have a metal casserole, brown the meat in a skillet; then proceed, using a fireproof earthenware casserole.)

Add olive oil if needed and brown the onion and garlic. Add the tomato; fry until the juice has evaporated. Add the Cognac and wine and cook over high heat until the liquid evaporates. Reduce the heat and add the salt, paprika, cinnamon, thyme, bay leaf and flour. Stir until the flour is browned. Put the meat back in the casserole. Add the boiling water, cover and simmer for 2 hours until the meat is tender.

If the sauce becomes too dry during cooking, add boiling water in small amounts. If the sauce is too thin when the meat is done, remove the meat and boil the sauce, uncovered, until thick enough. The consistency of the sauce will vary with the amount of juice released by the meat.

Half an hour before serving, put the prunes to boil in enough water to cover. Remove and strain when tender, about 30 minutes. Fifteen minutes before serving, boil the pine nuts in water to cover in a separate saucepan. Drain and add the pine nuts and prunes to the *estofado*.

The prunes are added only at the last moment to avoid oversweetening the sauce; the pine nuts are added just before serving in order to preserve their whiteness.

To serve, place the meat, prunes and pine nuts in a dish and strain the sauce over them.

Note: *estofado* is a convenient dish for the hostess-cook because it is particularly delicious if prepared several hours ahead and reheated just before being brought to the table.

BARBARA NORMAN
THE SPANISH COOKBOOK

Beef Game-Warden-Style

Boeuf à la Gardiane

To serve 4

2 lb.	beef rump or top round, cut into nut-sized pieces	1 kg.
2	onions, chopped	2
¼ lb.	lean bacon, chopped	125 g.
2 tbsp.	olive oil	30 ml.
	salt and pepper	
1	whole onion, stuck with 2 or 3 whole cloves	1
	bouquet garni	
1	small piece dried orange peel	1
½ cup	pitted green olives	125 ml.
½ cup	pitted black olives	125 ml.
4	medium-sized potatoes, coarsely diced	4
1 cup	water	¼ liter

In a large saucepan over moderate heat, fry the chopped onions and bacon in the oil until golden. Add the pieces of beef and lightly brown them. Season with salt and pepper. Then add the whole onion, the bouquet garni, orange peel, olives and potatoes. Moisten with the water, cover the pan and simmer very gently for 1 to 2 hours, or until the beef is tender and the juices are well reduced.

LOUIS GINIÉS
CUISINE PROVENÇALE

Beef Ragout

Ragoûts de Boeuf

Chipolata sausages are mildly seasoned pork sausages available at French food markets.

This type of beef stew may be prepared using red wine instead of stock—in which case it is called *boeuf à la bourguignonne*. The garnish for *boeuf à la bourguignonne* consists of slices of salt pork, blanched and browned, and small glazed onions and mushrooms.

To serve 6 to 8

4 lb.	boneless beef rump, chuck or rib, cut into 2-inch [5-cm.] cubes	2 kg.
4 tbsp.	lard or butter	60 ml.
2	onions, quartered	2
2	carrots, quartered	2
	salt and pepper	
¼ cup	flour	50 ml.
1 quart	beef stock	1 liter
1	bouquet garni	1
1	garlic clove, crushed	1
12	*chipolata* sausages, broiled (optional)	12
¾ lb.	mushrooms, sautéed (optional)	⅓ kg.
½ lb.	chestnuts, slit, parboiled for 10 minutes in water, peeled and cooked 30 minutes in beef stock (optional)	¼ kg.
½ lb.	salsify, parboiled until tender and stewed in butter (optional)	¼ kg.

In a large fireproof casserole, brown the meat in the lard or butter with the onions and carrots. Season to taste with salt and pepper.

When the meat and vegetables acquire a nice color, sprinkle on the flour, add stock to cover, and mix. Add the bouquet garni and garlic. Simmer gently, covered, for 1½ hours. Drain the meat and vegetables through a sieve and reserve the liquid. Discard the vegetables and arrange the meat pieces, side by side, in an earthenware casserole big enough to hold the meat and the garnish. Reduce the reserved liquid in a saucepan for 20 to 30 minutes over low heat, skimming regularly. Strain and pour the liquid over the ragout. Finish the cooking in a slow oven, preheated to 300° F. [150° C.], keeping the casserole covered, for 1½ hours. Half an hour before the meat is done, put on top of it a garnish of *chipolata* sausages, mushrooms, chestnuts or salsify, or the garnish for *boeuf à la bourguignonne* described at the beginning of the recipe.

PROSPER MONTAGNÉ
LAROUSSE GASTRONOMIQUE

Beef Daube

Boeuf en Daube

To serve 4 to 6

2 to 2½ lb.	beef chuck, cut into 1- to 2-inch [2½- to 5-cm.] cubes	1 kg.
3 tbsp.	olive oil	45 ml.
1 quart	dry red wine	1 liter
Seasoning mixture		
¼ lb.	lean salt pork without the rind, blanched in boiling water for 5 minutes, drained and diced	125 g.
3	garlic cloves, minced	3
3	whole cloves	3
1	piece fresh orange peel	1
2	bay leaves	2
½ tsp.	ground cinnamon	2 ml.
	salt and pepper	

Put a good layer of olive oil in a fireproof braising pot or *daubière*, then add the beef and the seasoning mixture. Toss the mixture over moderate heat to brown the meat lightly. When this is done, add the red wine and cook over low heat until the wine has reduced a little. Cover the pot and let the beef barely simmer for 6 to 8 hours. A good braised beef should cook all night and be eaten the next day at lunchtime.

C. CHANOT-BULLIER
VIEILLES RECETTES DE CUISINE PROVENÇALE

Country-Style Beef

Terrine à la Paysanne

To serve 4 to 6

2 to 2½ lb.	beef bottom round, thinly sliced	1 kg.
12	slices bacon	12
¼ cup	chopped fresh parsley	50 ml.
4	scallions, chopped	4
	mixed spices	
	salt and pepper	
1	bay leaf	1
2 tbsp.	brandy	30 ml.
¼ cup	water	50 ml.
	thick flour-and-water paste	

In a terrine, arrange alternating layers of beef slices and bacon, seasoning each layer with the parsley, scallions, a pinch of mixed spices, salt and pepper. When the terrine is half full, add the bay leaf and continue layering the ingredients, finishing with a layer of bacon. Add the brandy and water. Seal the terrine carefully by spreading a flour-and-water paste around the edges of the lid before setting it in place. Cook in a moderately slow oven at 325° F. [160° C.] for approximately 4 hours. Remove the terrine from the oven, break the seal to remove the lid, and skim off excess fat from the cooking liquid. Serve the beef straight from the terrine.

OFFRAY AINÉ
LE CUISINIER MÉRIDIONAL

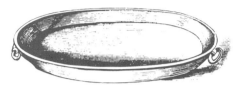

Spanish Beef Stew

Olives in the stew may sound bizarre, rather like the famous French roast chicken that is stuffed with a whole pound of garlic. Like the garlic in the chicken, the olives in the stew change magically in the long cooking to impart an elusive flavor. I confess that I am at a loss to describe this taste because I can think of nothing comparable. You'll just have to take it on faith that the combination results in a delicious and unusual dish.

To serve 4

2 lb.	boneless beef chuck, trimmed and cut into 2-inch [5-cm.] cubes	1 kg.
	flour	
3 tbsp.	olive oil	45 ml.
	salt	
	freshly milled pepper	
2	large onions, chopped (about 2 cups [½ liter])	2
1 cup	beef stock	¼ liter
½ cup	dry red wine	125 ml.
2	large garlic cloves, crushed	2
2	ripe tomatoes, seeded and chopped	2
2 tbsp.	fresh thyme (or substitute ½ tsp. [2 ml.] dried thyme)	30 ml.
1 cup	small green olives, pitted and rinsed	¼ liter

Dust the meat with flour, and heat the oil very hot in a heavy pot such as an iron Dutch oven. Brown the beef on all sides, sprinkling it with salt and pepper as you do so. Lower the heat, add the onions and cook, covered, until they are limp. Add the stock, wine, garlic, tomatoes, thyme and olives. Bring to a simmer and taste for seasoning. (The stew should be but lightly salted because the olives will take care of that. It is always best to adjust seasoning in a soup or a stew when it is finished and has reduced to its proper consistency.)

Cover, and either simmer the stew on a burner or in the middle of an oven, preheated to 350° F. [180° C.], for about 2 hours. Because there isn't a great deal of added liquid, the meat will need occasional stirring and basting with the sauce. If there is excess oil, skim the stew before serving.

Serve over mounds of steamed rice.

MIRIAM UNGERER
GOOD CHEAP FOOD

Mexican Braised Beef with Chili

Chili con Carne

There are many and various modifications of chili con carne, and one of the most important and agreeable is the use of green tomatoes in the summer and early autumn. As a matter of fact, the ideal chili con carne is made with green tomatoes instead of ripe ones, for they give it a peculiar piquancy and charm.

	To serve 6	
3 lb.	lean beef round, trimmed of fat, sliced ½ inch [1 cm.] thick and cut into ½-inch cubes	1½ kg.
2 oz.	beef suet, chopped (about ½ cup [125 ml.])	75 g.
4 or 5	medium-sized onions, thinly sliced	4 or 5
6	medium (or 12 small) green tomatoes, scalded, peeled and thinly sliced (or substitute ripe tomatoes, scalded, peeled and quartered)	6
1 cup	boiling water	¼ liter
2	garlic cloves	2
12 to 16	dry bread crusts, cut from 3 or 4 slices of firm-textured white bread	12 to 16
1 to 3 tbsp.	chili powder	15 to 45 ml.
1 tbsp.	cider vinegar or red wine vinegar	15 ml.
1 tbsp.	brown sugar	15 ml.
	salt	

Melt the suet in a large skillet, stir in the onions and cook to a golden brown. Take out the onions and add the beef. Sear the meat cubes quickly, fiercely, to seal their juices, then remove them to a dish and cover with foil to keep them hot. In a large fireproof casserole combine the fat remaining in the skillet, the onions, tomatoes and boiling water. Rub the garlic on the bread crusts and, as the mixture comes to a boil, add the crusts and steep them in the sauce for a few minutes.

Then, and then only, add the beef and season with chili powder, according to your taste. Let the mixture stew gently for 30 minutes, then stir in the vinegar and brown sugar, and

salt the chili to taste. Do not let the meat disintegrate, but test frequently and take the casserole from the heat as soon as the meat is tender. Serve at once.

LOUIS P. DE GOUY
THE GOLD COOK BOOK

Beef Stew

Étuvée de Boeuf

	To serve 6	
1½ lb.	beef rump or round, cut into 6 slices	¾ kg.
½ lb.	lean salt pork with the rind removed, blanched in boiling water for 5 minutes, drained and chopped	¼ kg.
1	large onion, chopped	1
¼ lb.	prosciutto, chopped	125 g.
	salt and pepper	
½ cup	dry white wine	125 ml.
2	tomatoes, peeled, seeded and coarsely chopped	2
1	garlic clove	1
1	bay leaf	1
½ to ¾ cup	beef stock	125 to 175 ml.
6	celery hearts, quartered, blanched in boiling water for 5 minutes and drained	6

Lightly fry the salt pork in a large fireproof casserole. Add the onions and cook for 2 to 3 minutes. Add the beef and prosciutto, and sauté over high heat until the beef is well browned. Season with salt and pepper, and moisten with the wine. Cover the casserole and place it over very low heat or put it in a slow oven—300° F. [150° C.]. One hour later add the tomatoes, garlic and bay leaf. Continue to cook for 3 hours in all, adding the stock when the juices reduce. When the meat is three-quarters cooked, after about 2 hours, add the garnish of celery hearts. To serve, skim off excess fat and arrange the stew in a hot serving dish.

URBAIN DUBOIS
ÉCOLE DES CUISINIÈRES

Meatballs Braised with Yogurt

Boeuf Abdullah

To serve 4

1 lb.	ground beef	½ kg.
1	medium-sized onion, chopped	1
8 tbsp.	butter	120 ml.
1	egg	1
2	thick slices stale, firm white bread with the crusts removed, soaked in milk and squeezed almost dry	2
	salt and pepper	
	toasted white bread crumbs	
1 cup	unflavored yogurt	¼ liter
¾ cup	chopped fresh mushrooms	175 ml.

In a large skillet, fry the onion in some of the butter until transparent. Remove from the heat and cool a little. Mix together the beef, onion, egg, bread and seasoning. Shape into small balls, flatten slightly, roll them in the bread crumbs and brown slowly in the remaining butter. Add the yogurt and mushrooms, and simmer for 30 minutes. Serve hot.

IRFAN ORGA
COOKING WITH YOGURT

Beef Pyramids in Beer Sauce

The seasonings in ready-made bottled tomato catsup, one of the ingredients in this dish, vary considerably from brand to brand. You may want to substitute fresh or canned tomatoes, puréed through a sieve.

To serve 6

3½ lb.	lean boneless beef rump or round, about 2 inches [5 cm.] thick	1¾ kg.
	salt and pepper	
	flour	
2 tbsp.	butter	30 ml.
2	large onions, thinly sliced	2
2	large red peppers, halved, seeded, deribbed and sliced	2
12	fresh mushrooms, coarsely chopped	12
1½ cups	light beer	375 ml.
1½ tbsp.	catsup	22 ml.
1 tbsp.	prepared mustard	15 ml.

Trim all fat off the meat. With a sharp knife, slice the meat lengthwise into two strips about 3 inches [8 cm.] wide. Cut a diagonal slice off one end of one strip. Starting at the point, cut diagonally in the opposite direction to make thick triangular pieces of meat. Continue cutting until the whole roast is cut in triangles or "pyramids."

Sprinkle each piece of meat with a pinch of salt and pepper, and dredge in flour on all sides. Melt the butter in a large frying pan or skillet and brown the meat lightly, turning carefully to retain the pyramid shapes. Add the onions, peppers and mushrooms to the pan and brown lightly. Pour the beer over all. Stir in the tomato catsup and the mustard. Cover tightly and simmer slowly for 1 to 1½ hours, or until the meat is tender. If more sauce is desired, add another ¾ cup [175 ml.] of beer during cooking. To serve, stand up the pyramids of meat on a warm platter, and pour the sauce and vegetables over all.

ALBERT STOCKLI
SPLENDID FARE

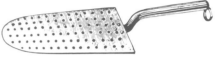

Lemon Beef

Citromos Marhahús

To serve 4

2 lb.	lean beef chuck, sliced 1 inch [2½ cm.] thick and cut into 1-inch cubes	1 kg.
1 cup	beef stock	¼ liter
4	slices lean bacon	4
1 tbsp.	rendered bacon fat	15 ml.
1 tbsp.	flour	15 ml.
1 cup	sour cream	¼ liter
1½ tbsp.	fresh lemon juice	22 ml.
1 tsp.	finely grated lemon peel	5 ml.
½ tsp.	sugar	2 ml.
1 tbsp.	chopped tarragon leaves	15 ml.

Simmer the cubed beef in the stock until tender, about 45 minutes. Use a heavy Dutch oven or similar pot with a cover so you will not have to add more liquid. Remove the meat from the pot, cool the stock and degrease it.

In a large skillet fry the bacon until crisp. Remove the bacon and crumble it, but leave the fat in the skillet. Add the beef to the hot fat and cook, covered, for 5 minutes.

In a separate pan make a roux with the additional tablespoon [15 ml.] of bacon fat and the flour. Stir constantly and cook to a golden brown. Whip the cooled stock into the roux, then whip in the sour cream, lemon juice, lemon peel, sugar and tarragon. Pour the lemon sauce on the beef and place in a serving casserole. Sprinkle the beef with the crisp bacon.

GEORGE LANG
THE CUISINE OF HUNGARY

Casseroled Beefsteak

Bistec en Cazuela

To serve 6

3 lb.	beef rump or round, sliced into 6 small steaks	1½ kg.
	salt and freshly ground pepper	
1 cup	fresh Seville orange juice	¼ liter
4 tbsp.	lard or vegetable oil	60 ml.
3	medium-sized onions, finely chopped	3
2	garlic cloves, finely chopped	2
½ tsp.	oregano	2 ml.
¼ cup	beef stock	50 ml.

Have the butcher flatten the steaks, or do it yourself with a meat pounder or the side of a cleaver. Salt and pepper the steaks on both sides. Place them in a bowl and pour in the orange juice. Cover and refrigerate overnight, turning them once or twice.

Lift the steaks out of the *adobo* (marinade) and pat them dry. Reserve the *adobo*. Heat the lard or oil in a large heavy skillet, and sauté the onions and garlic with the oregano. When the onions are tender, but not browned, push them to one side and sauté the steaks until lightly browned on both sides. Add the *adobo* and beef stock. Cover and cook for about 7 to 10 minutes or until the steaks are tender.

ELISABETH LAMBERT ORTIZ
THE COMPLETE BOOK OF CARIBBEAN COOKING

Cabbage Ragout

To serve 4

1 lb.	beef rump or round steak, sliced 1 inch [2½ cm.] thick and cut into 1-inch cubes	½ kg.
½ cup	flour	125 ml.
	salt and freshly ground black pepper	
2 tbsp.	lard	30 ml.
1	medium-sized onion, sliced	1
1¼ cups	dry cider	300 ml.
⅔ cup	water	150 ml.
1¼ cups	thickly sliced fresh mushrooms	300 ml.
4	ribs celery, chopped	4
1	green pepper, halved, seeded, deribbed and sliced	1
1½ to 2 lb.	cabbage, cored and thickly sliced	¾ to 1 kg.

Mix the flour with salt and pepper, place it in a paper or plastic bag and shake the pieces of meat in it to coat them.

Melt the lard in a large saucepan, add the meat and fry with the onion until the meat is lightly browned and the onion barely colored. Add the cider and water, cover the pan and simmer for 1 hour. Add the mushrooms, celery and green pepper. Stir well and continue cooking for 20 minutes more. Lay the cabbage slices on top, cover again and cook until the cabbage is tender, about 20 minutes.

PAMELA WESTLAND
A TASTE OF THE COUNTRY

Braised and Broiled Oxtail with Chestnut Purée

Queue de Boeuf à la Purée de Marrons

To make the chestnut purée that accompanies this dish, start with about 2 pounds [1 kg.] of fresh chestnuts. Slit across into the base of each one. Parboil the chestnuts for 10 minutes, drain, cool and peel them. Simmer the peeled chestnuts in milk to cover for about an hour. Purée the mixture, adding a knob of butter and a little strained oxtail braising liquid.

To serve 3 or 4

2 to 2½ lb.	oxtail, cut between the joints into 2-inch [5-cm.] pieces	1 kg.
1½ cups	beef or veal stock	375 ml.
⅔ cup	dry white wine	150 ml.
2	turnips, chopped	2
1	large onion, chopped	1
2	carrots, chopped	2
	salt and pepper	
	dry bread crumbs	
3	eggs, lightly beaten	3
6 tbsp.	butter, melted	90 ml.

Blanch the oxtail pieces by bringing them to a boil in cold water and simmering them for 10 minutes. Drain the pieces and place them in a fireproof casserole with the stock, wine and vegetables. Cover and simmer over very low heat or in an oven, preheated to 300° F. [150° C.], for 3 hours, or until the meat is tender and begins to come away from the bones.

Let the oxtail pieces cool in the braising liquid. Remove them, discard the vegetables, and strain and degrease the braising liquid. Season the oxtail pieces with salt and pepper, roll them in the bread crumbs, dip them in the beaten eggs and roll them in the bread crumbs again. Sprinkle the pieces with melted butter. Broil them 3 to 4 inches from a broiler, preheated to its highest setting, for 25 to 30 minutes, turning the pieces frequently. Arrange the oxtail pieces on a warmed platter and serve with the heated braising liquid and chestnut purée.

URBAIN DUBOIS
NOUVELLE CUISINE BOURGEOISE

Old-fashioned Oxtail Stew

La Terrine à l'Ancienne

The technique of sealing a pot with flour-and-water paste is explained in the recipe for Provençal Braised Beef, page 116.

To serve 8

2	oxtails, cut into 2-inch [5-cm.] pieces	2
	salt and pepper	
2	carrots, quartered	2
4	large onions, halved	4
1	bouquet garni	1
8 tbsp.	butter	120 ml.
½ cup	brandy	125 ml.
3	garlic cloves	3
⅔ cup	flour	150 ml.
1½ quarts	red Burgundy	1½ liters
2 cups	beef stock	½ liter
2 to 2½ lb.	fresh mushrooms	1 kg.
1 lb.	lean salt pork with the rind removed, blanched in boiling water for 5 minutes, drained and cut into lardons	½ kg.
	flour-and-water paste (optional)	

Dry the oxtail pieces well; season them with salt and pepper. Then, in a large sauté pan, sauté the oxtail pieces with the carrots, onions and the bouquet garni in 4 tablespoons [60 ml.] of butter until they are a good brown color. Add the brandy and ignite. When the flames die, add the garlic and flour. Mix well. Add the wine and the beef stock, mix again and bring to a boil. Transfer to a casserole, place in an oven, preheated to 325° F. [170° C.], and cook, covered, for 2 hours.

Transfer the oxtail pieces to another casserole—one that you can use on top of the stove. Strain the cooking liquid through a sieve into a bowl and set aside to cool. Discard the vegetables. In a separate pan gently sauté the mushrooms with the salt pork in the remaining butter. Add them to the casserole with the oxtail. Skim off any fat that has risen to the surface of the strained cooking liquid. Then transfer the liquid to a saucepan and reduce until it has the consistency of a light-bodied sauce.

When the sauce is ready, pour it over the oxtail pieces, put the casserole on the stove and bring to a boil. Seal by putting a layer of aluminum foil tightly over the top of the casserole, and covering the casserole with its lid; or seal by the traditional method: put the lid on the casserole and close the seam with a flour-and-water paste. Put the casserole in an oven, preheated to 350° F. [180° C.], for 2 hours.

Serve very hot from the casserole with spaghetti au gratin on the side.

ÉDOUARD NIGNON
LES PLAISIRS DE LA TABLE

Braised Oxtail

La Queue de Boeuf à la Bourguignonne

To serve 6

2 lb.	oxtail, cut into 2-inch [5-cm.] pieces	1 kg.
¼ cup	olive oil	50 ml.
2	onions, halved	2
4	carrots	4
6	shallots	6
1	pig's foot	1
1	calf's foot	1
1	bouquet garni	1
2 cups	chicken or veal stock	½ liter
	salt and pepper	
Wine marinade		
2 cups	dry red wine	½ liter
¾ cup	dry white wine	175 ml.
2	carrots, sliced	2
1	onion, chopped	1
3 or 4	shallots, sliced	3 or 4
	thyme, bay leaf and peppercorns	
2	garlic cloves, crushed	2
3 tbsp.	oil	45 ml.

Mix together the marinade ingredients, add the oxtail and marinate for 24 hours. Drain the oxtail pieces, pat them dry. In olive oil in a heavy fireproof casserole, lightly brown the oxtail together with the halved onions and whole carrots and shallots. Add the pig's foot, calf's foot and the bouquet garni. Cover with the stock and approximately ¾ cup [175 ml.] of the strained marinade mixture. Bring to a simmer on top of the stove, then cover and cook in a warm oven, preheated to 300° F. [150° C.], for 3 to 3½ hours.

When the cooking is completed, remove the meat from the pot. Bone the pig's and calf's feet, cut the meat into large cubes and place on a warmed platter with the oxtail pieces. Strain the braising liquid, pressing the vegetables to extract all their juices. Reduce the volume of the juices, if necessary, until the liquid has a light, syrupy consistency. Adjust the seasoning and pour this sauce over the meat before serving.

ALEXANDRE DUMAINE
MA CUISINE

Braised Stuffed Oxtail

Queue de Boeuf Farcie Braisée

For instructions on how to bone an oxtail, see page 64. Only the first six joints are boned; the rest of the tail can be used to make the stock. The beef marrow called for in the stuffing should be pried out of the bone by the method shown on page 11. The marrowbone may be used in the stockpot.

To serve 4

1	large oxtail, boned	1
2½ to 3 quarts	beef stock	2½ to 3 liters
2	medium-sized onions, coarsely chopped	2
3 to 4	small carrots, coarsely chopped	3 to 4

Herb marinade

1 tsp.	finely crumbled mixed dried thyme, oregano and winter savory	5 ml.
1 tbsp.	olive oil	15 ml.
1 cup	dry white wine	¼ liter

Marrow stuffing

6 oz.	beef marrow, chopped	175 g.
½ lb.	lean beef chuck, chopped	¼ kg.
2	garlic cloves, puréed	2
1½ cups	fresh bread crumbs	375 ml.
½ tsp.	finely crumbled mixed dried herbs	2 ml.
3 to 4 tbsp.	finely chopped fresh parsley	45 to 60 ml.
1	large fresh truffle, coarsely chopped, or truffle peel, finely chopped (optional)	1
	salt and pepper	
⅛ tsp.	ground allspice	½ ml.
2 tbsp.	Cognac	30 ml.
1	egg	1

Marinate the oxtail by sprinkling the meat lightly on both sides with herbs. Put the oil and wine in a crock, add the meat, turn to coat the oxtail well and cover. Leave overnight in the refrigerator.

The firmness of the stuffing is important. If possible combine the ingredients in advance and chill the stuffing; otherwise be certain that both meat and marrow are chilled, then thoroughly combine all the ingredients in a bowl using a fork (the warmth of your hands would soften the mixture).

Remove the oxtail from its marinade and spread it out, boned side facing up, on a square of muslin. Pile the stuffing in the center of the meat; fold the lower third of the oxtail flap up and over the stuffing. Draw together the edges of the tail where the flap has been folded. Then, run a trussing needle and a 3-foot [90-cm.] length of cotton string through the tail, tie the end of the string in a knot and sew up the tail in a spiral pattern, piercing the edges at approximately 1-inch [2½-cm.] intervals. Clip the string, leaving a generous length hanging free.

Wrap the oxtail gently but firmly in the muslin, twisting the cloth at one end and tying the end tightly. Loop the string three or four times around the length of the muslin; then tie the other end of the muslin.

Place the package in a close-fitting pot, pour over the marinade and enough warm, but not boiling, stock to cover well (if you do not have enough stock, add water). Bring to the boiling point and adjust the heat so that the liquid will just simmer for 2½ hours. Carefully lift all the fat from the surface two or three times during the last hour of poaching.

Remove the wrapped tail to a platter, clip the strings holding the muslin, unwrap the tail and leave the meat and muslin on a rack placed over a platter to drain while the stock is being reduced. The drained liquid can be poured into a bowl and chilled; thereafter the fat can be removed in one piece and the liquid added to the leftover stock.

Meanwhile, set the pot in which the tail was poached halfway off the burner and bring the stock in the pot to a light boil, maintained over just half of its surface. Skim repeatedly for about 30 minutes. Finally, with paper towels lift the floating fat from the surface. When no more traces of fat are visible and a skin no longer readily forms on the surface, turn the heat to high, bring the stock to a rolling boil and reduce to about half of its original volume.

Scatter the onions and carrots in the bottom of a snugly fitting *cocotte* or heavy fireproof earthenware casserole that will serve for braising the tail (add no fat, no liquid, no seasoning) and put the *cocotte,* covered, into a preheated 350° F. [180° C.] oven for about 30 minutes. Check the vegetables from time to time: they should sweat and become somewhat tender without coloring. Remove the lid and cook the vegetables for another 5 to 10 minutes, or until they just begin to stick to the bottom of the *cocotte* and there is a suggestion of golden edges appearing here and there.

Place the drained tail, sewn side down, on the bed of vegetables. Ladle over enough hot reduced stock to immerse the meat by from one half to two thirds. (Reserve the leftover stock for another use.) Cover the *cocotte* and put it over low heat—barely simmering—for 1 hour, basting every 10 to 15 minutes. Then continue cooking, uncovered, in a 325° F. [160° C.] oven for a further 1 to 1¼ hours. Again, baste every 10 to 15 minutes, taking care to scoop up vegetables along with the braising liquid, scattering them over the surface so that they, as well as the surface of the meat, acquire a rich, caramelized glaze.

Remove the oxtail carefully, with spatulas, to a heated serving platter. Clip the string around the oxtail at the knot, pulling gently from the other end while holding the meat in place, and remove the string. Serve the vegetables and braising liquid as an accompaniment in a warmed sauceboat.

RICHARD OLNEY
SIMPLE FRENCH FOOD

An Old New Mexican Stew

To serve 6 to 8

2½ lb.	beef chuck in 1 piece	1 kg.
2 quarts	water	2 liters
½ lb.	green beans, cut into pieces	¼ kg.
3	ears corn, cut into 2-inch [5-cm.] pieces	3
4	small zucchini or yellow squash	4
6	squash blossoms	6
½ cup	green scallion tops	125 ml.
½ cup	green garlic tops or 2 garlic cloves	125 ml.
½ cup	fresh coriander leaves	125 ml.
1 tbsp.	salt	15 ml.

In a large heavy casserole simmer the chuck in the water, uncovered, for approximately 2 hours or until it is tender. Then remove the meat and cut it into 1½-inch [4-cm.] cubes. If necessary, add more water to the casserole to make about 1 quart [1 liter]. Cook the beans, corn and squash in the water until the beans are tender. Add the meat and the rest of the ingredients, saving some of the greens for a garnish. Simmer for 25 minutes. Sprinkle the remaining greens on top and serve the stew from the casserole.

JAMES BEARD
JAMES BEARD'S AMERICAN COOKERY

Spiced Salt Beef

Saltpeter (see Tennessee Spiced Round, right) has been omitted from this recipe.

A larger piece of beef will need a proportionate increase in spices and in curing time. Allow 16 days in all for a 12-pound [6-kg.] piece.

To serve 6

5 to 6 lb.	beef round or rump, tied into 1 compact piece	2½ to 3 kg.
⅓ cup	brown sugar	75 ml.
½ cup	sea or kitchen salt	125 ml.
2 tbsp.	black peppercorns	30 ml.
1 tbsp.	whole allspice	15 ml.
2 tbsp.	juniper berries	30 ml.
1 cup	suet, shredded	¼ liter

First rub the beef all over with sugar. Leave it in a deep pot for two days in the refrigerator or in a very cool room or larder—the temperature should not go above 45° F. [7° C.]. Crush the other pickling ingredients together in a mortar, and rub the beef all over with this mixture once a day for

nine days (the process takes 11 days in all). The salt and other pickling ingredients will turn liquid, but continue to rub them into the meat just the same. Keep the pot covered.

To cook the beef, rinse it quickly to remove bits of spice. Put it into a close-fitting pot with about 1¼ cups [300 ml.] of water. Cover the top of the meat with shredded suet to keep it moist during the cooking time. Cover the pot with a double layer of wax paper or foil and then put on the lid, so that the juices cannot evaporate. Bake the meat in a very low oven, 275° F. [140° C.], for 45 to 50 minutes for each pound [½ kg.]. Leave it in the pot to cool undisturbed for 2 to 3 hours.

Drain off all the fatty liquid and remove the meat to a board. Cover it completely with wax paper and put a 2- to 4-pound [1- to 2-kg.] weight on top. Leave in the refrigerator or other cool place for 24 hours.

Serve the beef cold with horseradish sauce and, perhaps, a green salad or diced avocados with a vinaigrette, plus whole-grain bread and butter or baked potatoes.

JANE GRIGSON
GOOD THINGS

Tennessee Spiced Round

This dish is traditionally served at Christmas in Tennessee. The original version of the recipe calls for saltpeter (sodium nitrate), which often is added to meats to keep them red in color through the preserving process. The chemical has been omitted here because it has the disadvantage of hardening meat and, more importantly, may be hazardous to health.

To serve 30 to 40

10 lb.	beef top round	5 kg.
2 cups	dark brown sugar	½ liter
2 cups	salt	½ liter
4 tsp.	black pepper	20 ml.
⅛ tsp.	cayenne pepper	½ ml.
1 tbsp.	ground ginger	15 ml.
1 tbsp.	ground cloves	15 ml.
2 tsp.	ground cinnamon	10 ml.
1 tbsp.	freshly grated nutmeg	15 ml.
3	large onions, finely chopped	3
1 tbsp.	celery seeds	15 ml.
3 cups	finely chopped beef suet	¾ liter
1	bay leaf	1

Using heavy cotton string, tie up the beef in a compact round and place it in a small crock. Mix the brown sugar and salt, and rub them well into the beef. Mix the spices and rub them in also. Keep the meat in a cool, dark place and turn it every day for two weeks.

Drain off the accumulated juices and mix them with the onions, celery seeds and suet. Make numerous incisions on both sides of the round and stuff the mixture into them. Sew up the round tightly in clean cloth, place it on a rack in a soup kettle, add whatever juices may have escaped and pour on just enough water to cover it. Add the bay leaf and boil, covered, until the beef is tender, allowing 25 minutes per pound [½ kg.]. Cool the beef in the water in which it was boiled. Serve it cold and sliced thin.

SHEILA HIBBEN
AMERICAN REGIONAL COOKERY

Brine for Corning Meats

Saltpeter (see Tennessee Spiced Round, page 128) has been omitted from this recipe.

3½ quarts	water	3½ liters
1½ lb.	sea or coarse (kosher) salt	¾ kg.
1 lb.	dark brown sugar	½ kg.
1	bay leaf	1
1	sprig thyme	1
10	juniper berries, crushed	10
10	peppercorns, crushed	10

Bring all the ingredients to a boil and boil hard for 5 minutes. Leave the brine to cool. Clean a stoneware crock or plastic bucket and its lid with a solution of 1 tablespoon [5 ml.] baking soda to 1 gallon [4 liters] boiling water. Rinse well and leave to drain dry. Pour in the cold brine through a cheesecloth-lined strainer. Immerse the meat to be salted and keep it below the surface by laying a piece of boiled wood or a scrupulously clean plate on top. Cover and keep in a dry place, at a temperature below 60° F. [15° C.].

Salting time depends on the thickness of the meat: allow seven to 10 days for beef round or beef brisket or a sizable leg of pork; 36 to 48 hours for a duck (giblets removed). Pigs' feet are ready in 24 hours.

When removing pieces of meat from brine, always use clean tongs: this way the brine will stay good longer and new pieces of the same kind of meat can be put in to salt. Use separate pots for beef, pork, duck, etc.; they should never be salted together or in brine that might contain the sediments of another meat. It is possible to strain off the brine and reboil it, adding a refresher of about half the above quantities. Naturally the crock or bucket will need a complete cleaning. This should be done before mold appears.

JANE GRIGSON
GOOD THINGS

Pot-au-Feu

To serve 4

2 to 2½ lb.	boneless beef top-round or bottom-round roast, tied into a compact shape	1 kg.
2 to 2½ lb.	beef bones, sawed, not chopped, into pieces 2 to 3 inches [5 to 8 cm.] long	1 kg.
2½ quarts	water	2½ liters
1 tbsp.	salt	15 ml.
3	medium-sized carrots	3
2	medium-sized turnips	2
4	medium-sized leeks	4
3	medium-sized onions, 1 stuck with 2 cloves	3
1	small parsnip	1
1	rib celery	1

Place the bones in the bottom of a large, heavy pot and set the meat on top. Add the water and the salt. Place the pot on very gentle heat, without a lid so that you can be ready to skim the liquid when it boils. Slow heating of the liquid is essential for the clarity and savor of the broth. Meat penetrated gradually by heat releases scum, which will cloud the liquid if it is not removed. For the amounts indicated, aim to bring the water to the simmering point in half an hour.

The first scum will be dark and very dirty. Remove it, using a skimming spoon or a perforated spoon. When the liquid starts to boil again, add 3 tablespoons [45 ml.] of cold water to the pot. This cold liquid slows down the boiling and causes a new scum to rise to the surface; this will be lighter in color, less thick and less dirty than the first. Skim again and, once the liquid starts to boil again, add another 3 tablespoons of cold water. This produces a third lot of scum, this time almost white. Skim. When the liquid starts to boil once more, add another 3 tablespoons of cold water. The little scum that rises this time should be perfectly white and clean. Skim it. Then add the vegetables and skim off any scum that rises. Using a damp cloth, carefully wipe the inside edges of the pot so that no traces of scum remain. After this, set the pot to cook.

From start to finish, the cooking must be perfectly even. Very gentle simmering throughout the cooking time, with bubbles visible at only a single point on the surface of the liquid, is essential for the clarity of the liquid.

Cover the pot, leaving the lid slightly off-center to the width of two fingers; this is also with a view to the clarity of the broth. If simmering should cease for any reason, return the liquid to a simmer gently and slowly.

Cook the beef for 3 hours from the start of boiling, after the skimming is completed.

MADAME SAINT-ANGE
LA CUISINE DE MADAME SAINT-ANGE

Marrow Dumplings

To make 7 or 8 dumplings

1 oz.	beef marrow	50 g.
2 tbsp.	butter	30 ml.
2	small eggs, beaten	2
2	thick slices French bread with the crusts removed, soaked in a little boiled milk, strained and beaten to a paste with a fork	2
1 tsp.	finely chopped onion (optional)	5 ml.
1 tsp.	finely chopped fresh parsley	5 ml.
	salt	
	grated nutmeg	
1½ quarts	boiling beef stock	1½ liters

Beat the marrow and butter together to a creamy consistency. Add the eggs and, when they are well stirred, put in the bread paste. Stir in the onion, parsley and salt, and add nutmeg to taste. Form the mixture into small round dumplings. Drop these into the boiling stock and let them simmer for about 20 to 30 minutes. They may be served in soup, with roast meat, or with salad, as in Germany.

MRS. ISABELLA BEETON
THE BOOK OF HOUSEHOLD MANAGEMENT

Boiled Beef

Bollito di Manzo

To serve 6

3 lb.	beef brisket	1½ kg.
1 tbsp.	salt	15 ml.
1	rib celery	1
1	small onion	1
1	small bay leaf	1
3	plum tomatoes	3
4 or 5	peppercorns	4 or 5

Tomato and onion sauce

3 cups	coarsely chopped, peeled plum tomatoes	¾ liter
3	medium-sized onions (or 1 huge Bermuda)	3
3 tbsp.	olive oil	45 ml.
2 tsp.	salt	10 ml.
	freshly ground pepper	

Put the beef and all the other ingredients, except those for the sauce, in cold water to cover. Bring to a boil slowly,

uncovered, over low heat. When the water first boils, scoop off the froth that forms, lower the heat to a simmer, cover the pot and cook for about 3 hours. The meat should be tender, the broth a clear, light brown.

Meanwhile, to prepare the sauce, cut the onions in half, scoop out the center cores and slice the halves into the thinnest possible slivers. If using regular all-purpose kitchen onions, you may want to soak the slices for 5 or 10 minutes in cold water to make them milder tasting; drain the soaked slices well on paper towels.

Put the olive oil in a large skillet over medium heat. Add the onions and cook them until they are limp and transparent. Turn off the heat for a few minutes to allow the oil to cool, then add the tomatoes. Add the salt and a few grinds of the pepper mill to the sauce, and turn up the heat until the mixture boils. Then lower the heat and simmer, stirring occasionally, for 20 to 25 minutes, or until the tomatoes have practically disintegrated, the liquids have reduced almost by half and the color has darkened. Remove the sauce from the heat and cover the skillet to keep it warm.

Remove the meat from the broth and put it on a warmed platter. Strain the broth, and use it as a first course, with freshly boiled pastina, rice or cappelletti. Slice the meat and serve it, as a main course, accompanied by the sauce.

MARGARET AND G. FRANCO ROMAGNOLI
THE ROMAGNOLIS' TABLE

New England Boiled Dinner

To serve 6 to 8

4 lb.	corned beef brisket	2 kg.
1	medium-sized cabbage (about 1½ to 2 lb. [¾ to 1 kg.]), quartered and cored	1
6	turnips, quartered	6
6	small carrots	6
6	medium-sized potatoes	6
6	small beets	6

Ask the butcher for a piece of brisket only mildly corned. Wash it under running water and tie it up securely with cotton string. Cover it with cold water, bring it to a slow boil and cook for 10 minutes; remove the scum. Taste the water; if it is too salty, discard it and start again. If not, cover the pot and let the liquid simmer for 3 hours. Add the cabbage, turnips, carrots and potatoes; cook for 30 minutes more. Place the meat in the center of a hot platter, arrange the vegetables around it, including the beets, which have been boiled separately for 30 to 45 minutes and peeled.

SHEILA HIBBEN
AMERICAN REGIONAL COOKERY

Stuffed Flank Steak

Falda Mimlija

To serve 4

2 lb.	beef flank steak	1 kg.
2 or 3	onions, chopped	2 or 3
2	carrots, chopped	2
1	rib celery, chopped	1
1	kohlrabi, chopped (or substitute 1 turnip, chopped)	1
	Pork stuffing	
½ lb.	lean ground pork	¼ kg.
¼ lb.	ham or lean bacon, chopped	125 g.
4 to 6 tbsp.	fresh bread crumbs	60 to 90 ml.
1 tbsp.	finely chopped onion	15 ml.
1	hard-boiled egg, chopped	1
3	eggs	3
2 tsp.	freshly grated Parmesan cheese	10 ml.
	salt and pepper	

Ask the butcher to make a deep pocket in the steak. Combine the stuffing ingredients and use them to fill the pocket. Sew up the pocket opening. Put the steak in a large, heavy pan with the chopped vegetables and pour in enough boiling water to cover the meat. Return the water to a boil, cover the pan and reduce the heat. Cook slowly for about 2½ hours or until the steak is tender. Serve hot, cut in thick slices.

ANNE AND HELEN CARUANA GALIZIA
RECIPES FROM MALTA

Poached Tied Beef

Boeuf à la Ficelle

To serve 4 to 6

2 to 2½ lb.	beef tenderloin or sirloin in 1 piece	1 kg.
1½ to 2 quarts	veal stock or pot-au-feu broth	1½ to 2 liters

The beef fillet should be tied securely with cotton string around both its length and width, leaving a long end attached for use in lifting out the meat from the cooking pot.

Lower the beef into the stock or broth, suspending it in the liquid by tying the string to the pot handles. The beef should not touch the pot. Cook it over high heat for a few minutes, then lower the heat and simmer the meat until it is done; it should be delightfully rare on the inside and just colored by the broth on the outside. The cooking time is the same as for roasting a fillet: about 10 minutes per pound; a good-sized whole fillet will take 20 to 30 minutes.

Serve this deliciously different dish with coarse salt, boiled potatoes, with or without some of the broth, and mustard or horseradish if you wish.

JAMES BEARD
DELIGHTS AND PREJUDICES

Boiled Brisket of Beef

To serve 6

4 lb.	lean beef brisket	2 kg.
3 quarts	boiling water	3 liters
1	bay leaf	1
2	garlic cloves	2
1	medium-sized onion, studded with 6 whole cloves	1
2	ribs celery	2
2 tbsp.	vinegar	30 ml.
2 tbsp.	sugar	30 ml.
2 tsp.	salt	10 ml.
	freshly grated horseradish	

Combine the water, bay leaf, garlic, onion, celery, vinegar, sugar and salt in a large kettle. Cover and boil for 30 minutes. Add the beef. Cover and cook at a simmer for 4 hours, or until the meat is fork-tender, adding additional boiling water if necessary.

When the meat is done, remove and slice it, and arrange the slices on a hot platter. Serve with horseradish.

IDA BAILEY ALLEN
BEST LOVED RECIPES OF THE AMERICAN PEOPLE

Yorkshire Pan Pie

To serve 2 or 3

½ lb.	beef chuck steak, cut into cubes	¼ kg.
1 tbsp.	lard	15 ml.
1	large onion, finely chopped	1
3	carrots, sliced	3
2	tomatoes, sliced	2
2	leeks, sliced	2
	salt and pepper	
Dough		
1 cup	self-rising flour	¼ liter
⅓ cup	beef suet, chopped	75 ml.
	salt	
	water	

Melt the lard in a saucepan. Fry the onion and the meat until lightly browned. Add the carrots, tomatoes and leeks, and just enough water to cover, then simmer for 30 minutes. Season well with salt and pepper, and continue cooking gently for 15 minutes.

Mix together the flour and suet with a pinch of salt and enough iced water to make a firm dough. Roll out the dough and cut out a circle slightly smaller in circumference than the rim of the pan. Put this circle of dough over the meat and vegetables. Cover the pan and cook gently for 1 hour.

MARY NORWAK
THE FARMHOUSE KITCHEN

Farmhouse Pudding

For detailed instructions on how to steam a pudding, see the recipe for Beefsteak and Kidney Pudding, on page 133.

To serve 6 to 8

1½ lb.	ground beef	¾ kg.
3	onions, chopped	3
4 tbsp.	lard	60 ml.
3	carrots, grated	3
⅔ cup	chopped fresh parsley	150 ml.
½ cup	flour	125 ml.
2½ cups	beef stock	625 ml.
	salt and pepper	
	suet pastry rolled out ¼ inch [6 mm.] thick *(recipe, page 168)*	

In a large skillet over moderate heat, fry the beef and onions in the lard until they are light brown. Add the carrots and

parsley, stir in the flour and gradually add the stock. Cook and stir until the mixture is thick and boiling. Season with salt and pepper.

Grease a 1- to 1½-quart [1- to 1½-liter] pudding basin or mold and put a layer of suet pastry in the bottom. Place a layer of the meat mixture on the pastry; then fill the basin with alternate layers of meat and pastry, finishing with a layer of pastry. Cover with buttered wax paper, tie a cloth such as a dish towel over the top and steam for 1½ hours.

LIZZIE BOYD (EDITOR)
BRITISH COOKERY

Beefsteak, Kidney and Oyster Pie

An alternative way to make this pie is to precook the filling for 1 hour in a covered casserole and allow it to cool a little or completely, even overnight. Transfer the filling to the pie dish, cover with pastry and bake for 30 minutes at 375° to 400° F. [190° to 200° C.]. The method described below is better from the point of view of flavor, I think, but the alternative may suit your convenience, or your stove, better. It also gives you more exact control over the cooking meat; beef can vary a great deal in toughness, so oven time may vary.

Rabbit and some blanched salt pork, cut in pieces, may be substituted for steak and kidney. A longer cooking time will be required if the rabbit is mature; less time if it is very young and tender.

To serve 6

1½ to 2 lb.	beef chuck steak	¾ to 1 kg.
8 to 12 oz.	beef kidney	¼ to ⅓ kg.
12 to 18	live oysters	12 to 18
	salt and freshly ground black pepper	
2 tbsp.	butter	30 ml.
¾ cup	chopped onion	175 ml.
1½ tbsp.	flour	22 ml.
2½ cups	sliced fresh mushrooms	625 ml.
	beef stock	
	Worcestershire or soy sauce	
	short-crust pastry *(recipe, page 167)*	
1	egg, lightly beaten, or 1 tablespoon [15 ml.] milk	1

Shuck the oysters, taking the precaution of wrapping the hand you hold them with in a tea towel. Put them, along with their liquor, into a bowl. Then cut the steak into cubes and the kidney into chunky slices, discarding all fat and membrane. Season the meat with salt and pepper, and brown quickly in butter with the onion.

Stir in the flour and cook for a moment or two until it has absorbed the fat. Add the oysters and their liquor, the mushrooms and enough stock to make the sauce the consistency of thick cream (the mushrooms and meat will exude a certain amount of juice and make the sauce thinner). Season with salt, pepper and a dash of Worcestershire or soy sauce.

Transfer the mixture to a 1- to 1½-quart [1- to 1½-liter] pie dish. Lay a strip of pastry around the rim of the dish, then moisten the strip and lay on the pastry lid. Crimp the edges of the pastry, slit it in several places and, if desired, decorate it with pastry leaves. Brush the pastry lid with beaten egg or milk. Bake for 2 hours at 300° to 325° F. [150° to 160° C.]. Cover the crust with aluminum foil if it begins to overbrown.

JANE GRIGSON
GOOD THINGS

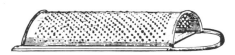

Beefsteak and Kidney Pudding

To ensure that the pudding cooks through evenly, the wrapped dish that contains it should be set on a trivet or rack in a pot containing enough boiling water to reach at least three quarters of the way up the sides of the dish —and the water should be kept at this level throughout the cooking time.

To serve 6

2 to 2½ lb.	beef round steak, sliced 1 inch [2½ cm.] thick and cut into 1-inch cubes	1 kg.
2	beef kidneys, trimmed of fat and membrane, and each cut into 8 pieces	2
	salt and black pepper	
Suet and milk pastry		
6 oz.	beef suet, shredded or finely chopped	175 g.
4 cups	flour	1 liter
1¼ cups	milk	300 ml.

Rub the suet well into the flour; add the milk and work the whole to a smooth paste; roll it out about ¼ inch [6 mm.] thick and it is ready for use.

Line a pudding dish with pastry, leaving a border on the crust to overlap the edges. Roll out and reserve the remaining pastry for the top crust. Then cover the bottom of the lined dish with a portion of the steak and a few pieces of kidney. Season with salt and pepper (some add a little flour to thicken the gravy, but it is not necessary), and then add another layer of steak, kidney and seasoning.

Proceed in this manner till the dish is full, then pour in sufficient water to come to within 2 inches [5 cm.] of the top of the dish. Moisten the edges of the top crust, cover the

pudding with it, press the two crusts together so that the gravy may not escape and turn up the overhanging edge of the pastry. Wring out a cloth in hot water, flour it and tie up the pudding inside it. Put it all into boiling water and let it boil for at least 4 hours. If the boiling water diminishes, always replenish with hot water, as the water should not be allowed to stop boiling. Remove the cloth and send the pudding to table in the dish, either on an ornamental plate, or with a napkin pinned round it. Serve quickly.

Beefsteak pudding may be very much enriched by adding a few oysters or mushrooms.

MRS. ISABELLA BEETON
THE BOOK OF HOUSEHOLD MANAGEMENT

Steak-and-Kidney Pie

This pie has numerous regional differences. In the West Country of Britain, just before serving, 1¼ cups [300 ml.] of heavy cream is poured into the pie through the pastry hole. The Ormidale steak pie from the Highlands of Scotland is flavored with 1 teaspoon [5 ml.] each of Worcestershire sauce, vinegar and tomato sauce. Still other versions add sliced mushrooms to the stewed filling, beneath the pastry covering. Even cooking techniques vary. In this recipe the meat is partly cooked before it is covered with the pastry.

To serve 6 to 8

1½ lb.	beef chuck steak, cut into small cubes	¾ kg.
½ lb.	beef or lamb kidney, trimmed of fat and membrane, and cut into small cubes	¼ kg.
¼ cup	flour, seasoned with salt and pepper	50 ml.
1 tbsp.	chopped fresh parsley	15 ml.
2 tbsp.	lard	30 ml.
¾ cup	onions, chopped	175 ml.
2 cups	beef stock	½ liter
	salt and pepper	
	suet pastry rolled out ¼ inch [6 mm.] thick (recipe, page 168)	
1	egg, lightly beaten	1

Dust the steak and kidney with seasoned flour and mix with the chopped parsley. Melt the lard, and fry the onions and meat in it until lightly browned. Cover with the stock, bring to a boil and simmer gently for 1 to 1½ hours. Correct the seasoning with the salt and pepper.

Put the meat in a deep, 1½-quart [1½-liter] casserole, cover it with pastry and brush the pastry with beaten egg. Bake in an oven, preheated to 400° F. [200° C.], for 1 hour or until golden brown.

LIZZIE BOYD (EDITOR)
BRITISH COOKERY

Meat Rolls in Potato Pastry

Meat Chaps

The garam masala called for in this recipe is an Indian spice mixture, available at stores that sell Indian foods.

To make 10 to 12 rolls

½ lb.	beef round or chuck, finely ground	¼ kg.
1 tbsp.	clarified butter	15 ml.
1	medium-sized onion, finely chopped	1
1	small piece ginger root, finely chopped	1
2 tsp.	finely chopped coriander leaves (dhania)	10 ml.
½ tsp.	ground turmeric	2 ml.
1 tsp.	salt	5 ml.
½ tsp.	chili powder (optional)	2 ml.
2	medium-sized tomatoes, sliced	2
1 cup	water	¼ liter
1 tsp.	garam masala	5 ml.
2 tsp.	mango pulp or fresh lemon juice	10 ml.
	vegetable oil for deep frying	
Potato pastry		
4	medium-sized potatoes, scrubbed but not peeled	4
½ tsp.	salt	2 ml.
3 tbsp.	bread crumbs	45 ml.
2	eggs, lightly beaten	2

Melt the butter in a saucepan and gently fry the onion, ginger and coriander; add the turmeric, salt—and the chili powder, if you are using it. Fry gently for 2 to 3 minutes. Add the tomatoes and let them get soft. Put in the ground meat and fry for 4 to 5 minutes over medium heat, stirring all the time, then pour in the water. Bring to a boil and turn down the heat to very low. Cover and cook for 45 minutes. Mix in the *garam masala* and mango pulp or lemon juice. When ready, the meat should be tender and perfectly dry; mash it a little with a spoon and let it cool.

Boil the potatoes in their skins in salted water. Remove them from the heat as soon as they are tender (not mushy). When quite cold, peel the potatoes, then mash them in a bowl and, with your hands, knead them on a lightly floured board for several minutes until they are as smooth as pastry. Place the bread crumbs on a plate. Take a small piece of potato pastry, flatten it on your hand and place some of the meat mixture in the center; then close up the pastry to form a roll with the meat inside.

When all the meat and potato is fashioned into rolls in this way, heat the oil in a deep skillet to 375° F. [190° C.]. Then dip each roll in the egg mixture and roll it in the bread crumbs. Fry the rolls two or three at a time in the fat.

When ready, the meat rolls should be uniformly golden brown in color. They are delicious eaten with chutney.

SAVITRI CHOWDHARY
INDIAN COOKING

Beef Stew with Rutabaga Crust

To serve 4 to 6

2 lb.	beef stew meat, sliced 1 inch [2½ cm.] thick and cut into 1-inch cubes	1 kg.
3 tbsp.	lard	45 ml.
3	medium-sized onions, thinly sliced	3
2 cups	light ale (or 2 parts ale to 1 part beef or veal stock)	½ liter
¼ cup	chopped fresh parsley	50 ml.
2	bay leaves	2
	salt and pepper	
¼ cup	Worcestershire sauce	50 ml.
1 to 1½ lb.	rutabagas, cut into chunks	½ to ¾ kg.
2 tbsp.	butter	30 ml.
1 tbsp.	grated horseradish	15 ml.
	bread crumbs	

Preheat the oven to 350° F. [180° C.].

Melt the lard in a heavy fireproof casserole on high heat and brown the pieces of meat all over. Remove them and set them aside. Lower the heat and cook two of the onions very gently in the lard until they are soft but not browned. Pour in the ale (and stock if used), add the parsley and bay leaves, season and bring to a boil. Replace the meat and add the Worcestershire sauce. Cover and cook in the oven for 1½ hours until the meat is tender and the sauce thick.

Meanwhile, boil the rutabaga chunks in salted water until they are tender (about 45 minutes). Drain them and set aside. Melt the butter in a saucepan over low heat and cook the remaining onion until golden. Turn off the heat, put in the cooked rutabaga and mash it with the onion and butter.

Take the lid off the casserole and remove the bay leaves. Scatter the horseradish over the top of the stew, and then spread the rutabaga mixture over the top as you would mashed potatoes on a shepherd's pie. Scatter the bread crumbs on top and put the dish back into the oven for 20 minutes, by which time it should be brown and crisp.

GAIL DUFF
FRESH ALL THE YEAR

Toad-in-the-Hole

The batter for Toad-in-the-Hole is made by the same method as that used for the Yorkshire Pudding in the recipe for Beef with Yorkshire Pudding and Horseradish Sauce on page 90. In this case, however, the batter should be heavier in consistency. Use 2 cups [½ liter] of flour, a pinch of salt, 3 eggs and 2 cups of milk; omit the cold water.

	To serve 6 to 8	
1¼ lb.	beef rump or round, sliced 1 inch [2½ cm.] thick and cut into strips 2 inches [5 cm.] long and 1 inch wide	⅔ kg.
4 tbsp.	lard	60 ml.
12 oz.	beef kidney, trimmed of fat and membrane, and cut into small pieces	⅓ kg.
	salt and pepper	
	Yorkshire pudding batter	

Fry the steak for a few minutes in half the lard. Season the kidney with salt and pepper.

Make the batter. In a fairly hot oven, preheated to 400° F. [200° C.], heat the remaining lard until smoking in a deep 2-quart [2-liter] pie dish or casserole. Pour in half the batter and bake 10 to 15 minutes or until the batter is set. Place the fried steak and the kidney on top of this batter, pour over the remaining batter and bake 40 minutes or until well risen.

LIZZIE BOYD (EDITOR)
BRITISH COOKERY

Rumpsteak Pudding

Le Pudding de Rumpsteak

For detailed instructions on how to steam a pudding, see the recipe for Beefsteak and Kidney Pudding, page 133.

	To serve 4	
1 lb.	beef rump or round steak, sliced ½ inch [1 cm.] thick and cut into ½-inch dice	½ kg.
2 tbsp.	butter	30 ml.
	salt and pepper	
½ cup	*fine Champagne* or other brandy	125 ml.
	Suet and egg pastry	
2 cups	flour	½ liter
1	egg	1
	salt	
¼ to ½ cup	warm water	50 to 125 ml.
5 oz.	beef suet, grated or shredded	150 g.

Prepare the pastry by mixing the flour, the egg and a pinch of salt, then add enough of the warm water to make a crum-bly mix. Roll out and sprinkle with one third of the beef suet. Fold the pastry into three layers and leave at room temperature for 10 minutes. Roll out and sprinkle over a further one third of the suet. Fold again into three layers and leave it for another 10 minutes. Repeat with the rest of the suet. Roll out this pastry into a layer ½ inch (a little over 1 cm.) thick.

Using the rim of your pudding basin or a 1-quart [1-liter] charlotte mold as a cutting edge, cut out a circle from the pastry and set the circle aside. Roll out the remaining pastry to line the basin or mold and let it overlap the rim.

Sauté the diced rump steak in the butter, and season with salt and pepper. Place the meat in the pastry-lined basin or mold. Add the Cognac. Cover with the circle of pastry, and seal tightly by pinching together the cover and the pastry overlapping the basin.

Wrap the basin or mold in a large kitchen towel by tying the four corners together. Place it on a rack in a pan of simmering water. Steam, covered, for 3 to 4 hours. Serve directly from the basin: cut the pudding and serve each person with both meat and pastry.

ÉDOUARD DE POMIANE
LE CODE DE LA BONNE CHÈRE

Tamale Pie

	To serve 4	
1 lb.	ground beef chuck steak	½ kg.
3 cups	water	¾ liter
3½ tsp.	salt	17 ml.
1 cup	cornmeal	¼ liter
3 tbsp.	shortening	45 ml.
1	medium-sized onion, chopped	1
1	small green pepper, halved, seeded, deribbed and chopped	1
½ tsp.	chili powder	2 ml.
4	medium-sized tomatoes, sliced	4

Bring the water with 1½ teaspoons [7 ml.] of the salt to a boil. Slowly add the cornmeal in a steady stream, stirring constantly. Cook over low heat, stirring frequently, for 10 minutes or until the cornmeal thickens and leaves the sides of the pan. Remove from the heat.

Melt the shortening in a skillet. Add the onion and the green pepper, and cook over low heat until they are limp but not brown. Add the meat and continue cooking until it is brown. Stir in the chili powder and the remaining salt. Remove the pan from the stove.

Spread half the cooked cornmeal over the bottom of a medium-sized casserole, cover with a layer of tomatoes, then add all the meat mixture. Add a second layer of cornmeal and top that with the remaining tomato slices. Bake in an oven, preheated to 375° F. [190° C.], for 25 minutes.

THE EDITORS OF AMERICAN HERITAGE
THE AMERICAN HERITAGE COOKBOOK

Beefsteak Tartar

To serve 2

½ lb.	lean boneless beef, preferably tenderloin, top round or eye of round, ground 2 or 3 times	¼ kg.
2	egg yolks	2
2 tbsp.	salt	30 ml.
2 tbsp.	freshly ground black pepper	30 ml.
2 tbsp.	capers, rinsed and drained well	30 ml.
2 tbsp.	finely chopped onions	30 ml.
2 tbsp.	finely chopped fresh parsley	30 ml.
8	anchovy fillets, soaked in water for 10 minutes and patted dry	8

Traditionally the beef for beefsteak tartar is chopped or ground very fine, and served as soon as possible thereafter. Shape the beef into two mounds in the center of separate serving plates. Make a well in the middle of each mound and carefully drop an egg yolk in each well.

Serve the salt, black pepper, capers, onions, parsley and anchovy fillets in small separate saucers. The beef and other ingredients are then combined at the table to individual taste. Serve with dark bread and butter.

FOODS OF THE WORLD/THE COOKING OF GERMANY

Raw Beef

The technique of chopping beef is shown on pages 40-41.

To serve 6 as an hors d'oeuvre

¼ lb.	beef tenderloin or round steak	125 g.
2	potatoes, cooked and diced	2
1	medium-sized beet, cooked and diced	1
2 tsp.	finely chopped red onions	10 ml.
2 tsp.	capers, rinsed in cold water, drained and finely chopped	10 ml.
1	egg yolk	1

Chop the meat finely with a sharp knife and shape into a patty. Place the patty on a small round dish, make a well in the center of it and slip the egg yolk into the well. Surround the patty with potatoes, beets, onions and capers, in separate heaps. Mix all these ingredients together at the table.

INGA NORBERG
GOOD FOOD FROM SWEDEN

Texas Chili con Carne

The volatile oils in hot chilies may make your skin smart and your eyes burn: wear rubber gloves when handling them and avoid touching your face.

To serve 6 to 8

3 lb.	lean boneless beef chuck, trimmed of excess fat, sliced ½ inch [1 cm.] thick and cut into ½-inch cubes	1½ kg.
6	dried *ancho* chilies, each about 2 inches [5 cm.] long	6
8	dried hot chilies, each about 2 inches [5 cm.] long	8
3½ cups	boiling water	875 ml.
½ lb.	beef suet, cut into ½-inch [1-cm.] bits — about 2 cups [½ liter]	¼ kg.
3	medium-sized bay leaves, finely crumbled	3
1 tbsp.	cumin seed	15 ml.
2 tbsp.	coarsely chopped garlic	30 ml.
4 tsp.	dried oregano	20 ml.
3 tbsp.	paprika	45 ml.
1 tbsp.	sugar	15 ml.
1 tbsp.	salt	15 ml.
3 tbsp.	yellow cornmeal	45 ml.
1 tsp.	cayenne pepper (optional)	5 ml.
2 cups	dried pinto beans (1 pound [½ kg.]), freshly cooked	½ liter
3 cups	raw unprocessed long-grain rice (1½ pound [¾ kg.]), freshly cooked	¾ liter

Under cold running water, pull the stems off the *ancho* and red chilies. Tear the chilies in half and brush out their seeds. With a small, sharp knife cut away any large ribs. Crumble the chilies coarsely, drop them into a bowl and pour the boiling water over them. Let them soak for at least 30 minutes, then strain the soaking liquid through a sieve set over a bowl and reserve it. Set the chilies aside.

In a heavy 5- to 6-quart [5- to 6-liter] casserole, cook the beef suet over moderate heat, stirring frequently until it has rendered all its fat. With a slotted spoon, remove and discard the suet bits. Pour off all but about 4 tablespoons [60 ml.] of the fat remaining in the pot.

Add the beef cubes to the casserole and, stirring constantly, cook over moderate heat until the pieces of meat are firm but not brown. Add 2 cups [½ liter] of the reserved chili-soaking liquid and bring it to a boil over high heat. Drop in the bay leaves and reduce the heat to low. Simmer partially covered for 1 hour, stirring the mixture from time to time.

Meanwhile, place the cumin seeds in a small ungreased skillet and, sliding the pan back and forth frequently, toss the seeds over low heat for 10 minutes. Drop the seeds into an electric blender and blend at high speed for 30 seconds. Turn off the machine, add the *ancho* and red chilies, the remaining chili-soaking liquid, the garlic, oregano, paprika, sugar and salt, and blend again at high speed until all of the ingredients are reduced to a smooth purée.

When the meat has cooked its allotted time, stir in the chili purée and simmer partially covered for 30 minutes. Then, stirring constantly, pour in the cornmeal in a slow stream and cook over high heat until the chili comes to a boil and thickens slightly. Taste the chili for seasoning and add the cayenne pepper if desired.

Serve the chili con carne directly from the casserole, or from a heated tureen or serving bowl. Mound the pinto beans and rice in separate bowls and present them with the chili.

FOODS OF THE WORLD
AMERICAN COOKING: THE GREAT WEST

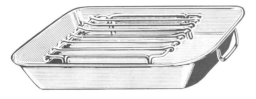

Brisket of Beef with Sauerkraut

	To serve 6	
3 lb.	beef brisket	1½ kg.
1	large onion, diced	1
	salt	
3 cups	sauerkraut	¾ liter
1	large potato, grated	1
1	large tart red apple, quartered and cored but not peeled	1
1 tsp.	caraway seeds	5 ml.
1 cup	dry red wine	¼ liter

Place the brisket in a 5-quart [5-liter] pot with the diced onion and salt to taste. Cover with boiling water, place the lid on the pot and bring to a hard boil. Boil 20 minutes, skim, re-cover the pot and simmer for 1 hour.

Remove the meat and slice against the grain into pieces ¼ inch [6 mm.] thick. Discard all except ½ cup [125 ml.] of the pot liquor. Return the sliced meat to the pot with the reserved pot liquor, the sauerkraut, grated potato, quartered apple and caraway seeds. Bring to a boil, cover, reduce the heat and simmer for ½ hour longer. Add wine and simmer until the meat is tender—about 15 to 30 minutes.

Serve hot, accompanied by whole, boiled potatoes garnished with parsley. Don't forget to pass the mustard.

SHANER GREENWALD
TREASURED JEWISH RECIPES

Pasta with Beef and Eggplant

Mostaccioli con Manzo e Melanzane

Mostaccioli, which literally means small mustaches, are medium-sized pasta tubes (about 2 inches [5 cm.] long) with diagonally cut ends. When mostaccioli are not available, rigatoni (large, ribbed pasta tubes) may be substituted.

	To serve 6	
2 lb.	top round of beef	1 kg.
8 tbsp.	olive oil	120 ml.
4	slices prosciutto, finely chopped	4
2	onions, chopped	2
1 cup	dry white wine	¼ liter
2½ lb.	tomatoes, peeled, seeded and diced	1 kg.
1¼ tsp.	salt	6 ml.
	freshly ground black pepper	
2 tbsp.	butter	30 ml.
5	fresh mushrooms, sliced	5
3	chicken livers, chopped	3
1 lb.	*mostaccioli* or rigatoni	½ kg.
1½ lb.	eggplant, peeled and cut into small strips	¾ kg.
¼ cup	Parmesan cheese, grated	50 ml.

Heat 2 tablespoons [30 ml.] of the oil in a large, deep, fireproof casserole. Stir in the prosciutto and onions, and sauté until soft. Add the beef to the casserole and brown it on both sides over high heat. Lower the heat, add the wine and cook, uncovered, stirring and turning the meat until the wine has evaporated. Stir in the tomatoes and season with 1 teaspoon [5 ml.] of salt and some freshly ground pepper. Cover the casserole and simmer, stirring often and basting the meat frequently, for 2 hours, or until the meat is tender.

In a large saucepan, melt the butter, and sauté the mushrooms and livers for 5 minutes. Sprinkle with ¼ teaspoon [1 ml.] of salt, stir, remove from the heat and keep warm. Remove the meat from the casserole, pour the sauce through a sieve into a bowl and degrease it. Dice the beef, and add the beef and sauce to the liver-and-mushroom mixture; blend well. Cook the *mostaccioli* or rigatoni *al dente*. Drain the pasta and place it in a heated bowl.

Sauté the eggplant strips in the remaining olive oil until tender and lightly browned. Sprinkle Parmesan on the pasta; toss. Add half of the sauce and toss again—well but gently. Serve in hot soup bowls, with strips of eggplant on top. Pass the remaining sauce and grated cheese at the table.

JACK DENTON SCOTT
THE COMPLETE BOOK OF PASTA

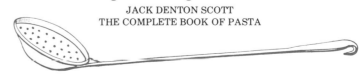

Thin Spaghetti and Meatball

Spaghettini e Polpettone

To serve 6

3 lb.	beef chuck, finely ground	1½ kg.
2	onions, finely chopped	2
4 tbsp.	olive oil	60 ml.
3	eggs, lightly beaten	3
2 cups	dry bread crumbs	½ liter
2 tbsp.	chopped fresh parsley	30 ml.
1 cup	freshly grated *Asiago* or Parmesan cheese	¼ liter
1 tbsp.	chopped raisins	15 ml.
2 tsp.	salt	10 ml.
2 tsp.	freshly ground black pepper	10 ml.
2 cups	tomato sauce (recipe, page 169)	½ liter
1½ lb.	spaghettini	¾ kg.

Cook the onions in 1 tablespoon [15 ml.] of the oil until they are soft and yellow but not brown. Place another tablespoonful of oil on a chopping board, put all of the meat on the oil and work the meat with your hands until it is soft and malleable. Add to the meat the beaten eggs, bread crumbs, parsley and half of the cheese, working them all in well. Now add the cooked onions, the raisins, the salt and a liberal grinding of pepper. Knead everything into the meat, forming it into one large ball and patting it into shape.

Pour the remaining 2 tablespoons [30 ml.] of oil into a large pot. Brown the big ball of meat over low heat, turning it as it becomes crisp so that all areas of the surface become brown and firm. Heat the tomato sauce and pour it over the meatball. Cover the pot and bake in a moderate oven, preheated to 350° F. [180° C.], for about 1 hour or until the meat is cooked through, basting liberally every 10 minutes.

Place the meatball on a warmed platter. Cook the spaghettini *al dente,* drain, and serve it in individual warmed soup bowls. Spoon some of the sauce that simmered with the meat over each serving. Serve the remaining cheese in a separate bowl at the table with the pasta. Follow with the whole meatball on its platter and carve at the table. Serve the remaining sauce in a sauceboat with the meat.

JACK DENTON SCOTT
THE COMPLETE BOOK OF PASTA

Bosnian Meatballs with Yogurt

Bosanske Cufte

To serve 4

1 lb.	ground beef	½ kg.
1	onion, chopped	1
4	eggs, 1 egg beaten lightly	4
½ cup	dry bread crumbs	125 ml.
	salt and freshly ground black pepper	
	flour	
3 tbsp.	butter	45 ml.
1½ cups	unflavored yogurt, beaten until smooth	375 ml.
1½ tbsp.	caraway seeds, finely ground in a blender or pulverized with a mortar and pestle	22 ml.

Preheat the oven to 350° F. [180° C.]. In a mixing bowl, combine the beef, onion, beaten egg, bread crumbs, salt and pepper. Blend thoroughly and shape the mixture into 12 small balls. Roll the meatballs in flour, then brown them in the butter in a large skillet. Drain the meatballs, then place them in a buttered baking dish, and bake uncovered in the oven for 30 minutes.

Thoroughly beat the 3 remaining eggs and slowly stir the yogurt into them. Add the caraway seeds. Season with salt and pepper. Pour the mixture over the meatballs and continue to bake until the egg-and-yogurt mixture is set.

PAULA WOLFERT
MEDITERRANEAN COOKING

Cultured Meat Balls

Terbiyeli Köfte

To serve 4

1 lb.	ground beef	½ kg.
1	onion, grated	1
3 tbsp.	raw unprocessed rice	45 ml.
	salt and pepper	
2 tbsp.	flour	30 ml.
3 cups	water	¾ liter
1 tbsp.	fresh lemon juice	15 ml.
2	eggs, beaten	2
1 tbsp.	chopped mint	15 ml.

Put the meat in a bowl, add the onion, rice, and salt and pepper to taste. Knead the mixture well. Form round meatballs the size of walnuts and place them on wax paper.

In a saucepan mix the flour with a little water to a smooth paste. Stir in the remaining water, then cook over low heat, stirring constantly. When the mixture starts bubbling, add the meatballs one by one and cook, uncovered, over medium heat for 45 minutes. Take the pan off the heat.

Add the lemon juice to the beaten eggs and beat for 1 minute. Gradually add a few tablespoons of the hot meatball sauce to the egg mixture and continue to beat. Then pour the egg mixture over the meatballs and sauce in the pan, and mix well, off the heat. Transfer the contents of the pan to a deep serving dish, sprinkle the mint on top, and serve.

NESET EREN
THE ART OF TURKISH COOKING

Dutch Beef Hash with Gingerbread

To serve 4

1¼ lb.	beef round or rump, sliced ½ inch [1 cm.] thick and cut into ½-inch cubes	⅔ kg.
	salt and pepper	
6 tbsp.	butter	90 ml.
1 tbsp.	oil	15 ml.
4	large onions, quartered	4
1	garlic clove, finely chopped	1
½ cup	flour	125 ml.
2	thick slices Dutch gingerbread cake (*ontbijtkoek*), cut into ½-inch [1-cm.] pieces (or substitute any firm-textured gingerbread)	2
2	whole cloves	2
2	bay leaves	2
½ tsp.	dried basil	2 ml.
¼ tsp.	ground cumin	1 ml.
	black pepper	
5 cups	beef stock	1¼ liter
1 tbsp.	tomato catsup	15 ml.
1 tbsp.	dry red wine	15 ml.
1 tbsp.	vinegar	15 ml.
	Worcestershire sauce or Tabasco (optional)	

Season the meat lightly with salt and pepper. Melt the butter with the oil in a heavy fireproof casserole set over moderate heat. Sauté the onions and the garlic until the onions are transparent. Add the meat and brown it lightly. Stir in the flour and sauté to a nut-brown color.

Add the cubes of gingerbread and the cloves, bay leaves, basil, cumin and pepper. Mix well. Add stock, tomato catsup,

wine and vinegar. Cover and simmer for 1½ hours over low heat, using a fireproof pad under the casserole to keep the beef from overcooking.

Add a little Worcestershire sauce or Tabasco for a more pungent taste. Serve with boiled rice or buttered noodles, and braised cabbage or red beans.

HUGH JANS
KOKEN IN EEN KASSEROL

Minced Meat and Lettuce Curry

Kheema Aur Bhagi

To make ghee, follow the instructions in the editor's note for Curried Beef, page 114.

To serve 2 or 3

½ lb.	leftover cooked beef, trimmed of fat and finely chopped (about 1 cup [¼ liter])	¼ kg.
1	small onion, finely chopped	1
1	garlic clove, finely chopped	1
1 tbsp.	*ghee* or other fat	15 ml.
2 tsp.	ground coriander	10 ml.
1 tsp.	ground turmeric	5 ml.
½ tsp.	pulverized dried chili or cayenne pepper	2 ml.
½ tsp.	ground ginger	2 ml.
½ tsp.	ground cumin	2 ml.
¼ tsp.	ground fenugreek	1 ml.
1	small lettuce, coarsely shredded	1
	salt	

Lightly fry the onion and garlic in the *ghee*. Add the spices and mix thoroughly. Continue the cooking for 2 to 3 minutes longer, then add the lettuce. Simmer for 10 minutes or so. Add the meat and the salt to taste; when the meat is heated through, the curry is ready.

E. P. VEERASAWMY
INDIAN COOKERY

Indian Corn Stew

To serve 4 to 6

1 lb.	ground beef	½ kg.
2 tbsp.	butter	30 ml.
1	onion, finely chopped	1
1	garlic clove, finely chopped	1
1	green pepper, halved, seeded, deribbed and coarsely chopped	1
3 cups	corn kernels, cut from about 6 large ears	¾ liter
3	tomatoes, peeled and coarsely chopped	3
1 tbsp.	Worcestershire sauce	15 ml.
2 tsp.	sugar	10 ml.
1½ tsp.	salt	7 ml.

Melt the butter in a large skillet, add the beef and sauté over high heat, stirring constantly until brown. Stir in the onion, garlic and green pepper, and cook for about 5 minutes. Add the corn, tomatoes and seasonings. Cover and simmer gently over low heat for about 30 minutes.

THE EDITORS OF AMERICAN HERITAGE
THE AMERICAN HERITAGE COOKBOOK

Beef and Onion Stew

Le Miroton

The original version of this recipe cooks the stew for 3 to 4 hours on the back of a wood-fired stove, where the heat is lower than any temperature attainable over a modern burner.

To serve 4

1 lb.	leftover boiled beef, cut into thin strips	½ kg.
4 tbsp.	butter	60 ml.
3	onions, sliced and separated into rings	3
⅓ cup	chopped fresh parsley	75 ml.
1	small bay leaf	1
1	sprig thyme (or 1 tsp. [5 ml.] dried thyme)	1
1 to 2 tsp.	red wine vinegar	5 to 10 ml.
1 tbsp.	Dijon mustard (optional)	15 ml.

In a large sauté pan or skillet, melt the butter and lightly fry the onions until they are golden. Do not allow them to brown. Then add the strips of meat, the parsley, bay leaf and thyme. Moisten with a little water and a sprinkling of vinegar. If desired, you can also add mustard to complement the taste of the meat. Simmer, covered, over low heat for 30 to 40 minutes. Serve straight from the pan.

CURNONSKY
A L'INFORTUNE DU POT

Beef Hash

Picadillo de Carne Cocida

To serve 6

2 to 2½ lb.	boiled beef brisket, coarsely chopped	1 kg.
2 tbsp.	unsalted butter	30 ml.
2 tbsp.	vegetable oil	30 ml.
2	green peppers, halved, seeded, deribbed and chopped	2
1	large onion, finely chopped	1
	garlic clove, chopped	
4	large tomatoes, peeled, seeded and chopped	4
1	bay leaf	1
¼ tsp.	ground cloves	1 ml.
	salt and freshly ground pepper	
1 tbsp.	white distilled vinegar	15 ml.

Heat the butter and oil in a large skillet. Add the green peppers and onion and cook until the onion is lightly browned. Add the garlic, tomatoes, bay leaf, cloves, salt and pepper, and cook gently for about 10 minutes. Add the vinegar and the beef, and cook until the meat is heated through.

In Cuba, this traditional dish is served with boiled white rice, black beans, fried ripe plantains and deep-fried eggs.

ELISABETH LAMBERT ORTIZ
THE COMPLETE BOOK OF CARIBBEAN COOKING

Beef with Eggplant and Tomatoes

Boeuf à L'Arlésienne

To serve 4 to 6

1½ lb.	leftover boiled beef, sliced ½ inch [1 cm.] thick	¾ kg.
2	medium-sized onions, finely sliced	2
4 to 5 tbsp.	olive oil	60 to 75 ml.
1 lb.	small eggplants, peeled and sliced into thin disks	½ kg.
4 or 5	medium-sized tomatoes, peeled, seeded and chopped	4 or 5
4	large red peppers, broiled, peeled, seeded, deribbed and cut into strips	4
	salt and pepper	
1 tbsp.	chopped fresh parsley	15 ml.
1	garlic clove, chopped	1

Arrange the beef slices in a gratin dish. Put the onions in a large skillet with the oil and cook slowly until they begin to soften. Add the eggplant and sauté for 7 to 8 minutes over moderate heat. Add the tomatoes and the red peppers. Season with salt and pepper, parsley and the garlic. Simmer for 20 minutes and pour the sauce over the beef. Bake in a moderate oven, preheated to 350° F. [180° C.], for 10 minutes.

AUGUSTE ESCOFFIER
MA CUISINE

Sautéed Beef, Lyonnaise-Style

Boeuf Sauté Lyonnaise

To serve 4

2 lb.	leftover boiled or braised beef, thinly sliced	1 kg.
2 tbsp.	butter	30 ml.
1 tbsp.	oil	15 ml.
	salt and pepper	
4	large onions, thickly sliced	4
1	bouquet garni	1
1	garlic clove	1
2 tbsp.	vinegar	30 ml.
1 tbsp.	chopped fresh parsley	15 ml.

Lightly fry the beef in a large skillet with 1 tablespoon [15 ml.] of butter and the oil. Season with salt and pepper. Set the pan aside and cover it to keep the beef warm while you slowly fry the onions, garlic and bouquet garni in a separate pan in the remaining butter.

When the onions are golden, add them to the beef. Warm the two together for 10 minutes, stirring twice, and finish the dish with a dash of vinegar and the parsley.

Various additions can be made to this dish: stewed tomatoes, sautéed sweet peppers, or the two together with sautéed potatoes. The new ingredients are added after the beef is finished; but then, naturally, the word "Lyonnaise" is deleted from the name of the dish.

H. HEYRAUD
LA CUISINE À NICE

Leftover Beef with Vegetables

Bubble and Squeak

Bubble and Squeak is usually thought of as a dish of fried leftover mixed vegetables—most often potatoes with cabbage or sprouts. The original dish always included boiled beef, either fresh or salted. This version comes from a handwritten family cookery book dated 1847.

To serve 4

1 lb.	leftover boiled beef, sliced ⅛ inch [3 mm.] thick and cut into ⅛-inch dice	½ kg.
1	cabbage	1
1	onion	1
1	carrot	1
4 tbsp.	butter	60 ml.
½ cup	beef stock	125 ml.
	salt and pepper	

Boil the cabbage, onion and carrot until just tender. Drain very well and chop finely. Melt the butter in a fireproof casserole and put in the beef to warm, taking care it does not dry up. Remove the meat and put in the vegetables. Cook them in the butter, moistened with a little stock, until very hot. Add salt and pepper, and serve the vegetables with the meat in a shallow dish, moistening them with a little more stock.

MARY NORWAK
THE FARMHOUSE KITCHEN

Leftover Beef with Gravy

Inky-Pinky

Meg Dods, writing in the early 19th Century, did not think it necessary to specify quantities for this recipe for leftover beef. The amounts given below are merely suggestions. The sippets she calls for are small pieces of fried bread or toast, made as described in the ingredients list.

To serve 2 or 3

½ lb.	leftover roast beef	¼ kg.
2	boiled carrots	2
1	onion	1
1 cup	beef stock	¼ liter
	vinegar	
	salt and pepper	
1 tbsp.	flour	15 ml.
	sippets made by browning 2 or 3 slices of bread in butter, then draining them on paper towels	

Slice the boiled carrots. Slice also the cold roast beef, trimming away the outside and the fat. In a large skillet, put an onion into a good stock (drawn from the roast beef bones, if you like) and let the carrots and beef slowly simmer in this. Add vinegar, salt and pepper. Thicken the gravy with the flour. Take out the onion and serve the beef hot, with sippets.

F. MARIAN MC NEILL
THE SCOTS KITCHEN

Leftover Beef with Scallions

Miroton Saint-Honoré

To serve 4

1 lb.	leftover boiled beef, sliced as thinly as possible	½ kg.
2 tbsp.	chopped fresh parsley	30 ml.
2 tsp.	chopped tarragon	10 ml.
1½ cups	sliced scallions	375 ml.
1 tsp.	chopped chervil	5 ml.
½ cup	capers, rinsed and drained well	125 ml.
2 cups	beef stock	½ liter

Combine the parsley, tarragon, scallions, chervil and capers. Put half of this mixture into a shallow ovenproof dish. Pour in half of the stock. On top of this arrange the beef slices. Add the rest of the seasonings mixture and the remaining stock, cover and cook in an oven, preheated to 350° F. [180° C.], for 30 to 40 minutes.

COMTE DE COURCHAMPS
NÉOPHYSIOLOGIE DE GOÛT

Sauté of Beef and Chestnuts

Boeuf Sauté "Père Gaspard"

This dish is usually made with beef that has been boiled in a pot-au-feu. To roast the chestnuts, make an incision in the base of each of them and place them in an oven, preheated to 400° F. [200° C.], for 20 minutes or until the skins split.

To serve 4

1 lb.	leftover boiled beef, sliced 1 inch [2½ cm.] thick and cut into 1-inch cubes	½ kg.
2 tbsp.	butter or lard	30 ml.
1	medium-sized onion, diced	1
2 tbsp.	flour	30 ml.
2 cups	hard cider	½ liter
5 tbsp.	beef or veal stock	75 ml.
	salt and pepper	
	bouquet garni made of parsley, celery, thyme and a bay leaf	
1	garlic clove, crushed	1
48	large fresh chestnuts, roasted and peeled	48

Melt the butter (or lard) in a large ovenproof sauté pan and soften the onion. Add the beef pieces. As soon as they are well browned on all sides, remove them from the pan and add the flour. Lightly brown this, add the cider and stock, mix, and season with salt and pepper. Add the bouquet garni and garlic, and cook for 10 minutes. Put the chestnuts into the pan. Cook, covered, for 40 minutes, stirring from time to time, but taking care not to break up the chestnuts.

Return the pieces of beef to the pan, put the lid on and cook in a moderate oven, preheated to 350° F. [180° C.], for 20 minutes. Remove the bouquet garni and serve the sauté in a large, deep dish.

PROSPER MONTAGNÉ AND A. GOTTSCHALK
MON MENU—GUIDE D'HYGIÈNE ALIMENTAIRE

Dry Curry of Cold Meat

Chundole

To make ghee, follow the instructions in the editor's note for Curried Beef, page 114.

To serve 4

1 lb.	cooked beef or mutton (preferably underdone), cut into ½-inch [1-cm.] cubes	½ kg.
1 tbsp.	ghee or other fat	15 ml.
2 tbsp.	chopped onion	30 ml.
½ tsp.	finely chopped garlic	2 ml.
3	fresh or pickled chilies, each halved lengthwise, stemmed and seeded	3
½ tsp.	finely chopped fresh or pickled ginger	2 ml.
2 tsp.	ground turmeric	10 ml.
¼ tsp.	pulverized dried red chili or cayenne pepper	1 ml.
	salt	
	fresh lemon juice	

Warm the ghee in a sauté pan and add the onion, garlic, halved chilies and ginger. Cook over low heat until the onion is soft, but not brown. Now add the turmeric and pulverized chili. Mix well, cook slowly for 2 to 3 minutes, then add the meat. Stir lightly and cook until the meat is warmed right through. Add salt and lemon juice to taste.

E. P. VEERASAWMY
INDIAN COOKERY

Red Flannel Hash

To serve 6 to 8

2 lb.	leftover corned beef, coarsely chopped	1 kg.
4 to 6	medium-sized potatoes, boiled and coarsely chopped	4 to 6
1	medium-sized onion, finely chopped	1
	freshly ground black pepper	
¼ tsp.	grated nutmeg	1 ml.
4 to 6 tbsp.	butter or lard	60 to 90 ml.
4	medium-sized fresh beets, boiled and coarsely chopped	4
½ cup	heavy cream or boiling water (optional)	125 ml.

Combine the potatoes and onions with the meat and add a few good grinds of black pepper and nutmeg. Blend well and allow the mixture to rest in the refrigerator for several hours or overnight. When you are ready to cook the hash, melt just enough butter or lard in a heavy skillet to cover the bottom. Add the hash and the beets, and press down firmly. When the hash begins to develop a crust on the bottom, turn it with a spatula so that some of the crust is brought to the top.

At this point many people add heavy cream or some boiling water, which enables the bottom crust to form more quickly. I prefer to cook the hash slowly to develop the crust, turning it several times. When it has crusted nicely, loosen it with a spatula, fold it once and turn it onto a platter. The hash can be served with poached eggs, toast and chili sauce.

JAMES BEARD
JAMES BEARD'S AMERICAN COOKERY

Boiled Beef Terrine

Bouilli en Terrine

To serve 4 to 6

2 lb.	leftover boiled beef, cut into small pieces	1 kg.
6	slices lean salt pork without the rind, blanched in boiling water for 5 minutes, drained and coarsely diced	6
1 tsp.	dried thyme	5 ml.
1	bay leaf, crumbled	1
6	large potatoes, thinly sliced	6
4	onions, sliced	4
	salt and pepper	
¾ cup	dry white wine	175 ml.

Scatter some diced pork in a 3-quart [3-liter] terrine and sprinkle some thyme and bay leaf over it. On top put a layer of boiled beef pieces, a layer of raw potato slices, then a layer of sliced onions. Season with salt and pepper. Repeat the layers, beginning with more pork and herbs, until you have filled the terrine. Finish with a layer of diced pork. Pour the white wine into the terrine and cook in an oven, preheated to 300° F. [150° C.], for 1 to 2 hours; you can never overcook this dish. It should be eaten very hot.

TANTE MARGUERITE
LA CUISINE DE LA BONNE MÉNAGÈRE

Beef Hash au Gratin

Hachis de Boeuf au Gratin

To serve 4 to 6

1 lb.	leftover boiled beef, coarsely chopped or diced	½ kg.
4 tbsp.	butter or lard	60 ml.
2	onions, chopped	2
2	tomatoes, peeled, seeded and finely chopped	2
1¼ cups	beef or veal stock	300 ml.
1 tbsp.	flour, mixed with 2 tbsp. [30 ml.] cold water	15 ml.
	salt and pepper	
	grated nutmeg	
2 tbsp.	chopped fresh parsley	30 ml.
1 tsp.	chopped garlic (optional)	5 ml.
3 tbsp.	dry bread crumbs	45 ml.
2 tbsp.	butter, melted	30 ml.

Heat the butter or lard in a saucepan over low heat and add the onions. When the onions are lightly colored, add the tomatoes and cook the mixture until the onions are soft. Add the stock and thicken it with the flour-and-water mixture to make a sauce. Boil for 2 to 3 minutes, then reduce the heat and add the beef. Season with salt, pepper, nutmeg, parsley and—if you wish—garlic.

Turn out the hash into a buttered gratin dish and shape the top into a dome. Sprinkle with the bread crumbs, moisten with melted butter and brown the hash under a preheated broiler for 3 to 4 minutes to finish it.

J. B. REBOUL
LA CUISINIÈRE PROVENÇALE

Beef Loaf My Way

The Pique seasoning called for here refers to a bottled sauce that was popular in the 1940s, when this recipe was first published, but that is no longer available. You can substitute Worcestershire or steak sauce.

To serve 8

3 lb.	lean ground beef	1½ kg.
3 tbsp.	finely chopped beef suet	45 ml.
2	medium-sized onions, finely chopped	2
2	large tomatoes, peeled and seeded	2
½ lb.	fresh mushrooms, coarsely chopped	¼ kg.
4 tbsp.	butter	60 ml.
1 lb.	green beans, halved lengthwise and roughly chopped	½ kg.
6	small, tender ribs celery with some leaves, thinly sliced	6
2	small carrots, coarsely grated	2
1	small garlic clove, crushed	1
2 tbsp.	finely chopped fresh parsley	30 ml.
1 tbsp.	finely cut fresh chives	15 ml.
	salt and freshly ground black pepper	
	thyme leaves	
½ tsp.	dry mustard	2 ml.
¼ cup	Pique seasoning	50 ml.
⅓ cup	soy sauce	75 ml.
2	large eggs, yolks separated from the whites	2
½ cup	milk	125 ml.
5 or 6	thin slices bacon	5 or 6
1 tbsp.	flour	15 ml.
1	bunch watercress	1

Melt the suet in an iron pan and lightly brown the onions in it. Add the tomatoes, breaking up the pulp. In a separate pan, sauté the mushrooms in 3 tablespoons [45 ml.] of butter for 4 to 5 minutes over low heat, stirring constantly.

Place the onions, tomatoes, mushrooms, beans, celery and carrots in a mixing bowl. Add the garlic, parsley, chives and beef, and stir lightly, tossing all of these ingredients over and over until they are thoroughly mixed. Season with salt, pepper, a good pinch of thyme leaves (no powdered thyme, please), the dry mustard, Pique seasoning and soy sauce, then toss again. Set the mixture aside.

Beat the yolks of eggs lightly with the cold milk, then add to the mixture. Prepare a glass baking dish, or any suitable pan having a tight-fitting cover, by lining it on the bottom and sides with the bacon. Lastly, beat the egg whites until stiff but not dry and fold them gently into the mixture. Shape the mixture into a loaf.

The ideal setup for cooking the loaf is a large cast-iron casserole into which the baking dish, with its cover, will fit. Otherwise, cover the dish and place it in a pan of boiling water in a hot oven, preheated to 400° F. [200° C.], replenishing the water as it boils away. Bake for about 2 hours, reducing the heat to moderate, 350° F. [180° C.], after 20 minutes.

Meanwhile, prepare a roux by blending the flour and the remaining butter over gentle heat until lightly browned.

When you uncover the baking dish, you will discover that the loaf has shrunk from the sides and is almost floating in a sea of rich, delicious sauce. Carefully drain off the sauce into a saucepan; skim off all but 2 tablespoons [30 ml.] of the fat and thicken with the roux. Then turn the loaf onto an ovenproof serving dish and peel off any bacon strips sticking to the sides of the dish, replacing them on the loaf. Put the serving dish in a very hot oven, 425 to 450° F. [220 to 230° C.] or under the broiler and brown the surface quickly without drying it. The bacon will dry off and crisp at the same time.

Serve in the hot dish, garnishing the loaf with a glazing of the sauce and sprigs of watercress. Pass the sauce, which will be abundant, in a heated gravy boat.

LOUIS P. DE GOUY
THE GOLD COOK BOOK

Boiled Beef Gratin

Boeuf Bouilli, Gratiné

To serve 4 to 6

1 lb.	leftover boiled beef rump or round, sliced ¼ inch [6 mm.] thick	½ kg.
½ cup	beef or veal stock	125 ml.
¼ cup	dry white wine	50 ml.
2 or 3	shallots, chopped	2 or 3
2	large onions, chopped	2
4 tbsp.	butter	60 ml.
1½ cups	chopped fresh mushrooms	375 ml.
1 tbsp.	flour	15 ml.
1 tbsp.	chopped fresh parsley	15 ml.
½ cup	bread crumbs	125 ml.

Trim the slices of beef to the same size and shape, and arrange them symmetrically in a shallow, fireproof baking dish. Moisten the meat with 4 tablespoons [60 ml.] of the stock and all of the wine. Cover and place on very low heat.

Fry the shallots and onions in the butter in a saucepan; when they are colored, add the mushrooms. After a few minutes, sprinkle the mixture with the flour and moisten with the remaining stock; the sauce should be fairly thick. Cook for 10 minutes. When the beef is hot, in about 15 minutes, cover it with the sauce, then sprinkle the parsley and bread crumbs over it. Bake the beef in an oven, preheated to 325° F. [160° C.], for 15 minutes. Serve in the same dish.

URBAIN DUBOIS
ÉCOLE DES CUISINIÈRES

Walnut Meat Loaf

To serve 8

2 lb.	ground beef	1 kg.
1	egg	1
⅓ cup	milk	75 ml.
2 tbsp.	finely minced onion	30 ml.
⅛ tsp.	pepper	½ ml.
1½ tsp.	salt	7 ml.
1½ tsp.	Worcestershire sauce	7 ml.
½ cup	tomato sauce *(recipe, page 169)*	125 ml.
¼ cup	water	50 ml.
	Black-walnut stuffing	
1 cup	coarsely chopped black walnuts	¼ liter
3 cups	soft bread crumbs	¾ liter
2 tbsp.	minced onion	30 ml.
1 tsp.	salt	5 ml.
⅛ tsp.	pepper	½ ml.
1½ cups	chopped celery	375 ml.
¼ tsp.	poultry seasoning	1 ml.
½ cup	milk, water or stock	125 ml.

Beat the egg. Add the milk and combine with the meat, onion, pepper, salt and Worcestershire sauce. On waxed paper, flatten out the mixture into a rectangle longer than it is wide and about ¾ inch [2 cm.] thick.

Combine the stuffing ingredients. Shape the stuffing into a roll on top of the meat, close to one lengthwise edge. Roll the meat so that it completely covers the stuffing. Place the loaf in a shallow baking pan and remove the wax paper.

Mix the tomato sauce with the water and pour the mixture over the meat loaf. Bake the loaf in an oven, preheated to 375° F. [190° C.], for 1 hour. Garnish with orange slices and toasted walnuts.

MARION BROWN
MARION BROWN'S SOUTHERN COOK BOOK

Ground Beef Loaf

To serve 8

2 lb.	lean ground beef	1 kg.
¼ lb.	lean salt pork, blanched in boiling water for 5 minutes, drained and chopped	125 g.
2	eggs, lightly beaten	2
1 cup	milk	¼ liter
3 tbsp.	butter, melted	45 ml.
1 tbsp.	prepared horseradish	15 ml.
2 tbsp.	finely chopped onion	30 ml.
¼ tsp.	pepper	1 ml.
1 tbsp.	salt	15 ml.
1 cup	soft bread crumbs	¼ liter
2	slices bacon	2

Mix the beef and salt pork with the eggs, milk, butter, horseradish, onion, seasonings and bread crumbs. Pack the mixture into a buttered 8-by-4-inch [20-by-10-cm.] loaf pan and cover the mixture with the bacon slices. Bake in an oven, preheated to 350° F. [180° C.], for 60 minutes, or until the meat loaf is browned and shrinks from the sides of the pan.

HELEN CORBITT
HELEN CORBITT'S COOKBOOK

Miss Daniell's Meat Loaf

To serve 6 to 8

1 lb.	ground beef	½ kg.
½ lb.	ground pork	¼ kg.
½ lb.	ground veal	¼ kg.
2 tbsp.	finely chopped onion	30 ml.
1 cup	fresh bread crumbs	¼ liter
¾ cup	milk or water	175 ml.
2 tsp.	salt	10 ml.
	pepper	
1	egg, lightly beaten	1
4	slices bacon	4
	tomato sauce *(recipe, page 169)*	

Mix the beef, pork and veal with the onion, bread crumbs, milk or water, seasoning and egg. Shape the mixture into a loaf or roll and put it into a shallow roasting pan. Lay the slices of bacon across the top. Bake in an oven, preheated to 350° F. [180° C.], for 1 hour. Serve hot with tomato sauce.

WILMA LORD PERKINS (EDITOR)
THE FANNIE FARMER COOKBOOK

Meat Loaf

I have at least six recipes for this in my notebooks, and I like them all but I never follow any of them. A select circle of meat-loaf fanciers has pronounced this version Best of Breed. It is a kissing cousin of the French *pâté de campagne* and, indeed, is very good cold.

To serve 4 to 6

1 lb.	ground beef chuck	½ kg.
½ lb.	ground veal stew meat	¼ kg.
½ lb.	ground pork shoulder	¼ kg.
2 tbsp.	rendered bacon fat	30 ml.
1	medium-sized onion, finely chopped	1
1	large garlic clove, finely chopped	1
2	slices day-old bread, trimmed	2
¼ cup	finely chopped fresh parsley	50 ml.
¼ cup	Cognac or bourbon	50 ml.
1	egg, lightly beaten	1
1½ tsp.	salt	7 ml.
½ tsp.	freshly ground pepper	2 ml.
¼ tsp.	ground allspice	1 ml.
½ tsp.	dried thyme	2 ml.
1	bay leaf	1
2 or 3	slices bacon	2 or 3

Preheat oven to 350° F. [180° C.]. Assemble all ingredients and put the meats into a large mixing bowl. Ground meat is easier to work at room temperature.

Heat the bacon fat, and sauté the onion and garlic until soft and transparent. Crumble the bread to fine soft crumbs (easy in a blender) and sprinkle over the meats. Scrape the onions into the meats, add the parsley, Cognac, egg, salt, pepper, allspice and thyme. Mix thoroughly with your hands; a spoon is tedious and an electric mixer overdoes the job, producing a rubbery texture.

Pack the meat-loaf mixture into a 1-quart [1-liter] oiled loaf pan (cheap aluminum-foil loaf pans are available in most supermarkets), lay the bay leaf on top, and cover the meat loaf with bacon slices. Set this in the preheated oven on the middle rack and bake it for 1½ hours. Leave the loaf in the pan, and put it in a warm place for 20 or 30 minutes before slicing; otherwise it will crumble terribly.

For a very firm texture to serve as a cold pâté, put another loaf pan on top of the meat loaf and weight for 4 or 5 hours with about 1 pound [½ kg.] of canned goods, evenly distributed. Seal tightly with aluminum foil and chill before serving, but the meat loaf should not be too cold or the flavor will be bland.

MIRIAM UNGERER
GOOD CHEAP FOOD

Veal

Marinated Veal Loin

Longe de Veau à la Marinade

In the original recipe (1651) the veal was roasted on a spit. The version below has been adapted for oven roasting. Directions for larding a roast appear on page 57.

To serve 4 to 6

2 to 2½ lb.	boneless veal loin roast	1 kg.
½ lb.	fresh pork fat, cut into lardons	¼ kg.
2 tbsp.	bread crumbs, or substitute 2 tsp. [10 ml.] flour	30 ml.
1 cup	beef or veal stock	¼ liter

Lemon and orange marinade

⅔ cup	vinegar	150 ml.
	salt and pepper	
½ tsp.	ground allspice	2 ml.
3	whole cloves	3
1	lemon, sliced	1
1	orange, sliced	1
1	onion, sliced	1
1	sprig rosemary or a few sage leaves (or substitute ½ tsp. [2 ml.] dried rosemary or sage)	1

Flatten the loin well with a meat mallet to help it absorb the marinade, then lard it with the pork fat. Mix all the marinade ingredients in a large bowl and marinate the meat for 2 to 3 hours at room temperature, turning it occasionally. Transfer the veal to a rack in a roasting pan and put it in a moderate oven, preheated to 375° F. [190° C.]. Strain the marinade and reserve.

Roast the veal for about 1 hour, basting frequently with the strained marinade. When the meat is cooked, transfer it to a warmed platter and place the pan over low heat. Mix the bread crumbs or flour with a little of the stock and add to the marinade in the pan to thicken it. Add the remaining stock and simmer the sauce for 10 minutes, basting the meat with sauce from time to time. Then pour the sauce over the meat. Garnish with mushrooms or asparagus and serve.

LA VARENNE
LE CUISINIER FRANÇOIS

Veal with Mustard

Morceau de Veau à la Moutarde

In the 18th Century this dish was made with orange-flavored mustard, now available at a few specialty food shops. Use Dijon mustard as a substitute. The technique of barding a roast is demonstrated on page 24.

To serve 6 to 8

2½ lb.	boneless veal rump or round roast	1 kg.
	prepared mustard	
	thinly sliced fresh pork fat	
2 tbsp.	water	30 ml.
3 tbsp.	heavy cream	45 ml.
	freshly ground pepper	

Spread the veal liberally with mustard, then wrap it in a thin bard of pork fat and tie up the veal with cotton string.

Put the veal into a small roasting pan with the water. Place in a moderate oven, preheated to 350° F. [180° C.]. Roast, uncovered, for 1¼ hours, basting frequently. Remove the veal and place it on a warmed platter.

Put the cream and freshly ground pepper into the roasting pan. Heat, while stirring. Pour into a sauceboat.

Remove the bard and serve the veal with the sauce separate. Fresh pasta makes a good accompaniment.

ROBERT COURTINE
BALZAC À TABLE

Perigord Veal Cutlets

Côtelette de Veau du Périgord

To serve 4

4	thick veal cutlets	4
	salt and pepper	
1	thick slice fresh pork fat, finely chopped	1
1	garlic clove, finely chopped	1
	finely chopped fresh chervil	
12	shallots, finely chopped	12

Flatten the cutlets, and sprinkle them with salt and pepper. Place them over a moderately hot charcoal grill. Mix together the pork fat, garlic, chervil and shallots with salt and pepper. When you turn over the cutlets after about 5 minutes, cover the cooked side with a generous layer of this mixture. The heat will melt the fat and, when the second side of the cutlet is cooked, the pork-fat garnish will be cooked. Serve promptly.

SUZANNE LABOURER AND X.-M. BOULESTIN
PETITS ET GRANDS PLATS

Veal Kebabs

To serve 4 to 6

2 lb.	boneless leg of veal, sliced 1 inch [2½ cm.] thick and cut into 1-inch cubes	1 kg.
⅓ cup	olive oil	75 ml.
¼ cup	dry white wine	50 ml.
2 tbsp.	fresh lemon juice	30 ml.
1 tbsp.	chopped fresh tarragon	15 ml.
	salt and pepper	

Mix the oil, wine, lemon juice and tarragon, with salt and pepper to taste, and pour over the veal cubes. Marinate at room temperature for about 3 hours. Drain. Thread the veal cubes onto skewers and broil them very slowly over coals for 20 minutes, or until nicely browned on all sides. Baste the kebabs frequently with the leftover marinade.

JULES JEROME BOND
THE OUTDOOR COOKBOOK

Veal Chops with Cheese

Côte de Veau Franc-Comtoise

To serve 8

8	thick veal chops	8
7 tbsp.	butter	105 ml.
	salt and freshly ground black pepper	
3½ cups	grated Gruyère cheese	875 ml.
2	eggs	2
¼ cup	heavy cream	50 ml.
	grated nutmeg	
½ cup	dry white wine	125 ml.

Melt the butter in a large sauté pan with an ovenproof handle. Add the veal chops and sear them on both sides over high heat. Reduce the heat, season with salt and pepper, cover the pan and cook gently for about 20 minutes, turning the chops once. Meanwhile, in a bowl mix together the cheese, eggs and cream. Season with salt, pepper and a pinch of nutmeg.

Drain off the cooking butter from the pan and reserve it. Put some of the cheese mixture on each chop, add the wine and put the pan, uncovered, into a moderately hot oven, preheated to 375° F. [190° C.], for 10 minutes. Baste the chops with the reserved cooking butter once or twice.

CURNONSKY
CUISINE ET VINS DE FRANCE

Stuffed Veal Roulades
Färsrulader

To serve 4 to 6

1 lb.	finely ground veal	½ kg.
1	medium-sized boiling potato, quartered	1
10 tbsp.	butter	150 ml.
½ cup	finely chopped onion	125 ml.
3 tbsp.	fine dry bread crumbs	45 ml.
⅔ cup	heavy cream	150 ml.
2 tbsp.	water	30 ml.
1½ tsp.	salt	7 ml.
½ tsp.	white pepper	2 ml.
1	egg	1
2 tbsp.	finely chopped fresh parsley	30 ml.
1 tbsp.	cornstarch	15 ml.
½ cup	very thinly sliced leek, white parts only	125 ml.

Boil the quartered potato in water to cover for 10 to 15 minutes, or until tender. Drain and mash with a fork. In a small skillet, melt 2 tablespoons [30 ml.] of the butter. Add the chopped onions and cook for 7 or 8 minutes, stirring frequently, until they are soft and transparent but not brown. Scrape the onions into a large mixing bowl and add the mashed potato, ground veal, bread crumbs, 5 tablespoons [75 ml.] of the cream, water, salt, pepper, egg, parsley and cornstarch. Mix well, then refrigerate for at least 1 hour.

Brush a large wooden pastry board (or another hard, smooth surface) with water, and pat or roll out the mixture to a 16-by-16-inch [40-by-40-cm.] square about ⅛ inch [3 mm.] thick. (Your hands or the rolling pin should be moistened with water to prevent the meat mixture from sticking.) With a pastry wheel or small, sharp knife, cut the meat into 16 squares of 4 by 4 inches [10 by 10 cm.] each. Put a thin layer of leek slices (about 1½ teaspoons [7 ml.]) on each square. Now, with the aid of a knife or—better still—a thin spatula, roll up each square, jelly-roll fashion. Ideally, the roulades should now be chilled for at least 1 hour, but they may, if necessary, be cooked immediately.

Heat 2 tablespoons [30 ml.] of the butter in a heavy 10- to 12-inch [25- to 30-cm.] skillet. Add the roulades, four at a time, turning them gently with a spatula so that they brown on all sides. When they are a rich brown, set them aside on a heated dish in a very cool oven—200° F. [100° C.]. Repeat the process, adding 2 tablespoons [30 ml.] of fresh butter for every four roulades. Pour the remaining heavy cream into the empty pan and boil it rapidly for 3 to 5 minutes, until it thickens, meanwhile scraping up the browned bits in the pan with a rubber spatula or a wooden spoon. Season to taste and pour the sauce over the waiting roulades. If you must, cover the dish with aluminum foil and keep warm in the oven—200° F. [100° C.]—for up to 15 minutes.

FOODS OF THE WORLD/THE COOKING OF SCANDINAVIA

Veal Scallopini with Cream, Calvados and Apples
Escalopes de Veau Normande

To serve 6

12	veal scallops, about 4 inches [10 cm.] in diameter and ½ inch [1 cm.] thick, not pounded	12
3	medium-sized golden or red Delicious apples	3
5 to 6 tbsp.	fresh lemon juice	75 to 90 ml.
1 tsp.	salt	5 ml.
1 tsp.	freshly ground pepper	5 ml.
½ cup	flour	125 ml.
4 tbsp.	butter	60 ml.
2 tbsp.	vegetable oil	30 ml.
⅓ cup	Calvados (French applejack)	75 ml.
1½ cups	heavy cream	375 ml.

Peel and core the apples, then cut them into ½-inch [1-cm.] cubes. Place these in a bowl, add the lemon juice and mix thoroughly so the apples are well coated. Set aside. Sprinkle the veal with salt and pepper, then with the flour, shaking off any excess. Heat the butter and oil in a large skillet about 15 inches [45 cm.] in diameter (or use two skillets). When hot, add the veal, a few pieces at a time, and sauté until lightly browned on both sides (approximately 4 minutes on each side, over medium heat).

When the scallops are cooked, arrange them on a platter and set it aside in an oven heated to 180° F. [85° C.]. Add the apples, lemon juice and the Calvados to the skillet. Stir and scrape up all the brown crusts in the skillet and cook over moderate heat, stirring frequently, for about 3 minutes. Add the cream and continue cooking until the mixture has turned to a rich ivory color. Reduce the heat and cook uncovered, stirring frequently, for almost 10 minutes, until the cream has reduced by about half and the sauce coats a spoon. Taste for seasoning; you will probably need to add about ½ teaspoon [2 ml.] of salt.

Spoon the sauce over the scallops and serve.

JACQUES PÉPIN
A FRENCH CHEF COOKS AT HOME

Veal Olives

Olivette di Vitello alla Pesarese

To serve 6 to 8

2 to 2½ lb.	veal round roast or boneless rump roast, cut crosswise into 18 scallops of equal size, each about ¼ inch [6 mm.] thick	1 kg.
	salt	
	flour	
1	egg, lightly beaten	1
	bread crumbs	
½ cup	oil	125 ml.

Ham stuffing

1½ cups	fatty, uncooked ham, finely chopped	⅓ kg.
6	anchovy fillets, soaked in cold water for 10 minutes, patted dry and finely chopped	6
1 tbsp.	capers, rinsed, drained well and finely chopped	15 ml.
1	large garlic clove, finely chopped	1
1 tbsp.	chopped fresh parsley	15 ml.
2 tbsp.	puréed tomato	30 ml.
½ cup	dry bread crumbs	125 ml.
	salt and pepper	
2 tbsp.	butter, softened	30 ml.

Flatten the scallops well with a meat mallet. Put the chopped stuffing ingredients in a mixing bowl, and add the puréed tomato and the bread crumbs. Season with salt and pepper, and mix in the butter to make a fairly stiff paste.

Place the scallops on a work surface, season lightly with salt and put some of the stuffing mixture in the middle of each scallop. Roll up each scallop, and close it with one or two wooden picks or tie it with cotton string so that the stuffing will not come out. Then dredge these veal "olives" with flour, dip them in the egg and roll them in the bread crumbs. Heat the oil in a skillet, arrange the veal olives in the pan and cook them over moderate heat, turning frequently, for approximately 10 minutes until they are golden brown. Remove the picks or string before serving.

LUIGI CARNACINA AND LUIGI VERONELLI
LA BUONA VERA CUCINA ITALIANA

Veal Chops with Cream

Côtelette de Veau à la Crème

To serve 4 to 6

6	veal chops	6
2 tbsp.	butter	30 ml.
½ cup	heavy cream	125 ml.
2 tbsp.	fresh lemon juice	30 ml.

Fry the chops in butter and transfer them from the pan to a warmed platter. Stir the cream and the lemon juice into the cooking butter. Allow the mixture to brown, then pour it over the chops.

SUZANNE LABOUREUR AND X.-M. BOULESTIN
PETITS ET GRANDS PLATS

Sautéed Veal Rib Chops

Côte de Veau

To serve 4

4	thick veal rib chops, about ½ pound [¼ kg.] each	4
¼ cup	chopped shallots	50 ml.
2 oz.	lean salt pork without the rind, blanched in boiling water for 5 minutes and drained	75 g.
4 tbsp.	butter	60 ml.
	salt and pepper	
½ cup	water, veal stock or dry white wine	125 ml.
1	egg yolk, lightly beaten	1
1 tbsp.	chopped fresh parsley	15 ml.
1 tbsp.	vinegar	15 ml.

In a large sauté pan or skillet, sauté the shallots and salt pork in the butter. As soon as the shallots begin to turn golden, add the chops and brown them gently, turning from time to time. Cover the pan. When the chops are cooked, after about 30 minutes, remove them to a warmed platter.

Skim the fat from the pan juices, season the juices with salt and pepper, and add the water, stock or wine. Let the liquid reduce over high heat for 2 to 3 minutes, then remove the pan from the heat. Stir a spoonful of the sauce into the beaten egg yolk. Then stir this mixture into the sauce in the pan to thicken it. Warm the sauce over low heat, but do not let it boil, lest it curdle.

Before serving the chops, sprinkle over them the chopped parsley and the vinegar. Serve the sauce separately.

MAURICE BÉGUIN
LA CUISINE EN POITOU

Fried Breaded Veal Scallops

Wiener Schnitzel

To serve 4

4	veal scallops or cutlets, 6 oz. [180 g.] each, cut ¼ inch [6 mm.] thick	4
	salt	
3 tbsp.	flour	45 ml.
1	egg, beaten	1
3 tbsp.	dry bread crumbs	45 ml.
1 quart	oil	1 liter

Trim and flatten the scallops or cutlets. Wipe them dry, salt and leave them to stand for about 10 minutes. Then dip the scallops or cutlets first in the flour, next in the egg and finally in the bread crumbs. Allow the scallops to dry for 15 minutes to set the coating. Fry them in ample hot oil at 375° F. [190° C.] until golden, about 1 minute on each side.

ELEK MAGYAR
KOCHBUCH FÜR FEINSCHMECKER

Veal Chops with Herb Sauce

To serve 4

4	thick veal chops	4
	salt	
6 tbsp.	unsalted butter	90 ml.
1 tbsp.	oil	15 ml.
½ cup	dry white wine	125 ml.
Herb sauce		
1 packed cup	mixed greens (spinach, parsley or watercress predominating; chives, thyme or sorrel added for flavoring)	¼ liter
½ cup	heavy cream	125 ml.
1	egg yolk	1
	salt and pepper	

Purée the greens in a blender or food processor. In a bowl, mix the greens with the cream, egg yolk and seasoning, then set the herbed cream aside.

Trim the chops, dry them with paper towels and salt them. Fry the veal in 2 tablespoons [30 ml.] of the butter mixed with the oil for 15 to 20 minutes. Remove the meat to a warmed oven platter, drain off the excess fat from the pan and deglaze the pan with the white wine. Scrape the bottom of the pan with a wooden spoon, and cook the wine and the pan juices down until there remains only about 1 tablespoon [15 ml.] of thickened glaze.

Over low heat, whisk the herbed cream into the pan glaze. Stir constantly until the sauce thickens (a matter of moments). Remove the pan from the heat, and whisk in the remaining 4 tablespoons [60 ml.] of butter, cut in chunks. Taste for seasoning. Pour the sauce over the chops and dish out individual portions.

JUDITH OLNEY
SUMMER FOOD

Sautéed Veal Scallops with Marsala Sauce

Scaloppine al Marsala

To serve 4

1½ lb.	veal scallops, sliced ⅜ inch [9 mm.] thick and flattened to ¼ inch [6 mm.]	¾ kg.
	salt and freshly ground black pepper	
	flour	
2 tbsp.	butter	30 ml.
3 tbsp.	olive oil	45 ml.
½ cup	dry Marsala	125 ml.
½ cup	chicken or beef stock	125 ml.
2 tbsp.	butter, softened	30 ml.

Season the veal scallops with salt and pepper, then dip them in flour and shake off the excess. In a heavy 10- to 12-inch [25- to 30-cm.] skillet, melt 2 tablespoons [30 ml.] of butter with the oil over moderate heat. Add the scallops, three or four at a time, and brown them for about 3 minutes on each side. Then transfer them to a heated plate.

Pour off the fat from the skillet. Add the Marsala wine and ¼ cup [50 ml.] of chicken or beef stock and boil the liquid briskly over high heat for 1 or 2 minutes, scraping up any browned fragments clinging to the bottom and sides of the pan. Return the veal to the skillet, cover the pan and simmer over low heat for 10 to 15 minutes, basting the veal now and then with the pan juices.

To serve, transfer the scallops to a heated platter. Add the remaining stock to the sauce in the skillet and boil briskly. When the sauce has reduced considerably and has the consistency of a syrupy glaze, taste it for seasoning. Remove the pan from the heat, stir in the softened butter and pour the sauce over the scallops.

FOODS OF THE WORLD/THE COOKING OF ITALY

Veal Cutlets with Ham and Cheese

Kalbsschnitzel Cordon Bleu

To serve 4

8	veal cutlets	8
	salt and pepper	
4	slices Swiss or Gruyère cheese, slightly smaller than the cutlets	4
4	thin slices ham, slightly smaller than the cutlets	4
1	egg, beaten	1
¼ cup	flour	50 ml.
½ cup	fine dry bread or cracker crumbs	125 ml.
3 tbsp.	butter	45 ml.
1 tbsp.	oil	15 ml.

Pound the veal cutlets with a meat mallet or the edge of a plate to flatten them, working in salt and pepper. Trim the edges. Place one slice of cheese and one slice of ham each over four of the cutlets, so that neither cheese nor ham overlaps the edges of the veal. Brush the edges of the veal with beaten egg; top each cutlet with another; pound the edges to seal them. Roll each veal "sandwich" in flour, dip it first in egg, then in crumbs. Sauté in a mixture of butter and oil until well browned. Transfer to a casserole or roasting pan, and place in an oven, preheated to 375° F. [190° C.], baking for 20 to 35 minutes.

BETTY WASON
THE ART OF GERMAN COOKING

Sautéed Veal Scallops

Frittura Piccata

To serve 6

1¼ lb.	veal scallops, cut ¼ inch [6 mm.] thick	⅔ kg.
	salt and pepper	
	flour	
8 tbsp.	butter	120 ml.
2 tbsp.	fresh lemon juice	30 ml.
1 tbsp.	chopped fresh parsley	15 ml.

Flavor the scallops with salt and pepper, and dust them lightly with flour. Melt 6 tablespoons [90 ml.] of the butter in a large skillet and brown the meat over high heat for 3 minutes on each side. Put the meat on a warmed serving plate.

Mix the remaining butter with the meat juices in the pan and cook over high heat until the butter takes on a nut-brown color. Finish the sauce by adding the lemon juice.

Pour the sauce over the veal, sprinkle with chopped parsley and serve immediately.

GIANNI BRERA AND LUIGI VERONELLI
LA PACCIADA

Veal Chops with Anchovies and Gherkins

Côtelettes de Veau à la Provençale

The orange juice called for in this recipe is traditionally squeezed from a bitter-flavored Seville orange. You can substitute sweet orange juice by mixing 2 tablespoons [30 ml.] of it with 1 tablespoon [15 ml.] of lemon juice.

To serve 4

4	thick veal rib chops	4
8	anchovy fillets, soaked in water for 10 minutes and patted dry	8
4	gherkins, cut into small strips	4
	salt and pepper	
3 tbsp.	olive oil	45 ml.
2 tsp.	finely chopped garlic	10 ml.
¼ lb.	fresh pork fat, thinly sliced	125 g.
Bitter-orange sauce		
4 tbsp.	butter	60 ml.
	salt and coarsely ground pepper	
2 tbsp.	chopped fresh parsley	30 ml.
3 tbsp.	finely chopped shallots	45 ml.
1 tbsp.	olive oil	15 ml.
1 tsp.	finely chopped garlic	5 ml.
3 tbsp.	fresh bitter-orange juice	45 ml.

Cut each chop along the grain in two places. Insert an anchovy fillet and a gherkin strip into each slit. Season the chops with salt and pepper, and marinate them for 2 to 3 hours in the 3 tablespoons [45 ml.] of oil and the 2 teaspoons [10 ml.] of chopped garlic. Pat the chops dry and press slices of pork fat onto both sides of each chop. Sauté the chops gently in a large skillet for about 15 to 20 minutes on each side. Remove the chops and discard the pork fat. Degrease the pan juices. Deglaze with a little water.

To make the sauce, melt the butter in the skillet and add salt, coarsely ground pepper, parsley and shallots. Cook rapidly for a short time, then add the tablespoon [15 ml.] of oil and the teaspoon [5 ml.] of chopped garlic. Return the chops to the pan, add the orange juice and heat gently. There should be only a little sauce—just enough to coat the chops.

BERTRAND GUÉGAN
LA FLEUR DE LA CUISINE FRANÇAISE

Veal Scallops with Prosciutto

Saltimbocca

To serve 4

4	veal scallops cut from the leg, each ¼ inch [6 mm.] thick	4
1	garlic clove, crushed	1
	salt and pepper	
4	sage leaves	4
4	thin slices prosciutto	4
2 tbsp.	butter	30 ml.
½ cup	Marsala or dry sherry	125 ml.

Flatten the veal scallops with a mallet. Rub them with garlic, and season with salt and pepper. Put a sage leaf on each scallop and top with a slice of prosciutto; keep the prosciutto in place with wooden picks. Sauté in a large skillet in hot butter until the veal and prosciutto are golden brown. Add the Marsala or sherry, then let the meat cook slowly, uncovered, over low heat for 15 to 20 minutes. Baste occasionally. Serve the scallops with the pan gravy.

BERYL GOULD-MARKS
THE HOME BOOK OF ITALIAN COOKERY

Veal Cutlets Milanese

Côtelette alla Milanese

To clarify butter, start with one third more butter than the amount specified in the recipe. Melt the butter over low heat, remove the pan from the heat, and let it stand until the milk solids settle. Spoon off the clear yellow surface liquid and strain it. Discard the milk solids.

To serve 4

4	veal cutlets, about ½ inch [1 cm.] thick	4
1	egg, lightly beaten	1
	bread crumbs	
7 tbsp.	clarified butter	105 ml.
	salt	
1	lemon, quartered lengthwise	1

Cut the edges of the meat at intervals to prevent the cutlets from curling up while they cook. Then flatten the cutlets slightly with a meat mallet. Dip the cutlets in the egg and then coat them with bread crumbs, pressing firmly with the palm of your hand so the crumbs will adhere.

Heat the butter in a skillet just large enough to hold the meat in one layer. Fry the cutlets over high heat so that a crust forms on one side; take care not to move them about during the cooking or the crust will break off. Then turn the cutlets over and fry until the crust forms on the other side. Lower the heat and cook gently for another 5 to 10 minutes. Only now do you salt them; earlier salting would have drawn moisture from the meat, softening the crust and causing it to break away. When the meat is cut to test it for doneness, the inside should be slightly moist. Serve with wedges of lemon.

OTTORINA PERNA BOZZI
VECCHIA MILANO IN CUCINA

Veal Scallops with Fennel

Escalopes de Veau au Fenouil

To serve 4

4	veal scallops	4
	butter or lard	
8 to 12	scallions	8 to 12
	fennel leaves, finely chopped	
	fresh lemon juice	

Brown the veal scallops in butter or lard. Add the scallions, cover the pan and simmer for 7 to 8 minutes. Throw in a handful of chopped fennel leaves; stir, and then add a squeeze of lemon. Excellent.

ELIZABETH DAVID
SUMMER COOKING

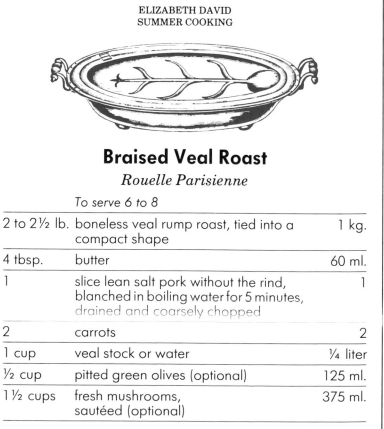

Braised Veal Roast

Rouelle Parisienne

To serve 6 to 8

2 to 2½ lb.	boneless veal rump roast, tied into a compact shape	1 kg.
4 tbsp.	butter	60 ml.
1	slice lean salt pork without the rind, blanched in boiling water for 5 minutes, drained and coarsely chopped	1
2	carrots	2
1 cup	veal stock or water	¼ liter
½ cup	pitted green olives (optional)	125 ml.
1½ cups	fresh mushrooms, sautéed (optional)	375 ml.

Butter a heavy fireproof casserole or *daubière*, and put in the veal with the salt pork and the carrots. Cover the casserole and place it over low heat. After 20 to 30 minutes the veal will be white and bathed in the stock produced by the meat juices. Continue cooking the veal slowly to evaporate this stock gradually.

After about 45 minutes to 1 hour, when only fat remains, remove the lid from the casserole and brown the veal over medium heat, turning it frequently. To prevent it from browning too much, moisten the veal frequently by adding the stock or water, 2 to 3 tablespoons [30 to 45 ml.] at a time. Cover the casserole again and cook the veal slowly over low heat for another 30 minutes.

When the meat has a good color and the cooking liquid is both fatty and gelatinous, remove the veal to a warmed platter. Strain the stock, then skim off the excess fat from the liquid and, if you wish, add the olives or mushrooms—or both—to the casserole. Pour a little of this sauce on top of the veal and serve the rest in a sauceboat. If you do not add the optional olive or mushroom garnish, serve the veal on a bed of sorrel, chicory, peas or mashed potatoes. Pour over a few spoonfuls of sauce and serve the rest separately.

TANTE MARGUERITE
LA CUISINE DE LA BONNE MÉNAGÈRE

Braised Veal

Fricandeau

For instructions on larding veal, see pages 56-57

	To serve 6 to 8	
3 lb.	veal rump or round in 1 piece, cut lengthwise along the grain	1½ kg.
½ lb.	fresh pork fat, cut into lardons and seasoned with salt and pepper	¼ kg.
	butter	
1 or 2	onions, sliced	1 or 2
1 or 2	carrots, sliced	1 or 2
	pepper	
2 cups	beef or veal stock	½ liter
1 cup	dry white wine	¼ liter
	salt	

Lard the meat and place it in a heavy fireproof casserole with a little butter. Set the casserole over medium heat. Turn the veal onto all surfaces for a few minutes without letting it brown. Add the sliced onion and carrot; season with pepper and add ⅓ cup [75 ml.] of stock and ⅓ cup of white wine. Raise the heat and boil to evaporate the excess liquid, but do not allow the veal to stick to the bottom of the casserole. When the cooking liquid has become syrupy, add the rest of the stock and the rest of the wine; then simmer, in the partially covered casserole, for 1¼ to 1½ hours. Baste the veal

as it cooks. Taste and complete the seasoning with salt and pepper if necessary.

Put the casserole in an oven, preheated to 425° F. [220° C.], and brown the fricandeau—that is, let it take on a brilliant, shiny, golden color—for 30 minutes. Baste frequently during this last procedure.

Place the fricandeau on a warmed platter, strain the sauce over it and serve hot, accompanied by sorrel, spinach or creamed chicory. Alternatively, the fricandeau may be served cold, coated with the jellied, strained pan juices.

ALI-BAB
ENCYCLOPEDIA OF PRACTICAL GASTRONOMY

Stuffed Veal Roast

Noix de Veau à l'Allemande

The caul used to wrap the veal and keep it moist as it cooks is the fatty membrane that surrounds a pig's stomach. You can order it from your butcher.

	To serve 6 to 8	
3 lb.	boneless veal rump or sirloin roast, slit lengthwise in 2 places	1½ kg.
4 tbsp.	butter	60 ml.
½ cup	veal stock	125 ml.
1	large piece caul	1
	Anchovy stuffing	
4 oz.	fresh pork fat, finely chopped	125 g.
3 or 4	anchovy fillets, soaked in cold water for 10 minutes, patted dry and finely chopped	3 or 4
2 tbsp.	finely chopped fresh parsley	30 ml.
	salt and pepper	
	grated nutmeg	
4 tbsp.	dried currants	60 ml.

To make the stuffing, mix thoroughly the pork fat, anchovies, parsley, salt, pepper, a little grated nutmeg and the currants. Fill the slits in the meat with the mixture. Close up the slits by pressing their edges together. Wrap the piece of veal in the caul and tie it up like a roast, with cotton string.

Put the butter in a large fireproof oval casserole set over moderate heat. When the butter has melted, put in the veal and brown it on all sides. Then cover the casserole, reduce the heat to low and cook for about 2 hours or until the meat is tender when pierced with a fork. If necessary, moisten the veal with stock, but use as little as possible.

Transfer the veal to a warmed dish. Degrease the sauce, reduce it to a coating consistency and pour it over the veal.

SUZANNE LABOURER AND X.-M. BOULESTIN
PETITS ET GRANDS PLATS

Pot-Roasted Veal, Swiss-Style

To serve 6

2 to 2½ lb.	boneless veal rump roast, rolled and tied	1 kg.
	salt and freshly ground black pepper	
	grated nutmeg	
2 oz.	prosciutto, Westphalian ham or *jambon de Bayonne*, cut into 6 thin slices	75 g.
¼ lb.	Gruyère cheese, cut into 6 thin slices	125 g.
¼ lb.	salt pork, blanched in boiling water for 5 minutes and drained, cut into long, thin strips	125 g.
8 tbsp.	butter	120 ml.
2	carrots, finely chopped	2
2	medium-sized onions, finely chopped	2
⅔ cup	dry white wine	150 ml.
1	garlic clove, crushed	1
3 tbsp.	brandy	45 ml.
30	small boiling onions, peeled	30
1 tbsp.	sugar	15 ml.
24	fresh white button mushrooms, thickly sliced	24
⅔ cup	heavy cream	150 ml.

For a really neat job, chill the veal thoroughly before slicing it, then let it come to room temperature before going ahead with the rest of the recipe.

Choose a long, thin cut of veal for roasting rather than a short one with a large diameter. Lay it on a board and, with a sharp knife, cut it into seven even-sized slices (that is, make six cuts) without separating the slices completely—just as you would a French loaf for garlic bread. Open the slices carefully and season generously between them with salt, freshly ground black pepper and a pinch of nutmeg.

Lay a slice each of ham and Gruyère cheese neatly in each cut. Pull the veal together again. Cover it with the salt pork and tie up securely with cotton string, first lengthwise and then horizontally in several places.

In a heavy fireproof casserole that will hold the meat comfortably, melt half of the butter and sauté the veal until it is nicely browned all over. Remove the veal from the casserole and keep it hot.

In the same fat, sauté the chopped carrots and onions until golden brown.

Meanwhile, combine the wine and garlic in a small pan and bring to a boil.

Lay the veal on top of the sautéed vegetables. Pour the brandy over it and ignite.

As soon as the flames have died down, add the boiling wine-and-garlic mixture to the casserole. Put a lid three

quarters on the pan and simmer over the lowest possible heat (diffused with a fireproof pad if you have one handy) for about 1 hour, or until the veal is tender but not overcooked.

Meanwhile, fit the onions into the bottom of a heavy pan that will take them in one layer (this is important; otherwise the onions will not glaze evenly). Add the sugar, 1 tablespoon [15 ml.] of butter, salt and freshly ground black pepper to taste, and just enough water to cover.

Bring to a boil and cook, uncovered, until the liquid has completely evaporated and the onions are a rich brown, tossing occasionally toward the end to glaze the onions evenly. Put aside. In another pan, sauté the mushrooms in 2 tablespoons [30 ml.] of butter for 4 to 5 minutes until tender and golden. Sprinkle with salt and freshly ground black pepper. Put the mushrooms aside.

When the veal is tender, remove it from the casserole; discard the strings and the pork fat and keep the meat hot on a heated serving dish while you finish the sauce.

Strain the sauce through a fine sieve, pressing some of the vegetables through as well. Return to the casserole; stir in the cream and reheat gently without boiling. Salt and pepper to taste. Combine the glazed onions and sautéed mushrooms in one pan and toss them together in the remaining butter for 2 to 3 minutes to heat them through.

To serve, garnish the veal with the onions and mushrooms. Spoon some of the sauce over the meat and vegetables, and serve the remainder in a heated sauceboat.

ROBERT CARRIER
THE ROBERT CARRIER COOKERY COURSE

Braised Veal Loin

Fricandeau

To serve 8 to 10

3½ lb.	boneless veal loin, cut with the grain into slices 1½ inches [4 cm.] thick	1½ kg.
¼ lb.	fresh pork fat, sliced ¼ inch [6 mm.] thick and cut into ¼-inch cubes	125 g.
2 oz.	fresh pork rind, chopped	75 g.
1	large onion, thickly sliced	1
1	large carrot, thickly sliced	1
1	bouquet garni	1
⅓ cup	dry white wine	75 ml.
2½ cups	chicken or veal stock	625 ml.

Cut two or three small gashes into one side of each veal slice and press into each one a pork-fat cube. Line a heavy, deep sauté pan with the pork rind, fatty side down, and cover with the onion, the carrot and the bouquet garni. Lay the slices of veal on top, side by side, with the larded surfaces uppermost. Cover the pan. Let the meat and vegetables sweat over low heat for 20 minutes. Then add the wine and continue to cook, uncovered. When the wine has been reduced by half, add ½ cup [125 ml.] of the stock. Reduce again until only about a tablespoon [15 ml.] of liquid is left. Add the rest of the stock—to reach the top of the meat—and bring it to a boil.

Cover the meat with a sheet of parchment paper or foil, and put the lid on the pan. Place the pan in an oven, preheated to 350° F. [180° C.], and simmer for 2½ hours, basting from time to time. When the meat is so tender that you can cut it with a spoon, transfer the veal to a warmed platter. Strain and degrease the stock, then reduce it, if necessary, to about a cupful. Pour it over the veal and serve.

MADAME SAINT-ANGE
LA BONNE CUISINE DE MADAME SAINT-ANGE

Veal Fricandeau

Fricandeau à l'Oseille

This dish is traditionally served with a creamed purée of sorrel, spinach or chicory.

For instructions on larding meat, see pages 56-57.

To serve 8 to 10

5 lb.	veal rump or round roast	2½ kg.
½ lb.	fresh pork fat, cut into lardons	¼ kg.
¼ lb.	lean salt pork with the rind removed, blanched in boiling water for 5 minutes, drained and thinly sliced	125 g.
¼ lb.	fresh pork rind	125 g.
3	carrots, chopped or sliced	3
2	large onions, chopped or sliced	2
1	bouquet garni	1
1 cup	water	¼ liter
	salt and pepper	
4 lb.	veal shank, sawed not chopped into ½-inch [1-cm.] pieces	2 kg.
½ cup	dry white wine or Madeira	125 ml.
1 cup	velouté sauce (recipe, page 168), made with veal stock	¼ liter

Without excessive trimming, split the veal lengthwise along its thinnest side. Do not slice all the way through: the meat should open like a book. Flatten the opened veal with a meat

mallet until it is uniform in thickness. Using a larding needle, lard the veal generously with strips of pork fat.

Line the bottom of a deep sauté pan or heavy casserole with the strips of salt pork and the pork rind, carrots, onions, bouquet garni and two or three pieces of the veal shank. Add the water, but do not include any stock. (This is important.) Season the veal with salt and pepper, and put it in the pan on top of the bones and aromatics. Spread the remaining pieces of bone over the veal. Press a sheet of buttered wax paper over the layer of bones and cover the pan tightly. Start cooking over fairly high heat, and—when the mixture reaches a boil—transfer to an oven, preheated to 375° F. [190° C.] and continue cooking.

There is no need to baste because the fats and water will evaporate and recondense on the bones covering the meat, automatically basting it. When the meat is tender—after about 2 hours—remove the veal and keep it hot. Remove the veal shank and deglaze the pan juices with white wine or Madeira. Reduce the liquid by half and add the hot veal stock. Strain the liquid through a fine sieve and degrease.

CURNONSKY
CUISINE ET VINS DE FRANCE

Veal in Milk

Il Vitello al Latte

To serve 6

2 lb.	boned veal shoulder, in 1 piece	1 kg.
5 tbsp.	butter	80 ml.
	fresh rosemary	
	fresh sage	
18	small boiling onions	18
	salt and freshly ground white pepper	
	grated nutmeg	
1½ quarts	milk	1½ liters

Spread 4 tablespoons [60 ml.] of the butter inside the bottom of a roasting pan, rub the veal with the rest of the butter and place the veal in the pan along with a few sprigs of rosemary and some sage leaves. Put the pan in an oven, preheated to 400° F. [200° C.], for 30 minutes. Turn frequently and baste the veal from time to time with the meat juices.

Remove the bouquet garni and put the veal in an ovenproof dish with a tightly fitting lid. Garnish the meat with onions and season it with salt, pepper and a pinch of nutmeg. Boil the milk and add enough to cover the ingredients. Put the lid on the dish and cook the veal in the oven at 350° F. [180° C.] for 2 hours. Remove the meat, slice and arrange it in a warmed, shallow serving dish. Sieve the cooking liquid and pour it over the slices of veal. Serve hot.

GIANNA BRERA AND LUIGI VERONELLI
LA PACCIADA

Braised Veal and Onions

Cul de Veau (Quasi) Sans Nom

To serve 10 to 12

4 to 5 lb.	veal sirloin or rump roast, including the bone	2 to 2½ kg.
2 tbsp.	Hungarian paprika	30 ml.
3	sage leaves, chopped	3
8 to 10	large onions, chopped	8 to 10
14 tbsp.	butter	210 ml.
	salt and pepper	
1	small bunch winter savory, tied together	1
1 cup	dry white wine	¼ liter

Mix the paprika and sage thoroughly into the onions. Melt the butter in an enameled cast-iron casserole over low heat. Add the onion mixture and toss gently, then place the veal on top. Salt and pepper it very lightly and add the savory. Cover the casserole and increase the heat to moderate. Allow the onions to sweat for about 30 minutes, taking care not to let them brown, since they would assume a harsh and bitter taste that would ruin the flavor of the dish; the onions and the veal should both be pale gold. Then transfer the casserole to an oven, preheated to 300° F. [150° C.]. Cook for about 1½ hours, moistening often with the wine. Veal rump, which is a white meat, needs to be fairly well done.

CURNONSKY
CUISINE ET VINS DE FRANCE

Veal Flemish-Style

Veau à la Flamande

To serve 4 to 6

2 lb.	veal round	1 kg.
4 tbsp.	butter	60 ml.
	salt and pepper	
1 cup	veal, chicken or beef stock	¼ liter
1 cup	dried prunes	¼ liter
1 cup	dried apricots	¼ liter
⅓ cup	raisins	75 ml.

Brown the veal in butter in a cooking pot. Season well and moisten with a little stock. Cover and allow to cook for about 1 hour, either over low heat or in an oven, preheated to 350° F. [180° C.]. Add the prunes, apricots and raisins. The liquid should cover the fruits completely; if it does not, pour in more stock. Cook for 30 minutes to 1 hour, or until the fruits are plump and tender, adding more stock if necessary.

SUZANNE LABOUREUR AND X.-M. BOULESTIN
PETITS ET GRANDS PLATS

Veal Breast with Mixed Meat Stuffing

La Pancetta Ripiena

The mortadella called for in this recipe is an Italian bologna obtainable from Italian food stores.

To serve 4

2 to 2½ lb.	boneless veal breast, with a pocket cut for stuffing	1 kg.
2½ oz.	prosciutto, thinly sliced	75 g.
2½ oz.	mortadella, thinly sliced and cut into strips 1½ inches [4 cm.] wide	75 g.
7 tbsp.	butter	105 ml.
	salt and pepper	
½ cup	dry white wine	125 ml.
4 to 5 tbsp.	veal stock	60 to 75 ml.

Mixed meat stuffing

½ lb.	lean pork, chopped	¼ kg.
1 oz.	prosciutto, chopped	50 g.
1 oz.	mortadella, chopped	50 g.
1	garlic clove, chopped	1
2 tbsp.	chopped fresh parsley	30 ml.
	salt and freshly ground white pepper	
	grated nutmeg	
2	eggs	2

To make the stuffing, mix together in an earthenware bowl the chopped pork, prosciutto, mortadella, garlic and parsley. Season with salt, pepper and a pinch of nutmeg, and bind the mixture with the eggs until it has a smooth consistency. Put a layer of this stuffing into the pocket formed in the meat. Put slices of prosciutto and mortadella in alternate layers over the stuffing. Spread on a second layer of stuffing and top it with slices of prosciutto and mortadella, and a third layer of stuffing if you have enough. Sew up the pocket with thick cotton thread to keep the stuffing in, and tie up the veal breast with crisscrossing string.

Coat the outside surfaces of the breast with half the butter. Melt the rest of the butter in a large fireproof casserole and put in the breast. Season with salt and pepper, and brown on both sides over high heat. Turn down the heat, cover the pan and continue to cook, moistening from time to time with a few tablespoons of mixed wine and stock.

When cooked, after about 2 hours, drain the meat, remove the string and thread, and place the breast on a hot platter. Strain the cooking liquid through a fine sieve. Reduce it, if necessary, to produce a syrupy sauce and pour it over the meat. Serve at once.

GIANNI BRERA AND LUIGI VERONELLI
LA PACCIADA

Stuffed Breast of Veal

If you have your butcher bone the breast of veal and make a pocket in it, be sure to ask him to give you the bones; you will use them as a rack on which to braise the meat. The bones, while serving as a rack to keep the meat off the bottom of the pan, also contribute a most distinctive flavor to the sauce.

To serve 6 to 8

4½ to 5 lb.	veal breast, boned, with a pocket cut for stuffing	2½ kg.
½ lb.	lean pork, ground	¼ kg.
½ lb.	lean beef, ground	¼ kg.
3 tbsp.	butter	45 ml.
½ cup	finely chopped shallots	125 ml.
1 lb.	spinach, parboiled, squeezed dry and chopped	½ kg.
½ tsp.	dried thyme	2 ml.
½ tsp.	dried marjoram	2 ml.
1½ tsp.	salt	7 ml.
¼ tsp.	freshly ground black pepper	1 ml.
½ cup	fresh bread crumbs	125 ml.
1	egg, lightly beaten	1
1	large onion	1
2	carrots	2
2 cups	water	½ liter

Preheat the oven to 400° F. [200° C.]. Pat the boned meat dry with paper towels and set it aside. Reserve the bones.

Place the ground meats in a medium-sized bowl, mix them together well and set aside.

Melt the butter in a small, heavy skillet over medium heat. When the butter is hot, stir in the shallots and let them cook for 2 or 3 minutes, or until they are transparent. Add the chopped spinach and, stirring with a wooden spoon, cook the mixture until it is dry and sticks slightly to the bottom of the pan. Remove the pan from the heat.

Add the mixture to the ground meats in the bowl. Add the thyme, marjoram, salt and pepper to taste, bread crumbs and beaten egg. Using a wooden spoon, mix the ingredients together until they are thoroughly combined. Pack the stuffing lightly into the pocket in the breast of veal.

To keep the stuffing in the pocket while the meat roasts, tie trussing cord around the veal in four to six places, ending each tie with a double knot before cutting the cord.

In a large roasting pan, arrange the bones like a rack. Set the stuffed veal on top of the bones. Add the onion and car-rots to the pan and cover tightly with aluminum foil. Place the casserole on the middle shelf of the oven and roast the veal for 30 minutes.

Add the water to the pan, cover the casserole and reduce the oven heat to 350° F. [180° C.]. Allow the roast to braise for 2 hours more.

To test for doneness, insert the tip of a sharp knife into the thickest part of the meat. If the juices run clear with no trace of pink, the veal is done; if not, cover the casserole, let the veal roast for about 10 minutes longer and test again. Transfer the veal to a large, heated serving platter. Cut away the trussing cords. Cover the meat loosely with aluminum foil and allow it to rest for 10 minutes before carving.

While the roast rests, skim the fat from the juices in the pan. Season the juices to taste with salt and pepper. Strain into a heated sauceboat and serve with the meat.

JOHN CLANCY AND FRANCES FIELD
CLANCY'S OVEN COOKERY

Stuffed Veal Roll, Transmontana

Trouxas de Vitela à Transmontana

To serve 6

3 lb.	veal breast, boned and trimmed	1½ kg.
3 oz.	*presunto*, prosciutto or smoked ham, finely chopped	100 g.
4 tbsp.	lard	60 ml.
6 tbsp.	finely chopped fresh parsley	90 ml.
1	garlic clove, finely chopped or crushed	1
	salt and freshly ground black pepper	
¾ cup	dry white wine	175 ml.

Open the veal breast as if it were a book and with a sharp knife, score the inside (bone side) crosswise, in lines about ⅛ inch [3 mm.] deep. Mix the *presunto*, 2 tablespoons [30 ml.] of the lard, 4 tablespoons [60 ml.] of the parsley, the garlic, 1 teaspoon [5 ml.] salt, and about ¼ teaspoon [1 ml.] pepper to make a paste. Spread this paste over the cut surface of the veal. Beginning at one of the narrow sides, roll up the veal tightly; skewer firmly or tie with cotton string. Season the meat surface with pepper and, lightly, with salt.

In a heavy, enameled casserole, slowly brown the veal on all sides in the rest of the lard. Add the wine, cover and simmer for 1 hour or until tender. Remove the veal to a carving board and allow to stand for 10 minutes before cutting into slices about ¼ inch [6 mm.] thick. Skim any excess fat off the pan juices. Taste the juices and add salt if necessary. Heat, add the remaining parsley and offer as a sauce for the veal slices. Serve with potatoes.

SHIRLEY SARVIS
A TASTE OF PORTUGAL

Shank of Veal with Masses of Garlic

Garrou de Veau en Pistache

To serve 6 to 8

3	veal shanks, cut into cross sections 1 inch [2½ cm.] thick	3
½ cup	walnut, olive or other vegetable oil, or 6 tbsp. [90 ml.] lard	125 ml.
3	large onions, thickly sliced	3
1	large carrot, thickly sliced	1
	bouquet garni	
½ cup	dry white wine	125 ml.
2 to 3 cups	veal stock, or enough to cover the meat	½ to ¾ liter
4	garlic bulbs	4
	salt and pepper	
	sliced brown bread	
	chopped fresh parsley	

Heat the oil or lard in a large braising pot. Brown the pieces of veal on both sides until they are a deep golden color. Remove the meat to a plate. Add the onions to the fat in the pot along with the carrots and bouquet garni. Toss them in the hot fat until golden brown. Tilt the pot and spoon off as much fat as you can.

Spread the vegetables evenly over the bottom of the pot and add the pieces of meat and the wine. Reduce over high heat. Add the veal stock. Slowly bring to a boil.

While waiting for the meat to boil, detach the cloves from the garlic bulbs and peel and crush them. Add them to the pot containing the veal. Salt and pepper to taste. Remove from the heat when the liquid boils and cover the meat with a layer of foil. Turn up the sides of the foil to form an inverted lid that will catch the steam and prevent it from diluting the sauce. Then cover with the pot lid and bake 1 to 1¼ hours in an oven, preheated to 325° F. [170° C.]. The meat is done when it pulls away from the bones and is easily pierced by a skewer that should also come out freely.

Remove the meat, vegetables and garlic cloves from the sauce; keep the meat and vegetables warm and reserve the garlic cloves on a separate dish. Discard the bouquet garni. Measure the sauce; there should not be more than 1½ cups [375 ml.] of very thick juice left. If there is more, pour the liquid into a pan and reduce it. (The sauce will need no thickening.) Return the onions and carrots to the sauce, if you desire; or purée them into the sauce, or strain the sauce clear—whatever you like best.

Toast the slices of bread lightly. Put the meat on a platter, pour the sauce over it and sprinkle with chopped parsley. Pass the bread with the meat and serve the garlic cloves separately so your guests can spread them on the bread.

MADELEINE M. KAMMAN
WHEN FRENCH WOMEN COOK

Veal Shank, Milanese-Style

Ossobuco alla Milanese

This dish is excellent served with a risotto alla Milanese: rice tossed in butter with onion, then cooked in dry white wine and chicken stock with a pinch of saffron, and mixed with grated Parmesan cheese.

To serve 6

6	slices veal shank, each 1½ inches [4 cm.] thick	6
8 tbsp.	butter	120 ml.
⅓ cup	flour	75 ml.
1	onion, chopped	1
1	carrot, chopped	1
1	rib celery, chopped	1
2	garlic cloves, chopped	2
1 tbsp.	chopped marjoram	15 ml.
1	small piece lemon peel	1
	salt and freshly ground white pepper	
½ cup	dry white wine	125 ml.
2	tomatoes, peeled, seeded and finely chopped	2
⅓ to ½ cup	veal stock	75 to 125 ml.
1 tbsp.	freshly grated lemon peel	15 ml.
1 tbsp.	freshly squeezed orange juice (optional)	15 ml.

Melt 6 tablespoons [90 ml.] of the butter in a skillet large enough to hold the veal pieces without crowding. Roll the meat in the flour and put it in the skillet over moderate heat to brown on both sides. Add the onion, carrot, celery, half the garlic, the marjoram and the piece of lemon peel, then season with salt and pepper. When the vegetables are lightly colored, pour in the wine and, over moderate heat, reduce it almost completely.

Add the tomatoes and approximately ⅓ cup [75 ml.] of stock. Cover the pan, lower the heat and simmer for 1½ hours. If necessary to prevent the juices from getting too thick, add a few more spoonfuls of stock.

A few minutes before the end of the cooking time, add the remaining garlic, the grated lemon peel, the remaining butter and, if liked, the orange juice (an optional but inspired variant, not from Milan). Stir the mixture and cook it lightly over moderate heat for a few minutes so that the flavors blend. Arrange the veal pieces in a ring on a warmed round platter, cover with the sauce and serve at once.

GIANNI BRERA AND LUIGI VERONELLI
LA PACCIADA

❧

Milanese Braised Veal Shank

Ossi Buchi alla Milanese

Osso buco, like most traditional dishes, is prepared with many variations. The author of this recipe proposes that this version, which contains no tomatoes, is the authentic one. To prepare risotto alla Milanese to accompany this dish, see the recipe for Veal Shank, Milanese-Style on page 158.

To serve 4

4	meaty veal shanks, 4 inches [10 cm.] long and 2 inches [5 cm.] thick	4
2 tbsp.	butter	30 ml.
2 tbsp.	flour	30 ml.
	salt and pepper	
1 cup	dry white wine	¼ liter
½ cup	hot beef stock	125 ml.

Gremolata

1 tbsp.	finely chopped fresh parsley	15 ml.
1	garlic clove, finely chopped	1
	yellow peel of 1 lemon, finely chopped	

Heat the butter in a heavy enameled casserole. Roll the shanks in seasoned flour and brown them thoroughly, turning them several times. Stand the shanks upright, so that the marrow in the bones will not fall out as the shanks cook. Pour the wine over them and cook uncovered for about 5 minutes. Add the hot stock, cover the pan and cook for about 1 hour, or until the meat is tender.

Ten minutes before serving, combine the parsley, garlic and lemon peel, and sprinkle the mixture over the bones. Cook 5 minutes longer. Check the sauce: if it is too thick, add a little more hot stock and butter, and blend well; if too thin, thicken it with about 1 tablespoon [15 ml.] of butter and ½ tablespoon [7 ml.] of flour kneaded into a smooth paste.

Risotto alla Milanese is the traditional accompaniment.

NIKA STANDEN HAZELTON
THE CONTINENTAL FLAVOUR

Veal Shank Stewed with Tomatoes and Garlic

Aillade de Jarret de Veau

To serve 4

1½ lb.	veal shank, cut lengthwise from the bone and sliced into strips 1 inch [2½ cm.] wide	¾ kg.
1 to 1½ tbsp.	lard or olive oil	15 to 22 ml.
	salt and pepper	
½ to ⅔ cup	veal or beef stock	125 to 150 ml.
3 tbsp.	fresh bread crumbs	45 ml.
1	garlic clove, finely chopped	1
	fresh lemon peel	
1 tbsp.	chopped fresh parsley	15 ml.

Tomato and herb sauce

2	medium-sized tomatoes, peeled and chopped	2
	salt and pepper	
	sugar	
	dried basil or marjoram	

First prepare a sauce from the tomatoes, stewed down to a pulp without the addition of any other liquid, but well seasoned with salt, pepper, sugar and dried basil or marjoram. Now brown the veal in lard or olive oil in a fireproof gratin dish or a heavy skillet. Season the meat, add the tomato sauce and the stock. Simmer uncovered on top of the stove for 15 minutes, then put the dish, with the lid on, in an oven at a very low setting, 275° F. [140° C.], for an hour. When the veal is tender, sprinkle over it the bread crumbs mixed with the garlic, a scrap of lemon peel and the parsley. Leave uncovered in the oven for another 10 to 15 minutes. There should be only a small amount of thickish sauce and the meat should have that sticky quality peculiar to stewed veal. Serve with rice.

ELIZABETH DAVID
FRENCH PROVINCIAL COOKING

Veal with Leeks

Sauté de Veau aux Poireaux

To serve 4

1 ¾ lb.	boned veal shank, cut into small cubes	875 kg.
½ cup	peanut oil	125 ml.
3 tbsp.	butter	45 ml.
	salt and pepper	
1 ¾ lb.	leeks, white part only, sliced	875 kg.
½ cup	dry white wine	125 ml.
1	bouquet garni	1
1 cup	milk	¼ liter
⅓ cup	raisins, soaked in cold water for 20 minutes and drained	75 ml.
1 tbsp.	fresh lemon juice	15 ml.

Heat the oil and butter in a heavy sauté pan large enough to hold the cubes of veal side by side. Season the veal cubes and sauté them in the pan over fairly high heat for about 15 minutes, turning them carefully until they are nicely colored. Reduce the heat to low, add the leeks and sweat them, covered, for 10 minutes without allowing them to color. Add the wine and the bouquet garni. Pour over the milk. Put on the lid, leaving the pan slightly uncovered, and cook for a further 30 minutes over low heat. When the veal is tender and the sauce is reduced to a coating consistency, remove the bouquet garni, add the raisins and the lemon juice. Adjust the seasoning and serve.

JEAN AND PIERRE TROISGROS
CUISINIERS À ROANNE

Veal Rolls with Bacon

Paupiettes de Veau au Bacon

To serve 4

1 lb.	veal round, cut in 4 slices ¼ inch [6 mm.] thick	½ kg.
12	slices bacon	12
	salt and pepper	
	flour	
2 tbsp.	butter	30 ml.
1	medium-sized onion, chopped	1
5	shallots, chopped	5
1 ⅓ cups	veal stock	325 ml.
1	bouquet garni of parsley and celery	1

Trim the veal of any fat or gristle, cover three quarters of each veal slice with bacon, season with salt and pepper, and roll up the veal slices with the bacon inside. Tie these *paupiettes* with cotton string and roll them in flour.

Dice the remaining bacon and cook in the butter along with any veal trimmings and the onion and shallots. When the onions are transparent, add the *paupiettes* and brown them. Add the veal stock and the bouquet, and simmer covered over very low heat for about 1½ hours.

Arrange the *paupiettes*, strings removed, on a platter. Strain the sauce over them and serve—accompanied by boiled potatoes that have been coarsely mashed with butter and browned under the broiler or in the oven; or serve plain mashed potatoes.

ALI-BAB
ENCYCLOPEDIA OF PRACTICAL GASTRONOMY

Veal Birds

Paupiettes de Veau

To produce fresh onion juice, chop an onion as finely as possible and squeeze in a dish towel; the juice will drip out.

To serve 6

12	veal scallops, sliced ¼ inch [6 mm.] thick, trimmed, flattened and cut into 4-by-2-inch [10-by-5-cm.] pieces	12
	trimmings from the veal slices, chopped	
2 oz.	salt pork with the rind removed, blanched in boiling water for 5 minutes, then drained and chopped	75 g.
½ cup	fine cracker crumbs	125 ml.
	salt and pepper	
	cayenne pepper	
1 tsp.	poultry seasoning	5 ml.
1 tbsp.	fresh lemon juice	15 ml.
1 to 2 tbsp.	fresh onion juice	15 to 30 ml.
1	egg, beaten	1
	water or veal stock	
	flour	
4 tbsp.	butter	60 ml.
2 cups	heavy cream	½ liter
12	small pieces toast	12
	fresh parsley	

Mix together the veal trimmings, salt pork and fine cracker crumbs. Season highly with salt, pepper, cayenne, poultry seasoning, lemon juice and onion juice. Moisten with the beaten egg and water or stock.

Spread each piece of veal with a thin layer of the mixture—avoid having the mixture come too close to the edges. Roll each slice and fasten with skewers. Sprinkle with salt and pepper, dredge with flour and fry in hot butter until the veal birds are golden brown.

Put the veal birds in a stewpan, add cream to half cover the meat, and cook slowly, turning the birds occasionally, for 20 minutes or until tender. Serve on small pieces of toast, straining the cream remaining in the pan over the birds and toast. Garnish with parsley.

FANNIE MERRITT FARMER
THE BOSTON COOKING-SCHOOL COOK BOOK

Hungarian Goulash

Szekely Gulyas

To serve 4 to 6

½ lb.	veal stew meat, trimmed of fat and cut into strips	¼ kg.
½ lb.	beef stew meat, trimmed of fat and cut into strips	¼ kg.
½ lb.	pork stew meat, trimmed of fat and cut into strips	¼ kg.
1	large onion, chopped	1
3 tbsp.	butter	45 ml.
5	medium-sized tomatoes, peeled and coarsely chopped	5
1	green pepper, halved, seeded, deribbed and chopped	1
	salt	
6	peppercorns	6
2	bay leaves	2
½ tsp.	capers	2 ml.
1 tbsp.	Hungarian paprika	15 ml.
1 tsp.	caraway seeds	5 ml.
½ cup	beef or veal stock	125 ml.
1½ lb.	sauerkraut	¾ kg.
1½ cups	sour cream	375 ml.

Fry the onion in the butter until brown and then add the tomatoes and green pepper. Cook for 15 minutes, very slowly, and then add the meat and seasonings. Add the stock and simmer, covered, for 30 minutes. Add the sauerkraut and cook for 1 hour longer. Before serving, add the sour cream.

ALICE B. TOKLAS
THE ALICE B. TOKLAS COOK BOOK

Veal Marengo

Potato flour, or potato starch, serves as a thickener for this classic stew. You can substitute 2 tablespoons [30 ml.] of all-purpose flour for 1 tablespoon [15 ml.] potato flour.

To serve 6 to 8

3 lb.	boned veal shoulder, sliced 2 inches [5 cm.] thick and cut into 2-inch cubes	1½ kg.
3 tbsp.	oil	45 ml.
1	medium-sized onion, chopped	1
½ cup	puréed tomato	125 ml.
1 tbsp.	potato flour	15 ml.
1 cup	dry white wine	¼ liter
2 cups	veal or beef stock	½ liter
1	garlic clove, crushed with 1 tsp. [5 ml.] salt	1
2	bay leaves	2
1 tsp.	dried thyme	5 ml.
	salt and pepper	
12	small white boiling onions	12
¼ lb.	fresh mushrooms, sliced	125 g.
3	tomatoes, peeled and quartered	3
	pitted ripe olives	
	finely chopped fresh parsley	

Preheat the oven to 350° F. [180° C.]. Heat the oil in a heavy casserole with a cover. Add the pieces of veal and cook, uncovered, over medium heat for 4 or 5 minutes. Add the onion to the veal and cook for 3 minutes.

Stir in the puréed tomato and the potato flour, and mix thoroughly. Gradually pour in the white wine and stock. Add the garlic, bay leaves, thyme, salt and pepper. Cover the casserole and transfer to the oven for 15 minutes.

Meanwhile, in a small skillet, cook the small onions until tender in the remaining stock and add them to the casserole with the mushrooms and tomatoes. Cook, covered, for another 30 minutes, or until the veal is tender. The length of time will depend upon the quality of the veal.

Just before serving, add the olives, and sprinkle the surface with parsley.

MAURICE MOORE-BETTY
COOKING FOR OCCASIONS

Veal with Garlic
Aillade de Veau

To serve 4

2 lb.	boneless veal cutlet or rump, sliced ¼ inch [6 mm.] thick and cut into 2-inch [5-cm.] squares	1 kg.
3 tbsp.	oil	45 ml.
1 tbsp.	soft fine bread crumbs	15 ml.
12	garlic cloves, peeled	12
½ cup	puréed tomatoes	125 ml.
	salt and pepper	
¾ cup	dry white wine	175 ml.

In a large skillet, brown the veal in the oil over moderate heat. Add the bread crumbs and garlic, then the puréed tomatoes. Season with salt and pepper. Stir in the wine. Cover and simmer over low heat for 1 hour. Serve with rice.

JEAN-NOËL ESCUDIER AND PETA J. FULLER
THE WONDERFUL FOOD OF PROVENCE

Williamsburg Veal Partridges

To serve 6

12	thin veal scallops, each weighing about 3 oz. [100 g.]	12
	flour	
3 to 4 tbsp.	vegetable oil or butter	45 to 60 ml.

Bread and herb stuffing

1 cup	dry bread crumbs	¼ liter
1	small onion, finely chopped and browned in butter	1
	salt and pepper	
½ tsp.	thyme	2 ml.
½ tsp.	marjoram	2 ml.
½ tsp.	basil	2 ml.
4 to 5 tbsp.	milk	60 to 75 ml.

Prepare the stuffing—made with the bread crumbs, the onion, salt, pepper and the herbs, all moistened with milk.

Lay about 1 tablespoon [15 ml.] of stuffing on each veal scallop, roll it up and skewer it together with two wooden picks stuck through diagonally to cross each other; keep the picks parallel with the rolls. Roll the veal rolls, or par-

tridges, in flour and brown in fat. As the veal partridges brown, place them in a baking dish.

Thicken the fat in the pan with flour, add enough hot water to make a smooth sauce. Pour the sauce over the veal, cover your baking dish and bake in a slow oven, preheated to 250° F. [120° C.], for 40 minutes. Serve with wild rice.

MRS. HELEN CLAIRE BULLOCK
THE WILLIAMSBURG ART OF COOKERY

Veal with Tuna Sauce
Vitello Tonnato

This dish should be cooked and fully assembled a day or two in advance and kept, covered, in the refrigerator so that the flavors will mingle. Remove the dish an hour before serving.

To serve 4 to 6

2 lb.	boned leg of veal	1 kg.
1	carrot, chopped	1
1	onion, chopped	1
1	rib celery, chopped	1
1	bay leaf	1
	salt	
3 or 4	peppercorns	3 or 4

Tuna sauce

3½ oz.	can tuna fish, preferably packed in olive oil	125 g.
3 or 4	anchovy fillets, soaked in cold water for 10 minutes and patted dry	3 or 4
¾ to 1 cup	olive oil	175 to 250 ml.
1 to 2 tsp.	fresh lemon juice	5 to 10 ml.
2 tbsp.	capers, rinsed and drained well	30 ml.
	pepper	

Tie the veal into a neat shape with string. Put it into a large pan and just cover it with water. Bring to a boil, skim, and add the vegetables, bay leaf, salt to taste and the peppercorns. Cover and simmer gently for 1½ to 2 hours, until the veal is tender. Remove the veal, allow it to cool, then slice it thinly. Arrange the slices, overlapping, on a deep platter.

To make the sauce, pound the drained tuna fish and the anchovy fillets to a paste in a mortar or purée them in a blender, and add enough oil by drops to make a thin mayonnaise. Add lemon juice to taste, the capers and pepper. Mix, correct the seasoning, then pour the sauce over the meat.

BERYL GOULD-MARKS
THE HOME BOOK OF ITALIAN COOKERY

Old-fashioned Veal Fricassee

Blanquette de Veau à l'Ancienne

To serve 4

2 lb.	veal breast or riblets, cut into pieces 2 inches [5 cm.] square	1 kg.
2 cups	small fresh mushrooms (about 6 oz. [200 g.])	½ liter
1 to 2 tbsp.	fresh lemon juice	15 to 30 ml.
¼ cup	water	50 ml.
5 tbsp.	butter	75 ml.
	salt and freshly ground pepper	
3	medium-sized carrots, cut into 1-inch [2½-cm.] lengths	3
2	medium-sized onions, 1 stuck with 2 or 3 whole cloves	2
	thyme or mixed spices	
1	bouquet garni of fresh parsley, 1 small rib celery and 1 bay leaf	1
20	small white boiling onions	20
1 tbsp.	flour	15 ml.
⅓ cup	heavy cream	75 ml.
3	egg yolks	3
	grated nutmeg	
	chopped fresh parsley	

Combine the mushrooms with most of the lemon juice, the water, 1 tablespoon [15 ml.] of the butter, and some salt and pepper. Boil them in a covered pan for 1 minute. Drain the mushrooms and set aside. Reserve their cooking liquid.

Arrange the pieces of veal in a heavy saucepan so that they take up a minimum of space. Pour in the mushroom cooking liquid and add enough cold water to cover the veal by about ⅓ inch [1 cm.]. Add salt. Bring the liquid to a boil over high heat and skim two or three times, adding small amounts of cold water each time the liquid returns to a boil. Add the carrots, the medium-sized onions, a large pinch of thyme or mixed spices and the bouquet garni, making sure that all are submerged. Regulate the heat to maintain a bare simmer, with the saucepan covered, for 1½ hours.

Meanwhile, put the boiling onions, with 2 tablespoons [30 ml.] of the butter, into a pan just large enough to hold the onions side by side in a single layer. Season the onions with salt and pepper, cover the pan and stew the onions gently for about 15 minutes, tossing them from time to time. They should be soft and slightly yellowed but not browned.

Strain the contents of the saucepan containing the meat through a large sieve placed over a bowl. Discard the onions and the bouquet garni. Put the bowl of liquid aside. Return the meat and carrots to their saucepan. Add the mushrooms and the boiling onions, and put the saucepan aside, covered.

Skim any fat from the surface of the liquid.

In another saucepan, melt the remaining butter over low heat, add the flour and cook for about 1 minute, stirring regularly without allowing the flour to brown. Pour in the cooking liquid from the meat all at once, whisking until it returns to a boil. Reduce the heat to maintain a simmer.

Over a period of about 20 minutes, skim off the light, fatty skin that repeatedly forms on the surface. Pour the resulting lightly thickened sauce over the meat and its vegetable garnish, and simmer, covered, for about 20 minutes.

Mix together in a bowl the cream and egg yolks. Add a little pepper and very little nutmeg. Slowly stir in a ladleful of the sauce and then, away from the heat, stir this mixture into the stew. Return the saucepan to medium-low heat, stirring constantly until the sauce is only thick enough to coat a spoon lightly; it must not approach a boil or it will curdle. Add a few drops of lemon juice; taste and add more if necessary. Sprinkle with chopped parsley; serve with rice.

RICHARD OLNEY
THE FRENCH MENU COOKBOOK

Shank of Veal, Bavarian-Style

Kalbshaxe auf Bayerische Art

To serve 4

1	large veal shank, trimmed of fat	1
1 quart	water	1 liter
1	carrot	1
1	turnip	1
1	onion	1
1	leek	1
1	rib celery	1
1	bouquet garni	1
1 tsp.	freshly grated lemon peel	5 ml.
	salt	
3 or 4	peppercorns	3 or 4
4 tbsp.	butter, melted	60 ml.

Combine the water, vegetables, bouquet garni, lemon peel, salt and peppercorns in a large pot, then add the cleaned and prepared veal shank, and bring to a boil over high heat. Skim off any scum that rises to the surface. Reduce the heat to low, cover and simmer for about 45 minutes. Remove the shank and, when it cools, brush it with butter, place it in a greased pan and brown it in an oven, preheated to 400° F. [200° C.], for 25 to 30 minutes. Baste the shank regularly with butter; it must be nicely colored. Transfer the shank to a warmed platter. Pour a little poaching broth into the pan, bring to a boil and pour over the shank as it is served.

GRETE WILLINSKY
KOCHBUCH DER BÜCHERGILDE

Veal Roll with Sauce

To serve 6

2½ lb.	veal breast in 1 piece, boned	1 kg.
	salt and pepper	
2	slices bacon or prosciutto	2
1	onion	1
1	garlic clove	1
1	carrot	1
3	sprigs parsley	3
1	rib celery	1

Egg and lemon sauce

8 tbsp.	butter	120 ml.
1 tbsp.	flour	15 ml.
1 cup	reserved poaching broth	¼ liter
2	egg yolks	2
1½ tbsp.	fresh lemon juice	22 ml.
	chopped fresh parsley	

Sprinkle the meat with salt and pepper, and place the bacon or prosciutto on the inner side of the meat. Roll the meat so that it forms a large sausage. Tie it with cotton string to keep its shape. Choose a large pan that will just hold the veal roll. Half fill the pan with water. Add the onion, garlic, carrot, parsley sprigs and celery. Add salt and pepper, and immerse the veal in the water, which should just cover the meat. Place the pan over high heat. When the water is boiling, reduce the heat to low, cover the pan and cook gently for about 1 hour, or until the meat is tender to the fork. If the water cooks off too much, add a little occasionally. When the meat is tender, remove it from the pan and set it aside. Strain the broth and discard the vegetables.

Melt the butter in a saucepan, add the flour and blend thoroughly. Add 1 cup [¼ liter] of the strained broth and cook for 5 minutes, stirring constantly. Add more broth if the sauce is too thick. Mix the egg yolks with a little broth and add to the sauce, stirring constantly. Pour the sauce into the large pan, then return the meat. Warm the meat (but do not boil the sauce) over low heat for 15 minutes. Remove the meat and slice it. Add lemon juice and chopped parsley to the sauce and serve poured over the meat.

ADA BONI
THE TALISMAN ITALIAN COOK BOOK

Veal Breast with Chard and Rice Stuffing
Poitrine de Veau Farcie

For instructions on how to prepare a breast of veal for stuffing, see pages 72-73. Instructions for making veal stock appear on pages 16-17.

To serve 6 to 8

3 lb.	veal breast, boned, with a pocket cut for stuffing	1½ kg.
6	hard-boiled eggs	6

Veal poaching stock

2 to 2½ lb.	veal bones	1 kg.
2	carrots, chopped	2
2	leeks, chopped	2
5 quarts	water	5 liters

Chard and rice stuffing

1¼ lb.	chard leaves (or substitute spinach leaves), ribs removed, parboiled for 5 minutes, drained and chopped	⅔ kg.
1 cup	raw unprocessed rice, cooked	¼ liter
2	slices stale bread with the crusts removed, soaked in warm water, then squeezed almost dry	2
4 oz.	lean salt pork, blanched in boiling water for 5 minutes, drained and chopped	125 g.
1	garlic clove, chopped	1
2	shallots, chopped	2
2	eggs	2
2 tbsp.	olive oil	30 ml.
	salt and pepper	

Simmer the veal bones, carrots and leeks in the water for 2 hours to make a veal stock. Strain and degrease.

Mix together all the stuffing ingredients, seasoning the mixture lightly with salt and pepper. Line the pocket in the veal with the stuffing, then lay the hard-boiled eggs end to end along the center of the pocket. Sew up the opening carefully, using fine cotton string and a trussing needle.

Heat the stock in a large heavy pot until it is tepid, then put the stuffed veal into the stock and gradually heat it to the boiling point. Simmer, covered, for about 1½ hours or until the veal is tender. Serve the veal either hot or cold, cut crosswise into ½-inch slices with a circle of hard-boiled egg at the center of each slice.

RAYMOND ARMISEN AND ANDRÉ MARTIN
LES RECETTES DE LA TABLE NIÇOISE

Veal Pudding, German-Style

Kalbfleisch Pudding

To serve 4

½ lb.	lean ground veal	¼ kg.
10 to 12	anchovy fillets, soaked in water for 10 minutes, drained and patted dry	10 to 12
3	egg yolks	3
5 tbsp.	butter	75 ml.
½ tbsp.	capers, rinsed and drained well	7 ml.
½ cup	heavy cream	125 ml.
10	rusks, grated	10
3	egg whites, stiffly beaten	3
	salt and pepper	

Grind the veal and anchovies together, then place them in a bowl and mix in the egg yolks, butter and capers. Add the cream and rusks, season with salt and pepper, and fold in the egg whites. Put the mixture in a greased 1-quart [1-liter] mold or pudding basin. Place the mold in a pan and set it in an oven, preheated to 300° F. [150° C.]. Pour enough hot water into the pan to reach two thirds of the way up the mold. Bake the pudding for 1½ hours or until a knife inserted into the center comes out clean.

JUTTA KÜRTZ
DAS KOCHBUCH AUS SCHLESWIG-HOLSTEIN

Veal Meatballs in Beer Sauce

Gehaktballen in Biersaus

To serve 4

1¼ lb.	ground veal	⅔ kg.
2	slices white bread, crusts removed	2
1 cup	beer	¼ liter
4 tbsp.	butter	60 ml.
1	small onion, chopped	1
1	garlic clove, crushed	1
1	egg, lightly beaten	1
	salt and pepper	
	grated nutmeg	
1 tbsp.	fresh lemon juice	15 ml.
1 tsp.	sugar	5 ml.
1 tbsp.	chopped fresh parsley	15 ml.

Soak the bread in ¼ cup [50 ml.] of the beer, then squeeze the bread dry. Melt 2 tablespoons [30 ml.] of the butter in a skillet, and sauté the onion and garlic over moderate heat until they are transparent. Mix the veal in a bowl with the soaked bread, the onion, garlic, egg, salt, pepper and a little nutmeg. Shape the mixture into eight patties and brown them all over in the skillet, using the remaining butter. Pour in the rest of the beer and the lemon juice. Add the sugar, cover and simmer for 30 minutes.

Using a slotted spoon, transfer the meatballs to a heated platter. Reduce the sauce by a quarter over high heat. Pour the sauce through a sieve over the meatballs and sprinkle with parsley.

Serve with French-fried potatoes, salad and cold beer.

HUGH JANS
VRIJ NEDERLAND

Veal Pudding, Spanish-Style

Budín de Ternera

To serve 4 to 6

1 lb.	ground veal	½ kg.
4 tbsp.	butter	60 ml.
⅓ cup	freshly grated Parmesan cheese	75 ml.
1	slice firm-textured, white bread with the crusts removed, soaked in milk and squeezed almost dry	1
1	red pepper, peeled, halved, seeded, deribbed and chopped	1
1	large tomato, peeled and chopped	1
4	eggs, lightly beaten	4
	salt	
	grated nutmeg	
1 to 2 tbsp.	dry bread crumbs	15 to 30 ml.
2 cups	béchamel sauce *(recipe, page 169)* or tomato sauce *(recipe, page 169)*	½ liter

Melt the butter in a saucepan (keeping aside a little for greasing the mold). Fry the veal lightly and put it in a bowl. Add the cheese, bread, pepper, tomato and eggs to the veal. Season with salt and a pinch of nutmeg, and mix well. Grease a 1-quart [1-liter] mold and sprinkle it with bread crumbs. Pour in the veal mixture and bake in a moderate oven, preheated to 350° F. [180° C.], for 1 hour. Turn the veal pudding out of the mold onto a warmed platter, and cover it with béchamel sauce or tomato sauce.

VICTORIA SERRA
TIA VICTORIA'S SPANISH KITCHEN

Veal-Sour Cream Meat Loaf

To serve 6

1½ lb.	ground veal	¾ kg.
½ lb.	ground pork	¼ kg.
2 tbsp.	grated onion	30 ml.
2	carrots, finely grated	2
1 tsp.	finely chopped fresh sage (or substitute ½ tsp. [2 ml.] dried sage)	5 ml.
1½ tsp.	salt	7 ml.
¼ tsp.	freshly ground black pepper	1 ml.
½ tsp.	freshly grated lemon peel	2 ml.
½ cup	sour cream	125 ml.

Preheat the oven to 350° F. [180° C.]. Mix all the ingredients together and pack them into a 9-by-5-by-3-inch [23-by-13-by-8-cm.] loaf pan. Bake in the oven for 1½ hours.

JEAN HEWITT
THE NEW YORK TIMES HERITAGE COOK BOOK

Veal Croquettes

Croquettes de Veau

To serve 6

1½ cups	leftover roast veal, trimmed of skin and gristle, and ground	375 ml.
3 cups	béchamel sauce (recipe, page 169)	¾ liter
1½ cups	fresh mushrooms, coarsely chopped and squeezed dry in a towel	375 ml.
	salt and pepper	
6	fresh tarragon leaves, finely chopped	6
2	egg yolks	2
2	eggs, lightly beaten	2
	fine dry bread crumbs	
2 tbsp.	fresh lemon juice	30 ml.

Make the béchamel sauce and cook the mushrooms in it for 2 minutes. Season with salt and pepper, and add the tarragon and the veal. Remove the pan from the heat and beat in the egg yolks. Spread the mixture on a baking sheet or marble surface to cool and thicken.

Form the mixture into oval croquettes the size of large eggs. Dip the croquettes into the beaten eggs and then roll them in the bread crumbs. Fry them in deep fat at 375° F. [190° C.] for 2 to 3 minutes or until crisp and golden brown. Drain them on paper towels and serve very hot, sprinkled with lemon juice. Serve with a green salad.

MAPIE, THE COUNTESS DE TOULOUSE-LAUTREC
LA CUISINE DE FRANCE

Veal Ring Soufflé Celestine

To serve 4 or 5

3 cups	chopped leftover roasted or braised veal	¾ liter
4 tbsp.	butter or lard	60 ml.
¼ tsp.	anchovy paste	1 ml.
⅓ cup	flour	75 ml.
½ cup	leftover veal gravy	125 ml.
¾ cup	hot scalded milk	175 ml.
¼ cup	dry sherry	50 ml.
1 tbsp.	finely cut fresh parsley	15 ml.
1 tbsp.	finely cut fresh chives	15 ml.
1 tbsp.	finely chopped onion	15 ml.
1 tbsp.	finely chopped green pepper	15 ml.
	salt and pepper	
	grated nutmeg	
	dried thyme	
3	eggs, yolks separated from the whites	3
2 tbsp.	cold milk	30 ml.
½ tsp.	finely grated lemon peel	2 ml.
	fine dry bread crumbs	

In a saucepan heat the butter or lard together with the anchovy paste. Blend in the flour and, when smooth, stir in the veal gravy, the scalded milk and the sherry, stirring constantly over low heat. When the mixture just begins to bubble, add the veal with the parsley, chives, onion and green pepper. Season to taste with salt, pepper, nutmeg and thyme. Boil for 3 to 4 minutes, stirring constantly.

Remove the pan from the heat, stir in the egg yolks, which have been mixed with the cold milk and then well beaten. Lastly, fold in the stiffly beaten egg whites, which have been flavored with the lemon peel.

Turn the mixture, sprinkled with the bread crumbs, into a generously buttered ring mold. Bake in a moderate oven, preheated to 350° F. [180° C.], for 45 to 50 minutes or until the soufflé is well risen, firm to the touch and a golden brown. Turn out the soufflé onto a heated platter; if you like, fill the center with creamed celery just before serving.

LOUIS P. DE GOUY
THE GOLD COOK BOOK

Baked Veal

To serve 3 or 4

½ lb.	leftover roast veal, ground	¼ kg.
5	bacon slices, finely chopped	5
1½ cups	dry bread crumbs	375 ml.
1 cup	veal gravy (or substitute velouté sauce, recipe, page 168)	¼ liter
½ tsp.	grated lemon peel	2 ml.
1	blade mace, pounded (or substitute ½ tsp. [2 ml.] ground mace)	1
	salt	
	cayenne pepper	
4	eggs, beaten	4

Mix the ground veal with the bacon. Add the bread crumbs, gravy and seasoning, and stir these ingredients well together. Add the eggs and mix the whole well together. Put into a greased ovenproof dish and bake in the oven at 350° F. [180° C.] for 45 minutes to 1 hour. When liked, a little good gravy may be served in a tureen as an accompaniment.

MRS. ISABELLA BEETON
THE BOOK OF HOUSEHOLD MANAGEMENT

Minced Veal and Oysters

To serve 4 to 6

1 lb.	leftover veal loin roast, trimmed and finely chopped	½ kg.
	salt	
	cayenne pepper	
	ground mace	
2 cups	white sauce (recipe, page 169)	½ liter
36	small oysters, shucked and their liquor reserved	36
	croutons, made by frying small pieces of bread in butter, or *fleurons* (flower shapes cut from puff pastry and baked)	

Sprinkle salt, cayenne pepper and mace over the veal. Heat the veal in the white sauce without allowing it to boil. At the moment of serving, mix with it the oysters plumped in their own strained liquor. Garnish the finished dish with pale fried croutons or with pastry *fleurons*.

One cup [¼ liter] mushrooms, finely chopped and stewed in a little butter for 10 to 12 minutes, may be mixed with the veal instead of the oysters; if the mushrooms are very small, they may be left whole.

ELIZABETH RAY (EDITOR)
THE BEST OF ELIZA ACTON

Standard Preparations

Short-Crust and Rough Puff Pastry

One simple formula produces dough for both plain short-crust pastry and for rough puff pastry. The difference is in how you roll it out.

To make enough pastry to line or cover an 8-inch [20-cm.] pie

1 cup	flour	¼ liter
¼ tsp.	salt	1 ml.
8 tbsp.	unsalted butter, cut into small bits and chilled	120 ml.
3 to 4 tbsp.	cold water	45 to 60 ml.

Mix the flour and salt in a mixing bowl. Add the butter and cut it into the flour rapidly, using two table knives, until the butter is in tiny pieces. Do not work for more than a few minutes. Add half the water and, with a fork, quickly blend it into the flour-and-butter mixture. Add just enough of the rest of the water to enable you to gather the dough together into a firm ball. Wrap the dough in plastic wrap or wax paper and refrigerate it for 2 to 3 hours, or put it in the freezer for 20 minutes until the outside surface is slightly frozen.

To roll out short-crust pastry: Remove the ball of pastry dough from the refrigerator or freezer and put it on a cool, floured surface (a marble slab is ideal). Press out the dough partially with your hand, then give it a few gentle smacks with the rolling pin to flatten it and render it more supple. Roll out the dough from the center, until the pastry forms a circle about ½ inch [1 cm.] thick. Turn the pastry over so that both sides are floured and continue rolling until the circle is about ⅛ inch [3 mm.] thick. Roll the pastry onto the rolling pin, lift it up, and unroll it over the pie dish. If using the pastry to line a pie pan, press the pastry firmly against all surfaces and trim the edges. If using the pastry to cover a pie, trim the pastry to within ½ inch of the rim. Turn under the edges of the pastry around the rim to form a double layer and press the pastry firmly to the rim with thumb and forefinger to crimp the edges.

To roll out rough puff pastry: Place the dough on a cool, floured surface and smack it flat with the rolling pin. Turn the dough over to make sure that both sides are well floured. Roll out the pastry rapidly into a rectangle about 1 foot [30 cm.] long and 5 to 6 inches [13 to 15 cm.] wide. Fold the two short ends to meet each other in the center, then fold again to align the folded edges with each other. Following the direction of the fold lines, roll the pastry into a rectangle again, fold again in the same way and refrigerate for at least 30 minutes. Repeat this process two or three more times before using the pastry. Always let the pastry dough rest in the refrigerator between rollings.

Suet Pastry

*To make enough pastry for a 1 to 1½ quart
[1 to 1½ liter] double-crust pudding*

4 cups	flour	1 liter
½ lb.	beef suet, finely chopped (about 2 cups [½ liter])	¼ kg.
	salt	
¾ to 1¼ cups	cold water	175 to 300 ml.

Using your fingers, combine the flour, suet and a pinch of
salt in a mixing bowl. Add the water, a tablespoon [15 ml.] or
so at a time, stirring with a fork until the dough has a firm
consistency. Knead well, then roll out on a floured surface to
the desired thickness.

Note: to make enough pastry for an 8- or 9-inch single-
crust pie, reduce the quantity of each ingredient to one
half of the amount shown.

Wine-Merchant Butter

Beurre Marchand de Vins

To make about 1 cup [¼ liter] butter

½ cup	dry red wine	125 ml.
1 tbsp.	finely chopped shallots	15 ml.
12 tbsp.	butter, softened	180 ml.
1 tbsp.	strained fresh lemon juice	15 ml.
1 tbsp.	finely chopped fresh parsley	15 ml.
	salt and freshly ground pepper	

Put the wine and shallots into a fireproof earthenware casserole or an enameled or stainless-steel pan. Simmer, uncovered, over low heat for 20 to 30 minutes, or until the liquid is
reduced by two thirds. Set aside to cool for 5 to 10 minutes. In
a bowl, stir together the butter, lemon juice and parsley, and
gradually whisk in the reduced wine-and-shallot mixture.
Add salt and pepper to taste. The butter should have a
creamy consistency; it should not be chilled before serving.

Velouté Sauce

To make 1½ to 2 quarts [1½ to 2 liters] sauce

4 tbsp.	butter	60 ml.
¼ cup	flour	50 ml.
2 quarts	veal or chicken stock	2 liters

Melt the butter in a heavy saucepan over low heat and stir in
the flour until this roux mixture is smooth. Cook, stirring
constantly, for 2 to 3 minutes. When the roux stops foaming
and is a light golden color, pour in the stock and whisk con-
tinuously until the mixture reaches a boil. Move the saucepan half off the heat, so that the liquid on one side of the pan
maintains a steady, but very light boil. Skim off fat and
impurities that form on the surface of the other, calm side of
the liquid. From time to time spoon off the skin. Cook for 30
minutes or until the sauce is the desired consistency.

Béarnaise Sauce

To make about 1 cup [¼ liter] sauce

½ cup	dry white wine	125 ml.
¼ cup	white wine vinegar	50 ml.
2	shallots, finely chopped	2
	cayenne pepper or 1 small dried red chili	
1	sprig tarragon	1
1	sprig chervil	1
3	egg yolks	3
16 tbsp.	unsalted butter, cut into small bits and brought to room temperature	240 ml.
1 tsp.	finely chopped tarragon	5 ml.
1 tsp.	finely chopped chervil	5 ml.
	salt and freshly ground pepper	

Put the wine, vinegar and shallots in a fireproof earthenware casserole, a heavy enameled saucepan or the top part of
a glass or stainless-steel double boiler set over hot, not boiling, water. Add a pinch of cayenne or the chili, and the sprigs
of tarragon and chervil. Place the pan over low heat and
simmer the mixture for 15 to 20 minutes, or until only 3 to 4
tablespoons [45 to 60 ml.] of syrupy liquid remain. Strain the
liquid into a bowl, pressing the juices from the herbs, then
return the liquid to the pan.

Reduce the heat to very low and whisk in the egg yolks.
After a few seconds, whisk in one third of the butter and
continue whisking until it is absorbed. Repeat this procedure twice more, whisking until the sauce begins to thicken.
Remove the pan from the heat and continue whisking: the
heat of the pan will continue to cook and thicken the sauce.
Stir in the chopped herbs and season the sauce with salt and
pepper to taste.

Tomato Sauce

When fresh ripe tomatoes are not available, use 3 cups [¾ liter] drained, canned plum tomatoes.

To make about 1 ½ cups [375 ml.] sauce

6	very ripe medium-sized tomatoes, chopped	6
1	onion, diced	1
1 tbsp.	olive oil	15 ml.
1	garlic clove (optional)	1
1 tsp.	chopped fresh parsley	5 ml.
1 tsp.	mixed basil, marjoram and thyme	5 ml.
1 to 2 tsp.	sugar	5 to 10 ml.
	salt and freshly ground pepper	

In a large enameled or stainless-steel saucepan, gently fry the diced onion in the oil until soft, but not brown. Add the other ingredients and simmer for 20 to 30 minutes, or until the tomatoes have been reduced to a thick pulp. Sieve, pushing the vegetables through with a wooden pestle or spoon. Reduce the sauce further, if necessary, to the required consistency and taste to check the seasoning.

Basic White Sauce

Use this recipe whenever béchamel sauce is called for.

To make about 1 ½ cups [375 ml.] sauce

2 tbsp.	butter	30 ml.
2 tbsp.	flour	30 ml.
2 cups	milk	½ liter
	salt	
	white pepper	
	freshly grated nutmeg (optional)	
¼ cup	heavy cream (optional)	50 ml.

Melt the butter in a heavy saucepan. Stir in the flour and cook, stirring, over low heat for 2 to 5 minutes until the mixture is a smooth paste. Do not let the mixture brown. Pour in all the milk, whisking constantly to blend the mixture smoothly. Raise the heat and continue whisking until the sauce comes to a boil. Season very lightly with salt. Reduce the heat to very low and simmer for about 40 minutes, stirring frequently to prevent the sauce from sticking to the pan. Add white pepper and a pinch of nutmeg if desired; taste for seasoning.

When the sauce has thickened and you cannot taste the flour, whisk again until the mixture is perfectly smooth. Add the heavy cream if you prefer a richer and whiter sauce.

Veal Stock

To make 2 to 3 quarts [2 to 3 liters] stock

1	veal shank bone, sawed into 2-inch [5-cm.] pieces	1
4 lb.	meaty veal trimmings (neck, shank or rib tips)	2 kg.
3 to 5 quarts	water	3 to 5 liters
4	carrots, scraped	4
2	large onions, 1 stuck with 2 or 3 cloves	2
1	whole garlic bulb, unpeeled	1
1	rib celery	1
1	leek, split and washed	1
1	large bouquet garni	1
	salt	

Put the meat and bones into a heavy stockpot. Add cold water to cover by 2 inches [5 cm.]. Bring to a boil over low heat, but start skimming off the gray scum that rises to the surface before the liquid reaches a boil. Keep skimming, occasionally adding cold water to keep the meat covered. Do not stir up the bones and meat; you may cloud the stock.

When no more scum appears, add the vegetables, bouquet garni and a dash of salt to the pot, pushing the vegetables down into the liquid so that everything is submerged. Again bring to a boil, reduce the heat to very low and cook, uncovered, at a bare simmer for 4 hours, skimming occasionally to remove any additional scum that rises to the surface.

Strain the stock by pouring the contents of the pot through a colander into a large bowl or clean pot. Discard the bones, veal pieces, vegetables and bouquet garni. Cool the strained stock and degrease it. If there is any residue at the bottom of the container after the stock cools, decant the clear liquid carefully and discard the sediment.

Beef Stock

Beef stock can be prepared in the same way as veal stock. Substitute 4 pounds [2 kg.] of oxtail or beef shank or chuck for the meaty veal trimmings, but use the veal shank bone—omitting the bone only if a less gelatinous stock is desired. Simmer the stock for at least 5 hours. Alternatively, an excellent beef stock may be obtained by simply straining the broth reserved from pot-au-feu (*demonstration, pages 68-69, recipe, page 129*).

Recipe Index

All recipes in the index that follows are listed by English titles except when a dish of foreign origin, such as sukiyaki, is universally recognized by its source name. Entries are organized by beef and veal and also by major ingredients specified in recipe titles. Sauces, marinades and stuffings are listed separately. Foreign recipes are listed under the country or region of origin. Recipe credits are on pages 174-176.

General Index/ Glossary

Included in this index to the cooking demonstrations are definitions, in italics, of special culinary terms not explained elsewhere in this volume. The Recipe Index begins on page 170.

Shanks, veal, 10; braised, 54; marrow from, 54; osso *buco,* 54
Short ribs, beef, 68, 82
Sirloin steak, 9; broiling time, 29; carving, 33; charcoal broiled, 26; for tartar, 80
Sirloin tip: high-heat roasting, 20; roasting temperature and time, 22; sectioning of, 13, 14
Skewering: kebabs, 34; steaks, 30
Standing rib, 8; carving, 20-21; combined-heat roasting of, 20-21; roasting temperature and time, 22; sectioning of, 13, 15
Steaks: broiling, 27, 28-34; broiling time for, 29; carving, 33; oiled before broiling, 30, 32; pan frying, 38-39; peppery crust and creamy coating for, 39; prepared for broiling, 30; sauces for, 35; searing, 27, 30, 31; stages of doneness, 28, 29; thickness of, 30; wine-and-marrow topping, 39. See also Broiling

Stock: beef, 53; cuts for, 16; gelatinous, 16-17, 49; veal, 16-17, 53
Stuffings: for breast of veal, 72; for hamburgers, 43; for meat rolls, 61; for oxtail, 64; as side dish, 72
Suet, 6, 78; pastry, 78
Swiss steak, 50
Tartar steak, 40, 80
T-bone steak, 9; broiling time, 29; carving, 33
Tenderloin, beef, 9; broiling time, 29; charcoal broiled, 26; high-heat roasting, 20; poached in pot-au-feu stock, 69; roasting temperature and time, 22; for tartar steak and Carpaccio steak, 80; tied for poaching, 69; whole, sectioning of, 13
Top-loin steak boneless, 9, 36, 39; charcoal broiled, 26
Top round, 9; for Carpaccio steak, 80; roasting temperature and time, 22
Tournedos, 13
Trussing. See Tying

Tying: beef tenderloin for poaching, 69; meat for pot-au-feu, 68; a roast, 14, 22, 24, 58; stuffed meat rolls, 61
Veal, 5, 6, 7; barding for roasting, 24; blanquette of, 70-71; boning breast of, 72; braising, 54, 61, 62-63; broiling time for chops and cutlets, 29; butter or oil for pan frying, 44; chopped by hand, 40-41; coated with mustard and cream, 24, 25; coating and scoring cutlets, 46-47; color of, 6, 12; cutlets, deep-fried, 37, 46-47; cuts for braising, 54; cuts for roasting, 24; fricandeau, 48, 55, 62; larding, 62; leftovers, use of, 88; marinating cutlets, 46; marrow from shank bones, 54; osso *buco,* 54; pan-fried, variations of, 45; poaching, 70-73; pot roast, 62, 63; pounding, 44; pressing scallops, 44; pudding, 88; refrigerating and freezing, 15; roasting, 19, 24-25; roasting time and temperature, 24; rolls, 44, 61; round

steak, 12; scallops, pan-fried, 37, 44-45; searing, 44; stock, 16-17, 53; stuffed breast, 72-73; temperatures and timings for frying, 44, 47; tying a roast, 24; wholesale and retail cuts, 6-7, 10-11
Vegetables: aromatic, 16, 50, 54, 58, 68; in braises, 50, 52, 54, 55, 58; for garnish, 55, 59, 63, 68, 69, 70, 71, 73, 74, 75; for hamburger stuffing, 43; for hash, 84-85; for kebabs, 34; mirepoix, 50; pinched, 58; root, 55
Velouté sauce, 70; cleansing, 70
Wine: bottom-round roast marinated in, 58; for braising, 53, 54, 58, 62; as deglazing liquid, 38; and marrow topping for steaks, 39; in poaching liquid, 67, 72; selection of, to serve with various dishes, 7
Wine-merchant butter, 35
Zest: *the scraped or grated, colored outer peel of citrus fruits, not including the bitter white pith underneath.*

Recipe Credits

The sources for the recipes in this volume are shown below. Page references in parentheses indicate where the recipes appear in the anthology.

Ainé, Offray, *Le Cuisinier Méridional.* Imprimeur-Libraire, 1855(94,100,122).
Ali-Bab, *Encyclopedia of Practical Gastronomy.* (English Translation). Translated by Elizabeth Benson. Copyright © 1974 by McGraw-Hill, Inc. Published by McGraw-Hill Book Company, N.Y. By permission of McGraw-Hill Book Co.(153,160).
Allen, Ida Bailey, *Best Loved Recipes of The American People.* Copyright © 1973 by Ruth Allen Castelli. Published by Doubleday Publishing Co. Reprinted by permission of Doubleday Publishing Co.(131).
American Heritage, the editors of, *The American Heritage Cookbook.* © 1964 American Heritage Publishing Company, Inc. Published by American Heritage Publishing Company, Inc., N.Y. Reprinted by permission of American Heritage Publishing Company, Inc.(135,140).
Anderson, Jean, *The Grass Roots Cookbook.* Copyright © 1977 by Jean Anderson. Published by TIMES BOOKS. Reprinted by permission of TIMES BOOKS, a division of Quadrangle/The New York Times Book Co., Inc.(105).
Armisen, Raymond & André Martin, *Les Recettes de la Table Niçoise.* © Librairie Istra 1972. Published by Librairie Istra, 15 rue des Juifs, 67000 Strasbourg. Translated by permission of Librairie Istra(164).
The Art of Cookery Made Plain and Easy. By a Lady. Published by James Donaldson, Edinburgh 1747 (106).
Bateman, Ruth Conrad, *I Love To Cook Book.* Copyright © 1962 by The Ward Ritchie Press. Published by The Ward Ritchie Press. Reprinted by permission of The Ward Ritchie Press(110).
Beard, James, *Delights and Prejudices.* Copyright © 1964 by James Beard. Published by Atheneum, N.Y. By permission of Atheneum(131). *James Beard's American Cookery.* Copyright © 1972 by James A. Beard. Published by Little, Brown and Company, Boston. By permission of Little, Brown and Company(93, 97, 128, 143).
Beeton, Mrs. Isabella, *The Book of Household Man-

agement (1861).* Reproduced in facsimile by Jonathan Cape Ltd., London(107, 130, 133, 167).
Béguin, Maurice, *La Cuisine en Poitou.* Published by La Librairie Saint-Denis, c. 1933(149).
Bocuse, Paul, *Paul Bocuse's French Cooking.* Copyright © 1977 by Random House, Inc. Published by Pantheon Books, Inc., N.Y. Reprinted by permission of Pantheon Books, a Division of Random House, Inc.(98).
Bond, Jules Jerome, *The Outdoor Cookbook.* Copyright © 1963 by Jules Jerome Bond. Published by Pocket Books. Reprinted by permission of Pocket Books, a Simon & Schuster Division of Gulf & Western Corporation(96,147).
Boni, Ada, *The Talisman Italian Cook Book.* Copyright, 1950, 1978, by Crown Publishers, Inc. Published by Crown Publishers, Inc., N.Y. By permission of Crown Publishers, Inc.(91,109,164).
Boyd, Lizzie (Editor), *British Cookery.* Copyright © British Farm Produce Council and British Tourist Authority. Published by Croom Helm (London). By permission of British Farm Produce Council and British Tourist Authority(132,133,135).
Bozzi, Ottorina Perna, *Vecchia Milano in Cucina.* © 1975 by Giunti Martello Editore, Firenze. Published by Giunti Martello Editore, Firenze, Italy. Translated by permission of Giunti Martello Editore(152).
Brera, Gianni and Luigi Veronelli, *La Pacciada.* © 1973 by Arnoldo Mondadori Editore, Milan, Italy. Published by Arnoldo Mondadori Editore, Milan. Translated by permission of Arnoldo Mondadori Editore(151,155,156,159).
Brissenden, Rosemary, *South East Asian Food.* © R. F. and R. L. Brissenden, 1970. Published by Penguin Books Ltd., London. By permission of Penguin Books Ltd.(117).
Brown, Marion, *Marion Brown's Southern Cook Book.* © 1951, 1968 by The University of North Carolina Press. Reprinted by permission of The University of North Carolina Press (92—Mrs. James H. Anderson, San Bernardino, California; 145—Mrs. Thomas Tyson, Burlington, North Carolina).
Bullock, Mrs. Helen Claire, *The Williamsburg Art of Cookery.* Copyright 1938, © 1966 by the Colonial Williamsburg Foundation. Published by Colonial Williamsburg. Reprinted by permission of Holt, Rinehart and Winston, Publishers(162).
Cannon, Poppy and Patricia Brooks, *The Presidents' Cookbook.* Copyright © 1968 by Poppy Cannon & Patricia Brooks. Published by Bonanza Books. Reprinted by permission of Harper & Row, Publishers, Inc.(111).

Carnacina, Luigi, *Great Italian Cooking,* edited by Michael Sonino. Published in English by Abradale Press Inc., N.Y. By permission of Abradale Press(98).
Carnacina, Luigi and Luigi Veronelli, *La Buona Vera Cucina Italiana.* © 1966 by Rizzoli Editore. Published by Rizzoli Editore, Milan. Translated by permission of Rizzoli Editore(149).
Carrier, Robert, *The Robert Carrier Cookery Course.* © Robert Carrier, 1974. © Illustrations, W. H. Allen & Co. Ltd., 1974. Published by W. H. Allen & Co. Ltd., London. By permission of W. H. Allen & Co. Ltd.(91,154).
Caruana Galizia, Anne and Helen, *Recipes from Malta.* Copyright © Anne and Helen Caruana Galizia 1972. Published by Progress Press Co. Ltd., Valetta. By permission of Anne and Helen Caruana Galizia(94,131).
Chamberlain, Narcisse and Narcissa G., *The Chamberlain Sampler Of American Cooking: In Recipes And Pictures.* Copyright © 1961 by Hastings House, Publishers. By permission of Hastings House, Publishers(91).
Chanot-Bullier, C., *Vieilles Recettes de Cuisine Provençale.* Published by Tacussel, Marseille. Translated by permission of Tacussel, Éditeur(91).
Chantiles, Vilma Liacouras, *The Food of Greece.* Copyright © 1975 by Vilma Liacouras Chantiles. Published by Atheneum, N.Y. By permission of Vilma Liacouras Chantiles(100).
Chowdhary, Savitri, *Indian Cooking.* Copyright © Savitri Chowdhary 1954, 1975. Published by André Deutsch Limited, London. By permission of André Deutsch Limited(134).
Chu, Grace Zia, *Madame Chu's Chinese Cooking School.* Copyright © 1975 by Grace Zia Chu. Published by Simon & Schuster, N.Y. Reprinted by permission of Simon & Schuster, a Division of Gulf & Western Corporation(102).
Claiborne, Craig, *The New York Times Menu Cook Book.* Copyright © 1966 by The New York Times. Published by Harper & Row, Publishers, Inc., N.Y. By permission of Harper & Row, Publishers, Inc.(101).
Clancy, John and Frances Field, *Clancy's Oven Cookery.* Copyright © 1976 by John Clancy and Frances Field. Published by Delacorte Press. Reprinted by permission of Delacorte Press/Eleanor Friede(157).
Clark, Morton Gill, *The Wide, Wide World of Texas Cooking.* © Morton Gill Clark. Published by Harper & Row, Publishers. Reprinted by permission of Harper & Row(110).
Corbitt, Helen, *Helen Corbitt's Cookbook.* Copyright © 1957 by Helen Corbitt. Published by Houghton Mifflin Company. Reprinted by permission of Houghton

Mifflin Company(145).

Courchamps, Comte De, *Néophysiologie du Goût.* 1849(142).

Courtine, Robert, *Balzac à Table.* © Éditions Robert Laffont, S. A., Paris 1976. Published by Éditions Robert Laffont, Paris. Translated by permission of Robert Courtine(147). *Mon Bouquet de Recettes.* © Les Nouvelles Éditions Marabout, Verviers 1977. Published by Les Nouvelles Éditions Marabout, Verviers. Translated by permission of Les Nouvelles Éditions Marabout(101).

Curnonsky, *A L'Infortune du Pot.* Copyright Éditions de la Couronne, 1946. Published by Éditions de la Couronne, Paris(140). *Cuisine et Vins de France.* Copyright © 1953 by Augé, Gillon, Hollier-Larousse, Moreau et Cie, (Librairie Larousse), Paris. Published by Librairie Larousse, Paris. Translated by permission of Société Encyclopédique Universelle(147, 155, 156).

Cutler, Carol, *The Six-Minute Soufflé and Other Culinary Delights.* Published by Clarkson N. Potter, Inc. Copyright © 1976 by Carol Cutler. By permission of Clarkson N. Potter, Inc.(107, 108).

Dannenbaum, Julie, *Julie Dannenbaum's Creative Cooking School.* Copyright © 1971 by Julie Dannenbaum. Published by E. P. Dutton & Co. Inc., N.Y. By permission of E. P. Dutton & Co. Inc.(90).

David, Elizabeth, *French Provincial Cooking.* Copyright © Elizabeth David, 1960, 1962, 1967, 1970. Published by Penguin Books Ltd., London. By permission of Penguin Books Ltd.(159). *Summer Cooking.* Copyright © Elizabeth David, 1955. Published by Penguin Books Ltd., London. By permission of Penguin Books Ltd.(152).

De Gouy, Louis P., *The Gold Cook Book (revised edition).* Copyright 1948, 1969 by the author (Louis P. De Gouy). Published by Chilton Book Company. Reprinted by permission of the publisher, Chilton Book Company, Radnor, Pennsylvania(123, 144, 166).

De Pomiane, Édouard, *Le Code de la Bonne Chère.* Published by Éditions Albin Michel, Paris, 1948. Translated by permission of Éditions Albin Michel(135).

Derys, Gaston, *L'Art d'Être Gourmand.* Copyright © by Albin Michel 1929. Published by Éditions Albin Michel, Paris. Translated by permission of Éditions Albin Michel (105).

Dubois, Urbain, *Ecole des Cuisinières.* Published by Dentu, Paris, 1876(123,144). *Nouvelle Cuisine Bourgeoise.* Published by Paul Bernardin, Libraire-Éditeur, Paris, 1888 (8th Edition)(125).

Duff, Gail, *Fresh All The Year.* © Gail Duff 1976. Published by Macmillan London Ltd., 1976. By permission of Macmillan London Ltd.(119, 134).

Dumaine, Alexandre. © 1972 Pensée Moderne. Published by Éditions de la Pensée Moderne, Paris. Translated by permission of Éditions de la Pensée Moderne(126).

Eren, Neset, *The Art of Turkish Cooking.* Copyright © 1969 by Neset Eren. Published by Doubleday and Company, Inc., N.Y. Reprinted by permission of Doubleday and Company, Inc.(118, 138).

Escoffier, Auguste, *Ma Cuisine.* © English text 1965 by The Hamlyn Publishing Group Limited. Published by The Hamlyn Publishing Group Limited, London. By permission of The Hamlyn Publishing Group Limited(140).

Farmer, Fannie Merritt, *The Boston Cooking-School Cook Book (The Fannie Farmer Cookbook).* Copyright © 1896, 1914 by Fannie Merritt Farmer. Copyright © 1915, 1924 by Cora D. Perkins. Published by Little, Brown and Company, Boston, 1924. Reprinted by permission of Little, Brown and Company(160).

Foods of the World, *American Cooking: The Eastern Heartland; American Cooking: The Great West; Pacific and Southeast Asian Cooking; The Cooking of Germany; The Cooking of Italy; The Cooking of Japan; The Cooking of Scandinavia.* Copyright © 1971 Time-Life Books Inc.; Copyright © 1971 Time Inc.; Copyright © 1970 Time Inc.; Copyright © 1969 Time-Life Books Inc.; Copyright © 1968 Time-Life Books Inc.; Copyright © 1976 Time-Life Books Inc.; Copyright © 1968 Time Inc. Published by Time-Life Books, Alexandria(91, 119; 136; 100; 115, 136; 150; 102; 101, 148).

Froud, Nina, *The World Book of Meat Dishes.* © 1965 by Nina Froud. Published by Pelham Books Ltd., London. By permission of Pelham Books Ltd.(115).

Fuller, Peta J. and Jean-Noël Escudier, *The Wonderful Food of Provence.* Copyright © 1968 by Robert Rebstock and Peta J. Fuller. Published by Houghton Mifflin Company. Reprinted by permission of Houghton Mifflin Company(162).

Giniés, Louis, *Cuisine Provençale.* Published by UNIDE, Paris, 1976. Translated by permission of UNIDE(92, 121).

Gööck, Roland, *Die 100 berühmtesten Rezepte der Welt.* © by Werner Hörnemann Verlag, Bonn 1971. Published by Werner Hörnemann Verlag, Bonn. Translated by permission of Werner Hörnemann Verlag(108).

Gould-Marks, Beryl, *The Home Book of Italian Cookery.* © Beryl Gould-Marks 1969. Published by Faber and Faber, London. By permission of Faber and Faber(152, 162).

Graves, Eleanor, *Great Dinners From Life.* Copyright © 1969 Time Inc. Published by Time-Life Books, Alexandria(97).

Greenwald, Shaner, *Treasured Jewish Recipes.* © 1969 by Hawthorn Books, Inc. Published by Hawthorn Books. Reprinted by permission of Hawthorn Books(137).

Grigson, Jane, *Good Things.* Copyright © 1968, 1969, 1970, 1971 by Jane Grigson. Copyright © 1971 by Alfred A. Knopf, Inc. Published by Alfred A. Knopf, Inc. Reprinted by permission of Alfred A. Knopf, Inc.(128, 129, 132).

Guégan, Bertrand, *La Fleur de la Cuisine Française,* Vols. 1 & 2. Published by Éditions de la Sirène, 1920. Translated by permission of Éditions Henri Lefebvre(151).

Hawkins, Arthur, *Cook It Quick.* © 1971 by Arthur Hawkins. Published by Prentice-Hall, Inc., Englewood Cliffs, N.J. Reprinted by permission of Prentice-Hall(99).

Hazelton, Nika Standen, *The Continental Flavour.* Copyright © Nika Standen Hazelton, 1961. Published by Doubleday and Company, N.Y. Reprinted by permission of Curtis Brown Ltd.(159).

Hewitt, Jean, *The New York Times Heritage Cook Book.* Copyright © 1972 by The New York Times. Published by G. P. Putnam's Sons, N.Y. Reprinted by permission of G. P. Putnam's Sons(166).

Heyraud, H., *La Cuisine à Nice.* Published by Imprimerie-Librairie-Papeterie, Nice, 1922(141).

Hibben, Sheila, *American Regional Cookery.* Copyright 1932, 1946, by Sheila Hibben. Published by Little, Brown and Company, Boston. Reprinted by permission of McIntosh and Otis(92, 128, 130).

Jans, Hugh, *Koken in een Kasserol.* © 1977 Hugh Jans. Published by A. W. Bruna & Zoons Uitgeversmij B. V., Utrecht. Translated by permission of A. W. Bruna & Zoons Uitgeversmij B. V.(139). *Vrij Nederland (Dutch Magazine).* Published by Vrij Nederland, Amsterdam. Translated by permission of Vrij Nederland and Hugh Jans(165).

Jensen, Ingeborg Dahl, *Wonderful, Wonderful Danish Cooking.* Copyright © 1965 by Ingeborg Dahl Jensen. Published by Simon & Schuster. Reprinted by permission of Simon & Schuster, a Division of Gulf & Western Corporation(112).

Jouveau, René, *La Cuisine Provençale.* Copyright © Bouquet & Baumgartner, Flamatt, Switzerland. Published by Éditions du Message, 1962, Berne. Translated by permission of Bouquet & Baumgartner(93).

Kamman, Madeleine M., *When French Women Cook.* Copyright © 1976 by Madeleine M. Kamman. Published by Atheneum Publishers, N.Y. By permission of Atheneum Publishers(158).

Kennedy, Diana, *The Cuisines of Mexico.* Copyright © 1972 by Diana Kennedy. Published by Harper & Row, Publishers, Inc., N.Y. Reprinted by permission of Harper & Row, Inc.(106).

Kürtz, Jutta, *Das Kochbuch aus Schleswig-Holstein.* © Copyright 1976 by Verlagsteam Wolfgang Hölker. Published by Verlag Wolfgang Hölker, Münster. Translated by permission of Verlag Wolfgang Hölker(165).

Laboureur, Suzanne & X.-M. Boulestin, *Petits et Grands Plats.* Published by Au Sans Pareil, 1928(147, 149, 153, 156).

Lang, George, *The Cuisine of Hungary.* Copyright © 1971 by George Lang. Published by Atheneum Publishers, N.Y. By permission of Atheneum Publishers(117, 124).

Laughton, Catherine C. (Editor), *Mary Cullen's Northwest Cook Book.* Copyright 1946, by Journal Publishing Company, Portland, Oregon. Published by Binfords & Mort, Publishers, Portland, Oregon. By permission of *The Oregon Journal*(118).

La Varenne, *Le Cuisinier François.* 1651(146).

Lin, Florence, *Florence Lin's Chinese Regional Cookbook.* Copyright © 1975 by Florence Lin. Published by Hawthorn Books. By permission of Hawthorn Books, Inc.(103,104).

Lo, Kenneth, *Chinese Food.* Copyright © Kenneth Lo, 1972. Published by Penguin Books Ltd., London. By permission of Penguin Books Ltd.(103).

MacMiadhacháin, Anna, *Spanish Regional Cookery.* Copyright © Anna MacMiadhacháin, 1976. Published by Penguin Books Ltd., London. By permission of Penguin Books Ltd.(120).

McNeill, F. Marian, *The Scots Kitchen.* Published by Blackie & Son Limited, London. Reproduced by permission of Blackie & Son Limited(141).

Magyar, Elek, *Kochbuch für Feinschmecker.* Printed in Hungary, 1967. Published by Corvina Kiado, Budapest. Translated by permission of Dr. Balint Magyar and Dr. Pal Magyar(150).

Mamma Pappas, *Louis Pappas' Famous Greek Recipes.* Published by Louis Pappas Riverside Restaurant at the Sponge Boat Docks, Tarpon Springs, Florida. By permission of Louis Pappas Riverside Restaurant(113).

Miller, Gloria Bley, *The Thousand Recipe Chinese Cookbook.* Copyright © 1966 by Gloria Bley Miller. Published by Grosset & Dunlap, N.Y. By permission of Gloria Bley Miller(104).

Montagné Prosper, *Larousse Gastronomique.* © Copyright The Hamlyn Publishing Group Limited, 1961. Published by The Hamlyn Publishing Group Limited, London. Reproduced by permission of The Hamlyn Publishing Group Limited(121).

Montagné, Prosper and A. Gottschalk, *Mon Menu — Guide d'Hygiène Alimentaire.* Published by Société d'Applications Scientifiques, Paris(142).

Moore-Betty, Maurice, *Cooking For Occasions.* © 1970 by Maurice Moore-Betty. By permission of David White, Inc.(161).

Muffoletto, Anna, *The Art of Sicilian Cooking.* Copyright © 1971 by Anna Muffoletto. Published by Doubleday and Company, Inc., N.Y. By permission of Doubleday and Company, Inc.(97, 99).

Nelson, Kay Shaw, *The Eastern European Cookbook.* © 1973 by Kay Shaw Nelson. Published by Dover Publications. By permission of Collier Associates, literary agents(120).

Nignon, Edouard, *Les Plaisirs de la Table.* Published by the author c. 1920. Translated by permission of Daniel Morcrette, B. P. 26, 95270 Luzarches, France(126).

Norberg, Inga, *Good Food From Sweden.* Copyright © 1939 by Inga Norberg. Published by William Morrow & Company. By permission of William Morrow & Company(136).

Norman, Barbara, *The Spanish Cookbook.* Copyright © 1969 by Barbara Norman. Published by Bantam Books, Inc., N.Y. By permission of Bantam Books, Inc.(120).

Norwak, Mary, *The Farmhouse Kitchen.* © Mary Norwak 1975. Published by Ward Lock Limited, London. By permission of Ward Lock Limited(90, 132, 141).

Oliver, Raymond, *La Cuisine — sa technique, ses secrets.* Published by Éditions Bordas, Paris. Translated by permission of Leon Amiel Publishers(98).

Olney, Judith, *Summer Food.* Copyright © 1978 by Judith Olney. Published by Atheneum Publishers, N.Y. By permission of Atheneum Publishers(150).

Olney, Richard, *Simple French Food.* Copyright © 1974 by Richard Olney. Published by Atheneum, N.Y. Reprinted by permission of Atheneum(113, 127). *The French Menu Cookbook.* Copyright © 1970 by Richard Olney. Published by Simon and Schuster, N.Y. By permission of John Schaffner, Literary Agent(114, 116, 163).

Orga, Irfan, *Cooking the Middle East Way.* © Paul Hamlyn Limited, 1962. Published by The Hamlyn Publishing

Group Limited, London. By permission of The Hamlyn Publishing Group Limited(111). *Cooking with Yogurt*. First published 1956 by André Deutsch Limited, London. By permission of André Deutsch Limited(125).
Ortiz, Elisabeth Lambert, *The Complete Book of Caribbean Cooking*. Copyright © Elisabeth Lambert Ortiz, 1973, 1975. Published by M. Evans and Company, Inc., N.Y. By permission of John Farquharson Ltd., Literary Agents(125, 140).
Ortiz, Elisabeth Lambert with Mitsuko Endo, *The Complete Book of Japanese Cooking*. Copyright © 1976 by Elisabeth Lambert Ortiz. Published by M. Evans and Company, Inc., N.Y. By permission of John Farquharson Ltd., Literary Agents(94, 104).
Pépin, Jacques, *A French Chef Cooks at Home*. Copyright © 1975 by Jacques Pépin. Published by Simon and Schuster, N.Y. Reprinted by permission of Simon & Schuster, a Division of Gulf & Western Corporation(148).
Perkins, Wilma Lord, *The Fannie Farmer Cookbook*. Eleventh Edition. Copyright 1896, 1900, 1901, 1902, 1903, 1904, 1905, 1906, 1912, 1914 by Fannie Farmer. Copyright 1915, 1918, 1923, 1924, 1928, 1929 by Cora D. Perkins. Copyright 1930, 1931, 1932, 1933, 1934, 1936, 1940, 1941, 1942, 1943, 1946, 1951, © 1959, 1964, 1965 by Dexter Perkins Corporation. Published by Little, Brown and Company, Boston. By permission of Little, Brown and Company(145).
Progneaux, Jean E., *Les Specialités et Recettes Gastronomiques Bordelaise et Girondines*. Published by Quartier Latin, La Rochelle. Translated by permission of Quartier Latin(110).
Ray, Elizabeth (Editor), *The Best of Eliza Acton*. © Longmans, Green & Co. Ltd., 1968. Introduction © Elizabeth David, 1968. Published by Penguin Books Ltd., London. By permission of Penguin Books Ltd.(167).
Reboul, J. B., *La Cuisinière Provençale*. Published by Tacussel, Marseille. Translated by permission of Tacussel, Éditeur(109, 143).
Romagnoli, Margaret and G. Franco Romagnoli, *The Romagnolis' Table*. Copyright © 1974, 1975 by Margaret and G. Franco Romagnoli. Published by Little, Brown and Company. By permission of Little, Brown and Co.(130).
Saint-Ange, Madame, *La Bonne Cuisine de Madame Saint-Ange*. Copyright 1929 by Augé, Gillon, Hollier-Larousse, Moreau et Cie. (Librairie Larousse), Paris. Published by Librairie Larousse, Paris. Translated by permission of Éditions Chaix(155). *La Cuisine de Madame Saint-Ange*. © Éditions Chaix, Grenoble. Translated by permission of Éditions Chaix(129).
Sandler, Sandra Takako, *The American Book of Japanese Cooking*. Copyright © 1974 by Sandra Sandler. Published by Stackpole Books, Harrisburg. By permission of Stackpole Books(95).
Sarvis, Shirley, *A Taste of Portugal*. Copyright © 1967 Shirley Sarvis. Published by Charles Scribner's Sons, N.Y. By permission of Shirley Sarvis(157).
Scott, Jack Denton, *The Complete Book of Pasta*. Copyright © 1968 by Jack Denton Scott. Published by William Morrow & Company, Inc., N.Y. By permission of William Morrow & Company, Inc.(137, 138).
Serra, Victoria, translated by Elizabeth Gili, *Tia Victoria's Spanish Kitchen*. Copyright © Elizabeth Gili 1963. Published by Kaye & Ward Ltd., London. By permission of Kaye & Ward Ltd. and Elizabeth Gili(165).
Sokolov, Raymond A., *Great Recipes from The New York Times*. Copyright © 1973 by Raymond A. Sokolov. Published by Quadrangle/Times Books. Reprinted by permission of Quadrangle/Times Books(99).
Steinmetz, Emma W. K., *Onze Rijsttafel*. © Unieboek/C.A.J. Van Dishoeck, Bussum. Published by C.A.J. Van Dishoeck, Bussum. Translated by permission of Unieboek/C.A.J. Van Dishoeck(96).
Stockli, Albert, *Splendid Fare*. Copyright © 1970 by Albert Stockli, Inc. Published by Alfred A. Knopf, Inc., N.Y. Reprinted by permission of Alfred A. Knopf, Inc.(124).
Tante Marguerite, *La Cuisine de la Bonne Ménagère*. Published by Éditions de L'Épi, Paris, 1929(143, 152).
Toklas, Alice B., *The Alice B. Toklas Cook Book*. Copyright 1954 by Alice B. Toklas. Published by Harper & Row, Publishers, Inc., N.Y. By permission of Harper & Row, Publishers, Inc.(161).
Toulouse-Lautrec, Mapie, the Countess de, *La Cuisine de France*. Copyright © 1964 by The Orion Press, Inc. Published by Viking Penguin, N.Y. Reprinted by permission of Viking Penguin(166).
Troisgros, Jean and Pierre, *Cuisiniers à Roanne. Les recettes originales de Jean et Pierre Troisgros*. Copyright © 1977 by Éditions Robert Laffont, S. A. Published by Éditions Robert Laffont, Paris. Translated by permission of William Morrow and Company, Inc.(160).
Ungerer, Miriam, *Good Cheap Food*. Copyright © Miriam Ungerer, 1973. Published by Viking Penguin Inc. Reprinted by permission of Viking Penguin Inc.(122, 146).
Uvezian, Sonia, *The Best Foods of Russia*. Copyright © 1976 by Sonia Uvezian. Published by Harcourt Brace Jovanovich, N.Y. Reprinted by permission of Harcourt Brace Jovanovich, Inc.(95).
Veerasawmy, E. P., *Indian Cookery*. Copyright © Arco Publications 1964. Published by Granada Publishing Limited, St. Albans. By permission of Herbert Joseph(114, 139, 142).
Wason, Betty, *The Art of German Cooking*. © Elizabeth Wason Hall 1967. Published by Doubleday and Company, Inc., N.Y. Reprinted by permission of Doubleday and Company, Inc.(119, 151).
Westland, Pamela, *A Taste of the Country*. Copyright © Pamela Westland, 1974. First published by Elm Tree Books, 1974. By permission of Hamish Hamilton(112, 125).
Willinsky, Grete, *Kochbuch der Büchergilde*. © by Büchergilde Gutenberg, Frankfurt am Main. Published by Büchergilde Gutenberg, Frankfurt am Main. Translated by permission of Büchergilde Gutenberg(163).
Wilshaw, Harold, *Cookbook for the Needy Greedy*. Copyright © Harold Wilshaw 1975. Published by New English Library, London. Reprinted by permission of New English Library Ltd. and Harold Wilshaw(105).
Wilson, José (Editor), *House and Garden's New Cook Book*. Copyright © 1967 by The Condé Nast Publications Inc. Published by The Condé Nast Publications Inc., N.Y. By permission of The Condé Nast Publications Inc.(93). *House and Garden's Party Menu Cookbook*. Copyright © 1973 by The Condé Nast Publications Inc. Published by The Condé Nast Publications Inc., N.Y. By permission of The Condé Nast Publications Inc.(95).
Wolfert, Paula, *Mediterranean Cooking*. Copyright © 1977 by Paula Wolfert. Published by Quadrangle/The New York Times Book Co. Inc., N.Y. By permission of Times Books(138). *Couscous and Other Good Food from Morocco*. Copyright © 1973 by Paula Wolfert. Published by Harper & Row, Publishers, Inc., N.Y. By permission of Harper & Row, Publishers, Inc.(96, 112).

Acknowledgments

The indexes for this book were prepared by Anita R. Beckerman. The editors are particularly indebted to Jeremiah Tower, London.

The editors also wish to thank: Pat Alburey, Royston, Hertfordshire, England; R. Allen & Co. Ltd., London; Jane Anderson, American Meat Institute, Washington, D.C.; Frank Arney, National Cattlemen's Association, Denver, Colorado; O. Bartholdi and Son Ltd., London; Janet Bartucci, Burson-Marsteller, New York, New York; Sara Beck, Dr. H. Russell Cross, David K. Hallet, Leonard Henning, United States Department of Agriculture, Washington, D.C.; Ginny Buckley, London; Dr. Raymond Cantwell, Dr. Steven Mutkowski, Cornell University, Ithaca, New York; Michael Carter, London; Central London Markets, London; B. J. Cutler, Washington, D. C.; Anne Dare, London; W. J. Duncum, Hatfield, England; Zaki Elia, London; Audrey Ellison, London; Irene Ertugrul, London; C. D. Figg, J. B. Kilkenny, R. J. Stollard, Meat and Livestock Commission, Bletchley, England; Dorothy Frame, London; Jack Freund, Silver Spring, Maryland; Samuel J. Gadell, Tyson's Locker Plant, Vienna, Virginia; Cyril Gilhespy, London; Diana Grant, London; Janet Hecker, Washington Gas Light Company, Washington, D.C.; Maggi Heinz, London; Karen Pearce Hills, London; Marion Hunter, Sutton, Surrey, England; H. Kenneth Johnson, Reba Staggs, Gay Starrak, Mark Thomas, National Live Stock and Meat Board, Chicago, Illinois; Dr. Robert Kelly, Virginia Polytechnic Institute and State University, Blacksburg, Virginia; Kerry Keysell, National Association of Veal Producers, Dorchester, England; M. Lemaire, École Supérieure de la Boucherie, Paris; Ruth Lynam, London; F. J. Mallion, College for the Distributive Trades, London; Larry Mirman, Mirman Brothers, Washington, D.C.; Jo Northey, London; Dr. Herbert Ockerman, Ohio State University, Columbus, Ohio; Elisabeth Lambert Ortiz, London; Martin Pumphrey, London; Dr. D. N. Rhodes, Meat Research Institute, Bristol, England; Elliot Staren, MacArthur Liquors, Washington, D.C.; Henry Sauter, Larimer's Inc., Washington, D.C.; Ursula Whyte, London; A. Wolsey, London.

Picture Credits

The sources for the pictures in this book are listed below. Credits for each of the photographers and illustrators are listed by page number in sequence with successive pages indicated by hyphens; where necessary, the locations of pictures within pages are also indicated — separated from page numbers by dashes.

Photographs by Alan Duns: cover, 11 —top left, 16-18, 22-25, 40, 41 —bottom, 43 —bottom, 48, 51 —top right and bottom, 54, 55 —bottom left and center, 56-62, 64-66, 68-71, 74 —top, 75 —top and bottom right, 78, 80-83, 84-85 —bottom, 86-88.
Photographs by Aldo Tutino: 12 —bottom center and right, 13-15, 20-21, 26, 29 —bottom, 30-33, 36, 38-39, 41 —top, 72-73.
Other photographs (alphabetically): Tom Belshaw, 4, 11 —top right and bottom, 28 —bottom. Bob Cramp, 42, 43 —top, 55 —bottom right, 63, 74 —top, 75 —bottom left and center, 76, 79, 84-85 —top. Paul Kemp, 28 —(4), 34-35, 44-47, 50, 51 —top left, 52-53. National Livestock and Meat Board, 12 —top.
Illustrations (alphabetically): Mary Evans Picture Library and private sources, 90-169. Whole Hog Studios, Atlanta, Georgia, 8-10, 11 —bottom left.

Library of Congress Cataloguing in Publication Data
Time-Life Books
    Beef and veal:
        (The Good cook, techniques and recipes)
    Includes index.
        1. Cookery (Beef) 2. Cookery (Veal) I. Title II. Series
TX749 T58   1979   641.6'6'2   78-10502
ISBN 0-8094-2852-0
ISBN 0-8094-2851-2 (lib. bdg.)
ISBN 0-8094-2854-7 (retail ed.)

Printed in U.S.A.